We found these notes supremely beneficial for clarifying the message of Romans, providing quality training for Bible study leaders and planting deep missionary convictions in young Christians.

Richard Coekin, Emmanuel Dundonald, Wimbledon

***Read Mark Learn*** has taught hundreds of us over the years to know our Bibles and our God better.

Rev. Hugh Palmer, Christ Church Fulwood, Sheffield

This is an exciting commentary on Romans, because it is the result of careful reflection on the meaning of the text and its theological implications, though very much designed to answer the questions of ordinary people. Those who want to use the material in a study group will find plenty of resources for engaging with the text, and a set of questions that will set everybody thinking about the true meaning of each passage.

Rev. Dr David Peterson, Oak Hill Theological College

**Also available from HarperCollins*Publishers:***

***Read Mark Learn:*** John's Gospel

✦ READ ✦ MARK ✦ LEARN ✦

# Romans

## St Helen's Church, Bishopsgate

**Marshall Pickering**

*An Imprint of HarperCollinsPublishers*

Marshall Pickering is an Imprint of

HarperCollins*Religious*
Part of HarperCollins*Publishers*
77–85 Fulham Palace Road, London W6 8JB
www.christian-publishing.com

First published in Great Britain in 2000 by Marshall Pickering

1 3 5 7 9 10 8 6 4 2

© 2000 St Helen's Church, Bishopsgate

St Helen's Church, Bishopsgate asserts the moral right
to be identified as the author of this work

A catalogue record for this book is
available from the British Library

ISBN 0 551 03252 9

Printed and bound in Great Britain by
Omnia Books Ltd, Glasgow

# CONTENTS

**Note**

Unless stated otherwise, all quotations are taken from commentaries on Paul's letter to the Romans. For details of these, please refer to the bibliography at the end of the book.

# FOREWORD

The **Read Mark Learn** Bible studies at St Helen's have, for very many years, been central to our training programme for young Christians. I regard RML, as it is called, as one of the most significant initiatives ever taken in our church life together.

From the beginning, with the Mark studies, and then with Romans, The Overview and John, this material for group work has proved itself in the equipping of countless men and women for effective Christian witness.

I remain full of admiration for the staff and leaders who have made this course what it is by their labour, and I am profoundly grateful that, for many hundreds of people, attendance at RML has been the start of a growing love for the accurate study and the businesslike application of God's holy word.

Dick Lucas
Rector Emeritus of St Helen's

# INTRODUCING
# 'READ MARK LEARN'

Blessed Lord, who has caused all holy Scriptures to be written for our learning: Grant that we may in such wise hear them, **read, mark, learn,** and inwardly digest them, that by patience and comfort of thy holy Word, we may embrace and ever hold fast the blessed hope of everlasting life, which thou hast given us in our Saviour Jesus Christ. Amen.

**Collect for the Second Sunday in Advent in the Book of Common Prayer**

## Beginnings

**Read Mark Learn** is the title of a collection of small group Bible studies which has been developed, over a number of years, at St Helen's Church, Bishopsgate, in the City of London.

The original studies, undertaken for the first time in 1976, covered the whole of Mark's Gospel in one year. In subsequent years, studies in Paul's letter to the Romans were devised for those who had previously studied Mark; the aim was to provide a thorough training in Christian doctrine. Finally, a third-year study was established, consisting of a complete overview of the Bible. Thus, over three years, members of the church have the opportunity of gaining a firm grasp of how to read and understand the Bible. They are firmly grounded in Christian doctrine and practice from the scriptures, and so they are equipped for a lifetime in the service of Christ.

After some years it was felt that a change was needed, and so material for studies in John's Gospel was written; this was published in 1999. As with Mark, the material for John and for Romans was written primarily for the leaders of small groups, to help them prepare, but it may, of course, be useful to any individual undertaking a study of these books of the Bible.

In all the **Read Mark Learn** studies there is a commitment to consecutive Bible study, with Bible passages being studied within the context of the scriptural whole. This is based on the conviction that when God's word is studied *in context*, God's voice is heard as His Holy Spirit speaks.

## Present arrangements

The format that we have found to work well is to have a pair of leaders for each small group, with eight to ten members in the group. The leaders are responsible for all the teaching over a period of three terms, each term running for about nine weeks.

Every member is expected to prepare for a study by reading the text carefully – there is no substitute for close and careful study of the text – and considering the discussion questions that have been handed out in advance. The leaders will do this preparation both individually and as a group, meeting together a week or so in advance of the study and using the study notes in this book. With the help of the suggested discussion questions, we study the passage that we will later teach. A key aspect of the leaders' preparation group is the time set aside for praying for each other and for the members of our groups.

## Training for leaders

We have found this preparation group to be a very helpful way of providing training for leaders, of supporting them in their ministry of leadership, and also, of course, of developing our understanding of the overall message of the book we are working on. In addition, there has been the long-term value of training people to lead House Groups in the future.

The strength of **Read Mark Learn** depends, in human terms, upon the calibre of the leaders. Without the leaders' considerable degree of commitment – as indicated above – the whole enterprise would fail. And so a high priority is given to training and encouraging leaders on a continuing basis. Information on the RML Leaders' Training Material may be found at the back of this book.

# INTRODUCING
# THE STUDY NOTES

These notes were, for the most part, written during the academic year of 1998/99. They were used by our RML leaders as they led studies in Romans throughout that year. It should be stressed, however, that this present set of notes represents the fruit of over fifteen years spent studying and teaching Romans at St Helen's. During that time, several sets of leaders' notes were compiled and each of these has made a substantial contribution to the notes as they now stand. Equally significant is the fact that all our RML teaching material is created by means of studying the passage in groups, feeding back and, together, correcting and revising our understanding. And so, although these notes are intended to help people understand the message of Romans, it is essential that members of Bible study groups adopt the approach of the Bereans in Acts 17:11, examining the Bible for themselves to see if our interpretation is correct.

These notes are not intended to be a formal commentary on Paul's letter to the Romans. Rather, the aim is to explain the heart of his teaching in each passage, showing how each part fits into his line of argument, in the letter as a whole, and also how it contributes to the achieving of his purpose in writing the letter. For more detailed comment on specific verses or on difficult issues we would point readers to the books listed in the Bibliography at the end of this book.

# Study passages

Romans has been divided into 23 passages, with a study for each passage and a review study at the end (for which preparatory questions only are given in this book). The divisions correspond mainly to the apparent building blocks of Paul's argument. But there are some exceptions: Study 3, for example, covers a long passage which could well be divided to give two studies (on 2:1–16 and 2:17–29) if time permitted, while Study 18 focuses on just two verses, at the beginning of ch. 12. The reason for this is that these verses represent a 'hinge' in Romans, and we have found that studying them separately provides a useful opportunity to review what has gone before, and also to understand the principles that underlie Paul's teaching in the rest of his letter.

Bible study leaders may feel, nevertheless, that some of the studies are too long for their groups. If this is the case, we would recommend that the group study the heart of the argument and that the leader summarises the surrounding material (particularly where much Old Testament background is involved).

# Section notes

Paul's letter has four main sections which contain the main body of his teaching, and these sit within a frame consisting of an introduction and a conclusion. In these notes we have included Section Notes which are intended to give an overview of each section and also an introduction to some of its most important themes.

# Study notes

Each study has the following headings:

**Context:** How the passage being studied fits in with the wider context of the whole letter.

**Structure:** How the text of the passage may be broken down into smaller parts. The main point of each part is stated and from the titles it should be apparent how each part relates to the overall main point of the passage.

**Old Testament background:** Romans contains many Old Testament ideas and concepts which Paul assumes we will understand. Here the most important ones are introduced.

**Text notes:** A brief commentary on the passage. More difficult verses are touched on, but the main aim is to see how Paul develops the main ideas.

**Key themes and application:** A summary of the key ideas raised in the passage is followed by some suggestions as to how these ideas apply, both to the first readers and to us today. A danger in application is that we tend to look for things to *do*, but in Romans much of the application will involve a change in our *thinking*. We should not underestimate the significance of such a change, for if we think differently about God, about His purposes and about ourselves, our whole lives will be influenced as a result.

**Unanswered questions:** These are included to help us consider how the logic of Paul's argument flows from one passage to the next.

**Aim:** The main point of the passage is taken as the aim of the study. The Bible study leader should enter the study itself with a clear aim and this aim ought to correspond to the main thrust of the passage.

**Suggested questions:** Suggested questions for leaders to use in the group study. These are only suggestions. They have been tried and tested in RML groups, but Bible study leaders will need to adapt them to suit their own groups. In addition to these questions, which leaders use to help them lead, there are preparation questions to help all members study the passage before coming to the group, and these may be found at the back of the book.

# INTRODUCING PAUL'S LETTER TO THE ROMANS

In the history of the church, Paul's letter to the Romans has been one of the most influential parts of the Bible. It was instrumental in the conversion of the great early theologian Augustine and crucial in Martin Luther's insights that led to the Reformation. Countless Christians, down the centuries, have come to a greater understanding of the glory of the gospel through reading and studying this epistle. But it is a long, sometimes complex letter, and this could easily put us off discovering its riches. The purpose of this Introduction, therefore, is to provide some background to Romans and also to give an idea of how the letter fits together, so that we will be encouraged to study this part of God's word more closely.

## General background to Paul's letter

The letter claims to have been written by the apostle Paul (e.g. 1:1; 15:15) and there is no good reason to doubt that he (with the help of his scribe, Tertius, see 16:22) was indeed its author.

It is also clear that the letter was written in the latter stages of Paul's third missionary journey. Chapter 15:23–29 tells us that, as he writes, Paul is planning to go to Jerusalem and then to Rome, and then eventually on to Spain. This final destination was because of his desire (expressed in 15:20) to 'preach the gospel where Christ was not known'. It seems likely that he wrote to the Romans while he was in Greece, before setting off on this three-stage journey (Acts 20:1–3). Subsequent to his letter, Paul did finally reach Rome where, although under guard, he preached the gospel for two years (Acts 28:11–31).

It is not certain how the church in Rome was founded, although 'the most likely scenario is that Roman Jews, who were converted on the day of Pentecost (see Acts 2:10), brought their faith in Jesus as the Messiah back with them to their home synagogues' (Moo, p. 4). But the majority of the Jewish Christians would most likely have left Rome at the order of the Emperor Claudius in AD 49 (reported in Acts 18:2). By the time Romans was written, in about AD 57, some Jews would have returned, but overall the church in Rome would have comprised a majority of Gentiles and only a few Jews, and this seems to be reflected in some of the concerns of Paul's letter.

# The purpose of Paul's letter

This has been the subject of much debate, for, unlike many of Paul's other letters, there seems to be no single issue that the letter as a whole is addressing. Nor is the church in Rome dominated by problems – various problems lay behind Paul's two long letters to the church in Corinth. Indeed, at both ends of his letter the apostle acknowledges the spiritual well-being of the Roman Christians (1:8; 15:14), so why does he write to them at such length? Three purposes emerge from the letter, although none by itself is adequate as an explanation.

### ♦ Paul is gathering support for his trip to Spain

Paul explicitly states this intention in 15:24. For his missionary trip to Spain he would have needed substantial support and 'it would be natural for Paul to try to enlist the help of the vital and centrally located Roman community' (Moo, p. 17). The rest of the letter, therefore, provides the background and the motivation for enlisting their partnership in his work, for only as the Romans understand the scope and wonder of the good news, of salvation for all people, will they fully support such an enterprise.

◆ **Tension between Jews and Gentiles in the church**
The Gentile majority and the Jewish minority are clearly not accepting one another as they should, but instead are looking down on one another for various reasons. Evidence for this comes in several passages. First, it appears that Jews may have been bragging about their spiritual heritage (2:17–20). Second, and more prominently, ch. 11 makes it clear that Gentile Christians are boasting over Jews because the gospel has largely been rejected by the Jews and is now spreading rapidly among the Gentiles (11:17–32). Third, Paul specifically addresses a Jew/Gentile point of conflict, in 14:1–15:13, as he urges them to avoid condemning or judging one another, in the situation where some Jewish Christians are still observing some food laws and festival days. In view of all this, Paul's careful explanation of the gospel – that it is powerful to save all people, both Jew and Gentile (1:16) – is the basis on which he urges the two groups to accept one another fully, so that each sees the other as part of the same Christian family. It is critically important that they do this, for their mutual acceptance will witness to God's work of building a united body of believers.

◆ **The importance of understanding the gospel**
It is striking that, although the Roman Christians have, as we learn, an international reputation for their faith and obedience (1:8; 16:19), Paul's message to them is essentially the gospel of salvation; he boldly reminds them of what they already know (15:15). Another purpose behind Paul's letter, therefore, seems to be that these Christians should *fully* understand the gospel that has saved them, the gospel that he is preaching.

These three strands could well be closely related. The Roman church will have a key part to play in the spread of the gospel, not only because they will provide support for Paul's trip to Spain, but also because they sit at the centre of the most powerful empire of the day. This church is in a position of the greatest influence in the known world, and it is therefore vital that its members be fully and accurately grounded in the gospel. They need correct understanding and, as a result of such understanding, their lives should witness to the power of the gospel of Christ – and in the first century nothing would have demonstrated this more vividly than the unity among Jewish and Gentile Christians.

## The implications for us

The urgent focus on the gospel in Romans has important implications for us, since our usual inclination may be to think that once we understand the gospel, we can move on to other matters in our Christian lives. Paul's inclination, however, is not to move on elsewhere but, rather, to go deeper into the gospel itself. Since we ourselves need to understand more and more the scope and magnitude of God's mercy, however long we have been believing, we should meditate on what Paul has written, trusting it and seeking to live in the light of it. Then, the things that Paul most desires to see – lives being transformed in obedience to God, a church that is genuinely united, the gospel being spread to all people and, above all, God being glorified – will start to become our highest priorities too.

John Calvin said that 'if we have gained a true understanding of this epistle, we have an open door to all the most profound treasures of scripture'. The aim of this study course is that, with the help of the Holy Spirit, we will grow towards such an understanding.

## Structure and outline of the letter

Romans is about the salvation that God has revealed in Jesus Christ. At its simplest, the letter fits together like this: following his introduction, Paul gives a short thesis for his argument in 1:16–17. He then sets up the problem, tells us the solution, *explains* the solution, draws out some of the implications, and signs off.

When studying Romans, it is easy to get lost in the detail and fail to see how the passage being studied fits into the big picture. The fuller outline given below is designed to give us a view of the big picture at the outset, before we start to look at the detail. The letter has four main sections, containing the substance of Paul's teaching, and these sit within a 'frame' formed by an introduction and a conclusion.

# An overview

The best way to get started in Romans is to read it! Set aside some time when you can read the whole book at one sitting. Read fairly rapidly, trying to get a feel for the book as a whole: the main themes, the structure, the language. (You may like to keep in mind the 'overview' questions, which are printed at the beginning of the prep questions at the end of this book.) The point of this exercise is to take in the big picture, so don't worry about understanding all the details at this stage. At the end, note down your first impressions. If you struggle to make mental notes, jot down a few very brief comments with references as you read, but don't lose your momentum.

# SECTION NOTES:
# Romans 1:1–17 and 15:14–16:27

These two sections bracket the rest of the letter to the Romans, making a frame for the main content of Paul's argument. Besides the formalities of greeting and valediction, they provide much insight into Paul's work and plans, and also explain his relationship with the Romans. Paul's purpose in these sections is to demonstrate his own commitment to the authentic gospel and so to give the Romans every reason to abide by it themselves.

The end of the opening bracket (vv. 16, 17) provides an introduction to the main part of the letter, as Paul presents his thesis concerning the saving power of God's gospel.

## Structure

| | |
|---|---|
| **1:1–7** | The gospel |
| | Greetings: from Paul, a servant of God's gospel to the Roman Christians |
| **1:8–15** | Background: Paul's long-term gospel commitment to them |
| **1:16–17** | Re: God's powerful saving gospel |
| | |
| **15:14–33** | Paul's ministry to the Gentiles |
| **16:1–16** | Greetings |
| **16:17–20** | Warnings |
| **16:21–23** | Messages |
| **16:25–27** | Glory to God who can establish you by this gospel |

# Key themes

### ◆ Paul' s role and work

In the opening words of his letter, Paul announces himself as 'a servant of Christ Jesus, called to be an apostle and set apart for the gospel of God' (1:1). He knows he has been called by God to take up a unique role as the apostle to the Gentiles (1:5; 15:16), and we learn that his aim is, therefore, to take the gospel to places where Christ is not known (15:20). There appear to be two main reasons why Paul should elaborate so much on his role and his work. First, he wishes to authenticate his ministry before the Romans, so that they will accept his message. And second, by explaining his ministry and mission to the Gentiles, he is giving the basis for his appeal to the Romans, that they should be willing to back his work of evangelism in the future; in particular, he hopes that they will support him as he takes the gospel on to Spain.

### ◆ Paul's relationship with the Romans

Paul's evident commitment to the Roman church (1:8–15) is rooted in his role as apostle to the Gentiles. His commitment is seen in his prayers (1:8–10), his desire to see them in order to strengthen them (1:11–12; 15:23), his encouragement at their faithfulness (1:8; 15:14) and his eagerness to preach the gospel among them (1:15). By showing his commitment he again gives them reason to accept his teaching. It is also clear, however, that he expects to receive encouragement and refreshment from them (1:12; 15:24, 32), and this leads him to appeal for support in his future plans (15:24, 30–31).

### ◆ The gospel

Paul begins his letter with a summary of the gospel. He does this so that the Romans may check the authenticity of the message he is proclaiming, and also so that they may be sure that they are abiding by the same message as the apostle. This leads them on to read the rest of his letter with confidence. The letter ends similarly with a briefer summary outlining what he has just been teaching. The key elements of the gospel, mentioned by Paul in both summaries, are these: it comes from God; its subject is Jesus; it was promised in the Old Testament; it is for all people; and it calls everyone to believe and obey.

# Paul's thesis (1:16–17)

These verses (1:16–17) sit slightly apart from the rest of the section, like a showcase in which Paul presents his thesis, the nub of his argument in the rest of the letter. Paul tells the Romans that he is not ashamed of the gospel because it is God's way of powerfully saving all who believe. The heart of the gospel, he says, is that it reveals a righteousness that comes from God. In this way he prepares the ground for the Romans to understand why all people need to be saved, which will be his subject in 1:18–3:20.

## Study I

# ROMANS 1:1–17

## Context

The apostle Paul is writing to the Christians who make up the church in Rome. He is hoping to visit them on his way to Spain, but first he must go to Jerusalem (15:24–28, see Introducing Paul's Letter to the Romans). This opening passage has links with the close of the letter (15:14–16:27, see Section Notes) and in both parts Paul points to the subject of his letter, which is the gospel. He explains his relationship to this gospel message, i.e. his God-given role of proclaiming it to the Gentiles, and his particular commitment, therefore, to the Gentile Romans.

Paul begins by spreading out the essentials of the gospel. This gives him the opportunity both to present his credentials as a preacher of the gospel and also to eliminate any confusion between himself and his readers as to the nature of the message – this is what he expects the Romans to be believing. He ends his introduction compellingly, declaring his confidence in the gospel as God's powerful means of salvation and so drawing his readers to read on and discover why this is such good news.

## Structure

1:1–7  From: Paul, a servant of God's gospel
       To: the Roman Christians
1:8–15 Background: Paul's long-term gospel commitment to the Roman Christians
1:16–17 Re: God's powerful saving gospel

# Old Testament background

**2 Samuel 7:8–16:** God promises David, Israel's greatest king, that He will establish an everlasting kingdom. In doing so He will be fulfilling the promises made to Abraham in Genesis 12 about reversing the effects of the Fall (Genesis 3). This kingdom will be ruled by one of David's descendants who will also be 'God's Son'. A description of God's powerful Son can be found in Psalm 2. This promised King or 'Christ' had not appeared by the end of the Old Testament, and so God's people were still waiting.

    **Habakkuk 2:4:** Habakkuk, writing just before the destruction of Jerusalem, asks how God, whose 'eyes are too pure to look on evil' (Habakkuk 1:13), can both punish evil and keep His promises of salvation to Israel. God's answer is that Habakkuk should wait: both will happen in the end. Evil will be destroyed and 'the righteous will live by his faith'. Salvation depends upon trusting God.

# Text notes

## 1–7 FROM: PAUL, A SERVANT OF GOD'S GOSPEL. TO: THE ROMAN CHRISTIANS

Although Paul follows the conventional structure, in the ancient world, for the start of a letter ('Paul, to the Romans, greetings'), he fills out his salutations in order to address some essential matters, namely why the Romans should pay attention to his message and what that message is.

◆ **Paul's credentials (v. 1)**
  Paul is serving Christ, his master, who called him to be an apostle (vv. 1, 5) and His authorized ambassador (Acts 9:15). He has been set apart by Christ Himself to carry the gospel, the 'good news', to others, a message that is not his own but God's.
◆ **The gospel (vv. 1–6)**
  One of our greatest errors is to place ourselves at the heart of the gospel we preach. Verses 1–5 turn such a selfish view upside down, as Paul gives a brief but dense description of the gospel he is proclaiming. The gospel …

1   ... *comes from God (v. 1):* The source of the good news is not humanity, nor even the apostle Paul, but God Himself.

2   ... *is not new (v. 2):* It was 'promised beforehand in the Holy Scriptures'. It is God's eternal plan, revealed to His people hundreds of years previously, in the Old Testament. Throughout history God has been working to fulfil His plan. We are wrong ever to think that Jesus is God's 'second plan', or that the Old Testament is about a God of anger and the New Testament about a God of love.

3   ... *is about Jesus (v. 3):* The reason why the gospel is 'regarding His Son' (rather than us and our needs) comes over in vv. 3–4, where Paul reveals the fullness of Jesus' identity in a sharp crescendo. He describes Jesus from two points of view: in earthly terms He was a descendant of David, in itself a fact that should arouse expectation about His messiahship (see OT notes on 2 Samuel 7:8–16), but in the spiritual realm, He has been declared to be the powerful Son of God by means of His resurrection from the dead. (Only a king who conquers death can reign for ever, as in 2 Samuel 7:13.) Thus He is, says Paul, 'Jesus *(the man)* Christ *(the promised Messiah)* our Lord *(the supreme ruler in the universe)*'.

4   ... *demands the obedience of faith (v. 5):* The appropriate response to such a figure is the absolute submission that Paul calls for in v. 5. He states that he has been set apart to call Gentiles to 'the obedience that comes from faith', a phrase that could mean 'the obedient life that stems from faith' or 'the obedient response that consists of having faith', i.e. trusting God. These two possibilities are not mutually exclusive: to put one's trust in Christ means following Him as Lord, but it is only possible to obey Him when one has first come to Him for rescue. Consider, as we read on, what this phrase means in the context of Romans.

5   ... *is for Jesus' name's sake (v. 5):* Once again our thinking is corrected. The goal of gospel proclamation is not our benefit, but that Jesus' name might be honoured.

6   ... *applies to everybody (v. 5):* The extent of Paul's ministry is to 'all the Gentiles'. The word used here, however, means 'nations', so that Paul's ministry is to all people rather than to the Gentiles as distinct from the Jews. The inhabitants of Rome, of course, fall within the terms of this remit (v. 6)!

## ◆ The Roman Christians (v. 7)

Paul's greeting to his readers contains ideas that will become major themes in his letter. God's love for these people (see 5:8) and His calling of them (see 1:5–6) are the basis for their identity as Christians, while grace (see 3:24) and peace (see 5:1) are prime aspects of Christian living.

## 8–15 PAUL'S LONG-TERM GOSPEL COMMITMENT TO THE ROMAN CHRISTIANS

If it was not Paul who first brought the gospel to them (see Introducing Paul's Letter to the Romans), how is he entitled to write to them? The answer lies in his ongoing personal commitment to all Gentiles, including these Christians in Rome.

## ◆ He prays for them (vv. 8–10)

Paul remembers them before God frequently and regularly, thanking Him for their faith and praying for them. His comment that their faith 'is being reported all over the world' reminds us that this church stands at the heart of the Roman empire, and so bears an unparalleled responsibility. Since their gospel message will be carried everywhere, it is vital that it should be correct.

## ◆ He longs to see them to encourage them (vv. 11–13)

Paul's purpose in visiting them is that both they and he may be built up as believers. There is no need to speculate as to the precise nature of the 'spiritual gift' he wishes to impart. Paul does not use the phrase for 'spiritual gift' that he uses in ch. 12 or in 1 Corinthians 12, and here he is non-specific, using the word 'some', so such speculation detracts from his meaning, which is quite clear. He longs that they may strengthen one another in their mutual faith. This reciprocal encouragement is explained well in the NASB: he wishes 'to be encouraged together with you, among you, each of us by the other's faith, both yours and mine'. So far his plans to see them have been frustrated, but nevertheless his desire is to 'have a harvest' among them. Although there would doubtless be outsiders whom he would wish to evangelize, the context demands that this 'harvest' refers principally to the fruit of his work among the Roman Christians, in encouraging their faith and making them strong (vv. 11–12).

◆ **He is eager to preach the gospel to them (vv. 14–15)**
Paul has said that his commission (vv. 1, 5) takes him to the whole world, across all linguistic, cultural and class barriers – literally 'to Greeks and Barbarians' – which is why he is so eager to proclaim the gospel to the Romans as well. Here we should sit up and take note. We would not expect that Christians who have been given such glowing references as those mentioned in v. 8 should need to hear the gospel. Surely they understand it already? It must be that Christians need to hear the gospel, too.

## 16–17 RE: GOD'S POWERFUL SAVING GOSPEL
These two crucial verses outline the central theme of the letter, summarizing the thesis that Paul will develop in the rest of his letter. They also explain why he feels 'bound' to the Gentiles and why he is so eager to preach the gospel to the Romans. Verse 16 is linked to v. 15 by the word 'for' (not shown in the NIV), which means that vv. 16–17 should be seen as a chain of logical clauses which explain the reason for Paul's ministry:

◆ **For Paul is not ashamed of the gospel … (v. 16)**
It is worth considering, as we read on, why Paul might be tempted to be ashamed of God's gospel or, literally, 'be disappointed by' what it delivers.

◆ **… because it is the power of God for salvation … (v. 16)**
When we think of God acting powerfully in order to save people, we think of events like the Exodus, but Paul is talking about the gospel. The gospel is the powerful means by which God saves people.

◆ **… for everyone who believes … (v. 16)**
Who is saved by it? Everyone who believes. The Jews have priority, but all the Gentiles are included. Chapters 9–11 will explain more about God's plans for both groups of people, and the role to be played by an individual's belief, or faith, will be explained in 3:27–4:5.

◆ **… For in the gospel a righteousness from God is revealed … (v. 17)**
The gospel reveals 'the righteousness of God' (a better translation). This is a major subject in Paul's letter (see Section Notes on 1:18–4:25 for comments on Paul's use of the word 'righteousness'),

and the words point us to the God-centredness of the gospel, teaching us that it is principally about God, what He is like and what He has done through Christ. The phrase 'the righteousness of God' could refer both to the righteous *state* that He confers on people and to the righteous *way* in which He saves people (by the death of Jesus on the cross), and we shall see that both are appropriate: He righteously makes people righteous. Why and how God does this, we shall see.

◆ **... a righteousness that is by faith from first to last ... (v. 17)**
The phrase 'by faith from first to last' (literally 'from faith to/for faith') has produced a plethora of interpretations. The options seem to be: (a) 'starting by faith and continuing by faith'; (b) 'through God's faithfulness, for man's faith'; or (c) 'faith and faith alone'. We think (a) is the most likely.

◆ **... as it is written: 'The righteous will live by faith' (v. 17)**
By quoting from Habakkuk (see OT notes) Paul shows that the gospel being revealed is consistent with OT revelation (cf. v. 2). God has always saved by faith, as we shall learn in 3:27–4:25. Furthermore, the gospel provides the answer to Habakkuk's question as to how God can remain just and, at the same time, keep His promises.

# Key themes and application

The focus of this opening passage is Paul's outline of the gospel.

◆ **The gospel is from God and about God**
The first essential issue with which Paul confronts us in Romans is that the gospel message is God-centred. It comes from Him and it is all about Him. Both truths have vitally important applications.

First, the gospel is not ours to alter in any way. It is a message that comes from God and we are to pass it on as it is given to us. This should encourage us in evangelism. We don't have to think of a new message for those who don't believe, we must merely be faithful to His message, which is Paul's message, outlined here. Also, we can leave God to be responsible for His gospel: if people are offended by it, it may be that they will take it out on us, but ultimately they should take it up with Him.

Second, as we consider the gospel we must acknowledge God as its subject. It is a message about Him – His character and His action through Christ. One of our greatest errors, therefore, is to place ourselves at the heart of our message, so that we suggest to friends that there is something missing in their lives, that there is a 'God-shaped hole' that only He can fill. We must beware of slipping into such a human-centred message, particularly when such a slant will always be more popular. To do this would be to misrepresent the message with which God has entrusted us. The gospel is His solution to His problem (a problem summarized by Habakkuk – see OT notes). If we want to see God working powerfully in His world, we should proclaim His message. 'Power evangelism' is the business of telling His gospel.

## ✦ The gospel is about Jesus and for Jesus

Equally at the centre of the Father's gospel is His Son. Again, we need to be reminded that the message is not about us but, rather, that it is about Jesus, the promised Messiah and Lord of all (see Text Notes). It is striking how easily we sideline Jesus in our evangelism, and yet in fact it is not possible to tell people the 'Evangel' (the gospel) without mentioning Jesus. Remembering His identity, and His absolute authority over all, we need to ask where we stand in relation to Him. Furthermore, telling people God's message about Jesus should be done not for our reward but for the honour of His name.

## ✦ The gospel demands a response of faith

People everywhere are called to the obedience of faith. It is important to recognize that the gospel does demand such a response. Very often the Christian message is presented in a 'take it or leave it' style because we are so keen not to offend, but in doing this we are being unfaithful to God's gospel and showing little appreciation of who Jesus is. We would do better to expect people to be offended by the call for them to obey God – or at least we should not be surprised if they do take offence. The gospel *is* radical and it *should* effect radical change.

## ✦ The gospel is for Jews and Gentiles

The gospel is for everyone. Consider different people groups: Muslims, Buddhists, Hindus, atheists, agnostics, the lost and lonely, the successful and happy, friends, family, colleagues, ourselves … Do we think, speak, act and pray as though the gospel were for all of them, equally? Paul's worldwide vision for the gospel exposes our parochial short-sightedness.

It is also worth considering the implications of Paul teaching this message to the Christians in Rome. We are easily tempted to think that we can move on from the basic gospel. Our confusion stems, possibly, from the false distinction we tend to make between coming to faith and the process of growing to maturity. Paul, though, has just one message, for unbeliever and believer alike, and it is God's gospel, about His Son. The message of Romans, therefore, is for us.

♦ **The gospel governs Paul's ministry**

Paul is often misrepresented as harsh and fanatical, and his teaching is explained away as being a product of his background and society. But the implication of this passage is that to reject Paul's teaching is to reject God's gospel and Christ's ambassador.

It is hard to ignore, in this preliminary part of his letter, Paul's deep concern for his readers and his personal commitment to them.

## Unanswered questions

♦ How does God's gospel reveal God's righteousness?
♦ Why is it 'by faith'?
♦ Why might we be tempted to be ashamed of the gospel?
♦ From what do we need to be saved?

## The aim of this study

To consider the extent to which our gospel message is the same as Paul's gospel message. Is ours, like his, centred on God and Jesus?

## Suggested questions

♦ If someone asked you what you believe as a Christian, what would you say? Or think of the last time you had the opportunity to tell someone the gospel. What did you say?

## 1–7 FROM: PAUL, A SERVANT OF GOD'S GOSPEL. TO: THE ROMAN CHRISTIANS

◆ What does Paul achieve by expanding his greeting in vv. 1–7?
◆ In these verses, Paul gives an outline of the gospel he serves. Draw up a table and fill in what he says about the gospel, its source, its background history, its content, the required response, to whom it applies, its goal.
◆ To what extent, in each category, and how does our message differ from his?

## 8–15 BACKGROUND: PAUL'S LONG-TERM GOSPEL COMMITMENT TO THE ROMAN CHRISTIANS

◆ What is Paul's aim in vv. 8–15? Why does he tell them these things?
◆ Why does Paul want to see them?
  – How will he seek to encourage them?
  – What does he mean, that he wants to 'have a harvest' among them? Why is this surprising in the light of v. 8? What are the implications of this for us?
  – Why does he want to preach the gospel among them?
◆ Summarize how we see Paul's ongoing commitment to the Roman Christians.

## 16–17 RE: GOD'S POWERFUL SAVING GOSPEL

*(NB: Verse 16, in the Greek, begins with the word 'for'.)*

◆ What is it about the gospel that makes Paul preach it un-ashamedly?
◆ How does Paul's description of what demonstrates the power of God contrast with our thinking? What can we learn from this?
◆ What is this powerful saving gospel about?
◆ What is the point of the quotation from Habakkuk?
◆ Trace Paul's argument from v. 15 to v. 17. Why does he want to preach the gospel to the Romans?
◆ Consider the first question again. How can Paul's teaching about the gospel help us in our evangelism? In what areas does our thinking most need to be changed?

# SECTION NOTES:
# Romans 1:18–4:25

In the first major section of his letter Paul explains the very heart of the good news revealed by the gospel – righteousness (or 'justification') by faith (1:16–17).

## Righteousness

In the original Greek the same root gives rise to four words meaning 'righteous' and 'just' (*dikaios*), 'righteousness' (*dikaiosyne*) and 'justify' (*dikaioo*); these words are all essential to our understanding of this section.

'Righteousness' is the attribute of acting consistently in a good and right way. As such, it finds its complete expression in the character of God Himself. God always acts rightly, in accordance with His nature and promises, and His perfection in this regard is the standard against which every person is measured.

The implications of this, for this section, are manifold. It means that God must punish sin and therefore must take action against the unrighteousness evident in us. Yet it also means that His promises to save a people must also stand.

The extraordinary good news of the gospel is about how God can make us righteous, without compromising His own righteousness.

Paul explains how it is that people can only be justified (made righteous) by faith and how God has made this possible through Christ.

The good news, about how God can make people righteous, is set against the backdrop of our utter condemnation and our total powerlessness to do anything to save ourselves. And so this section falls approximately into two halves, in which Paul explains first the problem and then the solution:

◆ **The problem: God's wrath at our unrighteousness**
The hopeless and helpless situation for all humankind (1:18–3:20)
◆ **God's solution: God justly makes people righteous**
We may all benefit from what He has done, by faith (3:21–4:25)

## Key themes

◆ **All humankind is unrighteous and condemned**
The case against humankind is both comprehensive and conclusive. Paul starts by speaking of all people everywhere, explaining our conscious, wilful rejection of our creator, and then turns to God's reaction to this rebellion: in the present, He condemns us to lives contaminated by malice and selfishness (1:18–32), and in the future we will face His wrath. Paul then focuses in on the Jews, who might seek to exclude themselves from this verdict on account of their religious pedigree, but shockingly he finds them equally guilty; they rightly face final condemnation on judgment day (2:1–3:8). This is Paul's conclusion regarding all humankind, in 3:9–20.
◆ **God is righteous**
The righteousness of God Himself (see above box) is a major theme in Romans. Paul asserts above all things that God is righteous and that this is demonstrated in two ways. First it is seen in judgment, as He condemns those guilty of rebellion (3:1–8). Then His righteousness is also seen in salvation. Chapter 3:21–26 outlines how God justly enables people to become righteous, by presenting Jesus Christ to atone for our sin, through His substitutionary sacrifice.

### ◆ God makes people righteous by faith, not by works

A critically important aspect of 'the problem' for humankind is that we are completely unable to make ourselves righteous. For the Jews it is a shock to be told this, that not only are they condemned for having broken the Law, but also that they cannot be made righteous by observing the Law. No-one can be good enough for God.

In the last part of the section (3:27–4:25) Paul explains that we can only be made righteous by faith; this is the only way that we can appropriate the benefits of what God has done through Christ. He teaches that faith involves trusting God's promises of salvation, and he points to Abraham as an example of how to do this. By referring to Abraham, Paul is demonstrating that there is no contradiction between the Old and New Testaments: righteousness by faith has always been God's way of saving His people.

As we come to the end of the section we see the heart of God's solution to the problem posed by 1:18–3:20. Although the whole of humankind, Jews as well as Gentiles, faces God's righteous wrath and condemnation, both Jews and Gentiles *can be* saved and made righteous by trusting in what God has done through the death of Jesus Christ. The approximate structure of the argument is shown below. Notice in particular the turning point at 3:21.

## Structure

**1:18–2:29** Jews and Gentiles are both unrighteous
    **3:1–8** God is righteous in judgment
    **3:9–19** No distinction: all have sinned
      **3:20** No righteousness by the Law

**BUT NOW ...**

  **3:21–22a** Righteousness by faith, apart from the Law
    **3:22–24** No distinction: all have sinned and all who believe are justified
    **3:24–26** God is righteous in salvation, through Jesus' death
**3:27–4:25** Jews and Gentiles alike are made righteous by faith

NB: 'The Law' *(nomos)* has several different meanings and only the individual context will determine which one applies. The NIV translates some occurrences of the word with a capital letter, but this does not correspond to any distinction in the Greek. Here are some examples of different meanings:

**3:19** 'whatever the law says' – meaning the whole of the Old Testament (and referring particularly to the quotations in vv. 10–18);

**3:20** 'observing the law' – meaning obedience to the commandments given to Moses in Exodus, Leviticus, Numbers and Deuteronomy;

**3:21** 'apart from law' – meaning apart from obedience to these commandments;

**3:21** 'the Law and the Prophets' – meaning the books of Genesis to Deuteronomy (and the books of the prophets).

# ROMANS 1:18–32

## Context

Paul begins his letter to the Roman Christians by telling them of his commitment to them and his desire to preach the gospel to them (1:11, 13, 15). He also gives an outline of what will be his main subject: God's gospel that is centred on Jesus. He ends his introduction by telling them that he is unashamed of this gospel because it concerns God's character and activity: it is the powerful means by which God saves everyone who believes. At this point in the letter a major question arises: 'From what do people need to be saved?' Verses 18–32 will start to answer that question.

## Structure

- **1:18** Paul's thesis: God is angry with humankind's unrighteousness
- **1:19–20** Humankind's rejection of God is inexcusable
- **1:21–32** God gives sinful humankind over to their own sin (this is explained in three repeated cycles: vv. 21–24, 25–27 and 28–32)

## Old Testament background

**God's revelation of Himself:** God reveals Himself to humankind as the one and only almighty creator and sustainer of everything. He is perfectly holy (Isaiah 6:1–5) and unable to tolerate evil

(Habakkuk 1:13); He has no equal and no-one can stand against Him (Isaiah 40:21–25). The OT 'story so far' tells us that rebellion against Him is inherently foolish and leads invariably to judgment.

**Israel's rebellion:** The heart of Israel's rebellion is seen in terms not of her wrongdoing but of her unfaithfulness to God (Hosea 1:2). This is because God's greatest concern for His people is that they should relate to Him, as seen in the first three of the ten commandments (Exodus 20). The idolatry into which Israel fell exemplifies her rejection of Him.

**God's wrath:** This is His active anger against the rebellion of humankind. From the time of the Fall onwards (Genesis 3:14–24), it is a major theme of the Old Testament. Sometimes it is seen immediately, as when an individual is killed for doing what is forbidden (e.g. 2 Samuel 6:6–7), and sometimes it is very dramatic, as in the destruction of an entire city (e.g. Genesis 19). As time goes on, however, it is expressed mostly as the promise of future judgment (e.g. Isaiah chs 1–3).

# Text notes

## 18 GOD IS ANGRY WITH HUMANKIND'S UNRIGHTEOUSNESS

### ◆ The wrath of God

Verse 18 is linked to the preceding verses by the word 'for'. Thus we are given the reason why God's saving gospel is needed: all humankind needs to be saved from God's wrath, His anger. This is an uncomfortable subject, but one on which we need to be clear. God is angry because of our wickedness, and this consists of our wilful refusal to acknowledge the truth about Him.

It is commonly held that we need to be saved from our sins, but the sobering truth is that we need to be saved from God Himself, for His anger is personal and active. Just as He reveals His righteousness (v. 17), so He reveals His wrath, and the purpose of both is to lead people to repentance and faith.

We are mistaken when we wonder how a righteous and loving God can be angry. The opposite of love is not wrath but indifference (just as the opposite of wrath is also indifference). We must not equate God's anger with our own, which is frequently out of control, selfish and irrational, i.e. fundamentally unrighteous. It is precisely because God is righteous that He is angry at our sin.

NB: We also see a hint of how God's solution addresses the problem. He is angry at our unrighteousness ('wickedness' in the NIV, v. 18) but His good news concerns a righteousness that comes *from* Him (v. 17).

## 19–20 HUMANKIND'S REJECTION OF GOD IS INEXCUSABLE

These verses explain the phrase that is central to Paul's argument: '[they] ... suppress the truth by their wickedness'. They make plain both the truth that people are suppressing and also why it matters that they do so.

◆ **God has revealed Himself in creation (v. 20)**
Verse 19 states an essential principle of revelation, that we can know about God because God has clearly revealed Himself to us through creation. The world around us tells at least two fundamental truths: that the God who created it is powerful and that He is worthy of worship.

◆ **People are without excuse (v. 20)**
Not only is the evidence in creation available to all, without exception, but also this evidence has been clearly seen and understood, which leaves us with no defence when we suppress this knowledge. This thought is difficult to take on board. We struggle to understand how it is that people know these things about God from the world around them, calling to mind those who don't, but Paul's point is clear enough. These things *are* understood, even if they are instinctively and immediately suppressed. It is important to be clear about the point that Paul is making: God's self-revelation in creation does not save people, but rather, because they do know better, it makes their rebellion culpable.

## 21–32 GOD GIVES SINFUL HUMANKIND OVER TO THEIR OWN SIN

Here Paul presents us with a devastating analysis of the essence and consequences of humankind's rebellion against their creator. Three times he identifies the same pattern: our rebellion, which involves the exchange of something good for something bad, as in vv. 23, 25 and 28, is followed by God's response, described in the phrase, 'He gave them over', as in vv. 24, 26 and 28.

### ◆ The nature of sin (vv. 21–23)

*Sin is rebellion against God:* The conventional understanding that sin is wrongdoing, i.e. an example of bad behaviour, completely misses the personal nature of our rebellion against our creator. We must distinguish between 'sin', meaning rebellion against God, and 'sins', meaning the outward manifestations of our rebellion.

Our rejection of God results in a change in the object of our affections. They do not stay in a vacuum, but are redirected. We turn our devotion elsewhere, to images (v. 23) and created things (v. 25). Paul's classic description of idolatry reminds us of Israel's worship of the golden calf in Exodus 32, but it applies no less, of course, to our present-day pursuit of possessions or our devotion to alternative ideologies. Ultimately, since all idolatry is a matter of our own decision, we are replacing God with ourselves.

*Sin is wilful:* People do not 'fall into sin' by accident, in unconscious rebellion. On the contrary, though they know the right response to the creator (v. 21), they deliberately reject Him. This rejection is made explicit in the active 'exchange' that is made when they give up their knowledge of God (vv. 23, 25, 28).

*Sin is stupid:* In the Old Testament, idolatry is not only forbidden (Exodus 20:4) but also ridiculed (Isaiah 44:9–20). The folly of our break for independence is exposed in the absurdity of the decisions we make, preferring mere images to the immortal God (v. 23), accepting a lie, rather than the truth (v. 25), and thinking it not 'worthwhile' to retain the knowledge of the creator who gave us everything. These preposterously 'bad deals' reveal the futility of our thinking and our darkened foolish hearts (v. 21).

### ◆ God's wrathful response – He gives them over (vv. 24–31)

The words 'therefore' (v. 24), 'because of this' (v. 26) and 'since' (v. 28) tell us that God's handing over of humankind is His specific response to our rebellion. There is a dreadful reciprocity in

His judgment against us: when humankind rejects God, God rejects humankind. It is possible to underplay God's role in this. He does more than merely leave us to ourselves; He actively hands us over to further rebellious acts. Handing us over means condemning us to be enslaved to our sinful selves.

When God hands us over, we are entirely corrupted: unclean ('uncleanness' is a better translation than 'sexual impurity' in v. 24, although v. 24b implies that sexual impurity is the result), wanting what is detestable (vv. 26–27) and unable to think rightly (v. 28). The end result is all the sins that are listed.

It may require a big change in our thinking if we are to recognize these sinful acts for what they are, not *the cause* of God's wrath, but *the present evidence for its reality* (v. 18). Paul writes about two categories:

*Sexual sins (vv. 24–27):* The focus on sexual sins should not surprise us. If God made humankind in His own image, male and female (Genesis 2:23–25), then humankind's rejection of God is bound to lead to the undermining of these primary relationships. Homosexuality is named, therefore, not because it is a greater sin than any other, but because it is the clearest evidence of a rejection of God's order in creation.

*Every kind of unrighteousness (vv. 28–31):* The list in these verses is overwhelming and comprehensive. There is no scale of 'better' or 'worse' sins – envy, for example, is placed next to murder. All kinds of sins are included, and the inventing of new ones is anticipated. It is a list in which everyone can find themselves, for all have committed some of these sins. And so the conclusion is unavoidable: all humankind is under God's wrath for their rejection of Him.

◆ **Wrath in the present and in the future (v. 32)**

In the Bible the primary focus of God's wrath is in the future, but in this passage it is an important feature of Paul's argument to demonstrate that it is also being revealed in the present, in all the sinful actions of humankind. Verse 32, however, reminds us of future wrath: those who sin deserve death. Thus the chronological pattern in this passage is as follows:

**Revelation by God**
**Rejection by humankind**
**God is angry**
**Handed over to sins**
**Death**

Paul is saying that we know our sins deserve such punishment, but this knowledge doesn't bring about any change in us at all (v. 32).

# Key themes and application

### ◆ God's wrath is being revealed

It is critical that we understand Paul's diagnosis of the human problem and so recognize our absolute hopelessness before God. If we don't do this, we ourselves won't understand the solution and our evangelism will slide into heresy. If, wrongly, we identify 'sins' as the problem with the world, then we will look for moral reform, teaching religion in order to help people live 'better lives'. If, on the other hand, we see our problem correctly, that God must punish our rebellion and that He has already handed us over in judgment, then we will realize that we are absolutely powerless to alter our plight. God's revelation in creation means there is no such thing as 'those who have never heard'; everyone knows enough to be found guilty. We are all sitting under God's righteous judgment because of our rejection of Him, our creator, and we all face the certainty of death. There is no solution unless God provides one: it is entirely up to Him to rescue us, and He will do so only if He chooses.

Our society completely fails to understand the helplessness of our situation. Most people acknowledge that something is wrong, but they suggest that we should try to make ourselves better. All solutions like this are a waste of time. The moral rearmament or 'back to basics' campaigns proposed by the media, the government and, often, the church address the symptoms rather than the disease. They very rarely mention our rebellion against our creator, and talk of His wrath is even rarer. Paul tells us that it is *too late* to do anything about our sins, because we are already under God's judgment.

◆ **Sin is rebellion against God**

Sin is the personal rejection of our creator rather than doing things that are wrong. An incorrect focus on the latter will encourage us to think that we are not very guilty because, in our own eyes, we commit few sins; we will compare ourselves favourably with others whose lives contain more sins than our own. Most people do not think of themselves as sinful, because they do not know what sin is. A right definition of sin teaches us that we are all rebels in God's world: we don't want God to be God over us. Again, our evangelism will reflect our understanding of this.

◆ **God responds to sin by handing humankind over to sins**

When we look at our world and see the sins described in vv. 26, 27 and 29–31, we should be able to understand that God has 'given us over'. It is ironic that the world sees many of these things as defining our freedom, when in fact we are slaves to them; we cannot but sin. Our sins do not demonstrate our independence from God, as some might suppose. They should be seen as evidence of the fact that He is angry at our rebellion against Him and, furthermore, as a warning signal of worse to come. Not only are we under judgment now, but we are also facing certain death.

## Unanswered questions

◆ 'Yes, but I'm not as bad as that!'
◆ 'Yes, but I'm a Jew – one of God's chosen people.'
◆ 'How is God going to solve this problem righteously?'

## The aim of this study

We should be devastated by the truth that all humankind is facing God's wrath because everyone has wilfully rejected Him.

## Suggested questions

◆ If you were to stop people on the street and ask them what they associate with sin and judgment, how might they answer? What do Christians generally think of sin and judgment (when not giving a 'textbook' answer)?

## 18 GOD IS ANGRY AT HUMANKIND'S UNRIGHTEOUSNESS
◆ How does v. 18 follow on from v. 17? (In the Greek, v. 18 begins with the word 'for'.) Why is God angry?

## 19–20 HUMANKIND'S REJECTION OF GOD IS INEXCUSABLE
◆ Why is God's anger fully justified?
◆ 'Surely God can't blame people who have never come into contact with the gospel?' How would Paul respond?

## 21–32 GOD GIVES SINFUL HUMANKIND OVER TO THEIR OWN SIN
◆ These verses give us a deep insight into the nature of sin. What are the hallmarks of our wickedness?
◆ How would Paul correct the following statements?
    – 'We fall into sin' (i.e. we can't really help ourselves)
    – 'Sinning means we are free'

◆ How does God respond to humankind's rejection of Him?
◆ Why does Paul include sexual sins? (What truth are people suppressing?)
◆ Why does Paul include such a long list of 'sins' in vv. 29–31? What does their existence tell us about our world? Of what are they a sign?

◆ How do we normally think God views sin?
    – How should this passage correct our thinking?
◆ How should we correct the following views?
    – 'The main problem with sin is that it messes up our lives'
    – 'In response to this passage we should stop sinning and live better lives'
◆ How should this passage affect what we say in evangelism?

**Study 3**

# ROMANS 2:1–29

## Context

Having outlined his gospel message and explained his commission to preach it, in 1:1–17, Paul has told the Romans of the devastating situation facing humankind. Everyone is under God's wrath (v. 18) because everyone has wilfully rejected their creator, refusing to glorify Him or give thanks to Him (v. 21), turning away from Him in favour of things in this world (v. 23) and exchanging His truth for a lie (v. 25). God's wrath is now manifested by His handing us over to our sinful desires, and the result is the mass of sinful thoughts and actions listed in vv. 25–31. We should infer that we have all been handed over; God is angry with everyone, we are all facing death (v. 32) and there is nothing we can do about it.

It is possible, however, that some may wish to exclude themselves from Paul's analysis. This would include any who think themselves better than others and especially the Jews, who would have good reasons for thinking so (see OT notes). So the apostle now devotes his attention to establishing that there are no exceptions.

## Structure

2:1–5   'You, who think yourselves better than others, will not escape judgment'

2:6–16   The nature of God's final judgment

2:17–29   The Law will not save the Jews because they disobey it

# Old Testament background

**The day of God's wrath:** God's promises of great blessing are accompanied by promises of a terrible future judgment. In the Old Testament the people of Israel suffered God's wrath many times. By far the worst was when the nation was exiled to Babylon, yet even this was only a foretaste of God's final judgment. This will be a terrible day when God will punish 'all the arrogant and every evildoer' (Malachi 4:1). Several other places in the Old Testament testify to the fact that God judges according to people's deeds – see Psalm 62:12 and Hosea 12:2.

**The Jews:** God promised Abraham that through his family the effects of the Fall would be reversed (Genesis 12:1–3). Abraham's descendants, rescued by God from slavery in Egypt, were given the extraordinary and unique privilege of being God's chosen people. Some key aspects of this relationship are:

*Circumcision:* Having promised that He would be the God of Abraham's descendants for ever, God commanded Abraham that he and every male descendant should be circumcised. This would be the outward sign of the covenant (or agreement) that He was making with Abraham. God has made it clear, however, that the outward sign is not enough: what counts is 'circumcision of the heart', a complete commitment to love, serve and obey the LORD (Deuteronomy 10:12–16).

*The Law:* At Mount Sinai the people of Israel are given the Law, which tells them how to live as God's rescued people. If they are to remain His treasured possession among the nations, set apart as His holy nation, they must obey this Law (Exodus 19:5). To understand the significance of the Law for the Jews, consider Psalm 119.

*'A guide for the blind' (2:19):* God had also promised, through Abraham, to extend His blessing to the rest of the nations (Genesis 12:3). Israel was to demonstrate a model relationship with God and, as 'a kingdom of priests' (Exodus 19:6), to represent Him to the world. Yet, despite all these privileges, Israel strayed from her God, repeatedly breaking His Law, as the Old Testament records, and causing His name to be profaned by the surrounding nations (Isaiah 52:5; Ezekiel 36:22).

# Text notes

## 1–5 'YOU, WHO THINK YOURSELVES BETTER THAN OTHERS, WILL NOT ESCAPE JUDGMENT'

Although Paul's thesis in 1:18–32 – that everyone is facing God's wrath against their sin – is in itself conclusive, it is not hard to imagine that many people, and particularly the Jews, would distance themselves from the accusation. Indeed, unlike those in 1:32, they would express their wholehearted disapproval of those who commit the sins of 1:29–31. The apostle now addresses such people and his verdict is unequivocal. It comes in three stages:

♦ **'You are condemning yourself' (v. 1)**
Far from setting yourself apart from those who face condemnation, to acknowledge that you know right from wrong is to hoist yourself with your own petard, for the simple reason that 'you who pass judgment do the same things'. The moralizer himself commits some of the sins in 1:29–31 but, by his own admission, he knows better and therefore has no excuse.

♦ **'You will not escape God's perfect judgment' (vv. 2–5)**
Throughout the Old Testament it is understood that when God judges, He does so with absolute justice – 'fully in accord with the facts' (Moo, p. 131). There is no loophole, therefore, for the person who 'plays God' in judging others (v. 1) and yet sins himself. God will not ignore any sins.

It is important to hold 1:18–32 in our minds here, remembering that the very existence of the moralizer's sins – which to us may appear very few – betrays the fact that God has 'given him over' for his wilful rejection of Him as his creator: he too is guilty of deliberate, self-centred idolatry.

♦ **'By not repenting, you are storing up wrath for yourself' (vv. 4–5)**
Having established the guilt of those who would deny his diagnosis, Paul goes on to challenge their refusal to repent. Verse 4 gives us an astonishing perspective on the present scenario facing humankind. Standing under God's wrath in the devastation of 1:18–32, we are also enjoying 'the riches of his kindness, tolerance and patience'. All we deserve is that God should destroy us instantly, but He delays final judgment, giving us time to

repent. By not repenting, we show our contempt for Him and thus make things worse for ourselves, literally 'treasuring up' wrath against ourselves. God's wrath is seen, therefore, both in the present, as He hands us over to our sinful desires (1:24) and, more dreadfully, in the future, on 'the day of God's wrath' (see OT notes) when He will judge with absolute and final justice.

## 6–16 THE NATURE OF GOD'S FINAL JUDGMENT
Having introduced the idea of the day of God's wrath, Paul expands on some of the underlying principles of His judgment.

◆ **Judgment will be according to our works (vv. 6–8)**
These verses must be taken in their context and read carefully. Paul is not saying that some will earn their way to heaven. His point is not that we are saved by our works, but that we are judged by our works, because they reveal the underlying attitude of our hearts. This has always been the case (see OT notes), and vv. 7–8 spell it out:
*To those who do good, He will give eternal life (v. 7):* Paul picks up the vocabulary of 1:21–23 in order to define what it is that doing good reveals. It reveals a right response to God's revelation of Himself, shown in giving Him glory and honour, and in holding on to Him as the immortal God instead of exchanging Him for images. Chapter 1 has told us that *no-one* does in fact respond like this, as is shown by people's persistence in doing evil (cf. 2:7); Paul's conclusion (3:10–20) will show even more clearly that v.7 is entirely hypothetical.
*For those who do evil, there will be wrath and anger (v. 8):* Correspondingly, 'following' evil betrays a rebellious heart that is defined in familiar terms. Instead of seeking God's glory (1:21), we seek our own, and we reject the truth of God in favour of a lie (1:25).

◆ **Judgment will be retributive (vv. 7–10)**
On judgment day, people will get exactly what they deserve. It is easy to take this aspect of God's judgment for granted, the fact that there will be no miscarriages of justice; God will reward those who have done good and punish those who have done evil.

◆ **Judgment will be impartial (vv. 9–11)**
Paul makes it clear that everyone will be judged in this way. He has the whole world in his sights, categorizing 'every human being' as either Jew or Gentile, and asserting that no favouritism will be shown towards God's historic people. It is hard for us to capture the shock that this statement would have given Paul's first readers: explaining the reason for it will take him until 3:20.

◆ **Having or not having the Law makes no difference … (v. 12)**
In the Greek v. 12 begins with the word 'for', which indicates the beginning of the explanation as to why Jew and Gentile will both be judged. This sentence may also be seen as Paul's main point, on which he will expand until the end of the chapter, with vv. 14–17 explaining how Gentiles perish apart from the Law and vv. 17–19 explaining how Jews are judged by the Law. For both Jew and Gentile, however, the outcome is the same …

*… because obedience to the Law is what counts (v. 13):* This is the principle that will underlie the argument in vv. 17–29, concerning the Jews. It also appears in vv. 14–16, where Paul points to the evidence that the requirements of the Law are written on the Gentiles' hearts. Both Jews and Gentiles disobey the Law.

*… because the Gentiles do know what is right (vv. 14–16):* Paul's argument here is not so much that Gentiles do not sin, but rather that they do not sin all the time. This testifies to the existence of their moral consciences – but they do not obey their consciences any more than the Jews obey the written Law. All Gentiles *do* sin and equally deserve to face God's wrath.

The words 'this will take place' (v. 16 in the NIV) do not appear in the Greek, nor do the parentheses around vv. 14 and 15. In v. 16 Paul finishes the line of argument begun in v. 13 by asserting that when the Gentiles stand before Jesus on the day of judgment, their consciences will have already told them whether their deeds were good or evil.

## 17–29 THE LAW WILL NOT SAVE THE JEWS BECAUSE OF THEIR DISOBEDIENCE

We should not dismiss the apparent arrogance of v. 17 without understanding the issues. The word 'brag' (NIV) comes from the

Greek word that is translated as 'rejoice' in 5:2. It has the root idea of boasting or glorying in something (either good or bad), and the Jews had plenty to brag about. We may think that Paul's conclusion is unavoidable, but for the Jews there is the essential issue of the Law. God had established a relationship with their ancestors which – they would argue – put them in a category entirely separate from the Gentiles (see OT notes).

◆ **'You privileged Jews break the Law and dishonour God's name'**
**(vv. 17–23)**
Although we can tell that Paul is preparing to turn on the Jews, we should note how vv. 17–20 accurately describe the privileges and role that God had given Israel (see OT notes). As a nation they were indeed in an extraordinary position, having God's Law to instruct them and having been called to be a light to the Gentiles (e.g. Isaiah 60:1–3). In v. 21, however, Paul's argument strikes home: they do not obey the Law that they are supposed to teach. Stealing, adultery and sacrilege ('robbing temples' in the NIV) are classic hallmarks of Israel's rebellious history (cf. Jeremiah 7:9; Hosea 2:1–13); they break the Law in which they boast and thus God's name is dishonoured. Far from being a light to the Gentiles, they, as a result of their rebellion, have caused the Gentiles to blaspheme God's name. As if to add irony to condemnation, it is the Law itself that predicts this (v. 24, quoting Isaiah 52:5).

◆ **'Your Law-breaking means you are not true Jews' (vv. 25–27)**
Verse 25, in the Greek, begins with the word 'for', and explains that the Jews are guilty in spite of having circumcision and the Law. A Jew would appeal to his circumcision as being a sign of his membership of God's people (see OT notes), but, Paul says, Law-breakers are uncircumcised. Circumcision was always coupled with an obligation to obey God (Genesis 17:1), so Israel's rebellion makes this membership badge invalid. Even more shocking, however, are the statements about the Gentiles: not only will a Law-keeping Gentile be seen as a true Jew, but also he will judge the circumcised Jewish Law-breaker. (We will understand more of this in chs 4 and 9–11.) These would have been devastating words for a Jew to read, for Paul appears to be

demolishing hundreds of years of Jewish heritage and privilege. He goes on to define the true people of God.

◆ **True Jews are circumcised in heart (vv. 28–29)**
Verse 28 should also begin with the word 'for', as Paul continues his argument that circumcision was never meant to be purely physical (see OT notes). He makes a clear distinction between two types:

*The false Jew:* He is characterized by outward, physical circumcision ('of the flesh'), according to the written code; this receives the praise of men. The Jews in general fall into this category.

*The true Jew:* He is characterized by inward circumcision of the heart (Deuteronomy 10:16), according to the spirit (Ezekiel 36:26), and this receives praise from God. And so, because of their Law-breaking and because of their dependence on the outward sign rather than on an inward devotion to God, the Jews have no excuse. They are in the same boat as the rest of humankind, facing the wrath of God, both now and on the day of judgment.

# Key themes and application

◆ **God's wrath is inescapable ...**
In this passage and right through to 3:20, it is as though Paul is cutting off escape routes for those who wish to avoid the conclusions of ch. 1. The application, therefore, is the same as the one he made in 1:18–32, that everyone is facing God's righteous wrath for their rebellion against Him. Paul now applies this specifically:

*... for anyone who thinks of himself as not that bad:* This lesson has to be learned by the person who disapproves of the activities of 1:29–31, thinking of themselves as good enough. In their case, not only is there no excuse and no escape, but also they are actually making things worse for themselves when judgment comes. Whenever, therefore, we shake our heads at the world around us, we are completely missing the point about our own wickedness and God's anger against us. Our excuses show our contempt for God's patience.

*... for the Jew:* The Jew would certainly be included in the above category. Many of us will be unaffected by Paul's point here, but

we must not underestimate how shocking this application would have been at the time. Nothing in Israel's long history of being God's people will save them from His judgment. People sometimes want to put the Jews in a different category and suggest that God will somehow treat them differently, but there is no warrant for this in scripture. Paul does write about God's long-term plans for the Jewish people, but there is no avoiding the truth of their condemnation.

Paul's argument is addressed specifically to the Jews; we cannot apply it directly to ourselves. We have already seen, in ch. 1, that we are condemned with the rest of humankind. There is, however, a reasonable secondary application for someone who ducks the issue in ch. 1, appealing to his religious privileges or experience. If we think that we will escape condemnation by virtue of belonging to a Christian family or having been baptized, or through membership of a particular Christian group at any time, we should feel the force of Paul's argument. We may have such privileges, but we still break God's laws and will therefore be condemned on judgment day.

*(... for those who haven't heard of Jesus):* This is a further implication of Paul's argument. People often question God's justice in judging the person 'in the Amazonian tribe, or brought up in an exclusively Muslim culture' who has heard nothing of the gospel. Paul is quite clear on this: the witness of conscience, added to that of creation, condemns everyone.

◆ **God's future wrathful judgment**

Someone might come to the end of ch. 1 and suppose that if God's judgment means only that He hands us over to do what we want, then it is no big deal. Indeed, that person might see himself as having a good time. Paul's teaching on future judgment changes everything. The idea that hell will mean having more of a good time is totally inaccurate. The future holds out wrath and anger, trouble and distress (vv. 8–9), and the longer we go on in our rebellion, the worse it will get (v. 5). A clear understanding of how terrible the future will be will give us a proper perspective on our present situation, and help us to see how much we need saving.

This is of particular importance in evangelism. We often try to tell our happy, successful, unbelieving friends that they need

Jesus, because of the difference He will make to their lives, whereas much more important is how He can affect their existence after death. If we don't tell people about God's future wrath, they will not see their need for a saviour.

◆ **The basis of God's judgment – what we do**

By understanding more about how God judges, we should understand even more clearly that there is no avoiding His just judgment. Our deeds convict us, because we all do evil. According to Paul, there is no such thing as an exception to the rule: when God judges our deeds, everyone is found wanting because no-one has lived up to His perfect standard of perfect good works. This means that all the saintly, charitable, kind and self-sacrificing people we think of as representing the very best of human philanthropy are in the same terrifying predicament. Their sins demonstrate that they are under God's wrath, that He has handed them over because of their rebellion against Him. Even more seriously, they will face His wrath on the day of judgment.

# Unanswered questions

◆ If God judges the Jews, surely He is undermining all that He promised them in the Old Testament. What about His commitment to them?
◆ Would it ever be possible to persist in doing good (v. 7)?
◆ How can God righteously save anyone?

# The aim of this study

We should realize that the danger ahead of everyone is God's future wrath, because He judges us on the basis of what we do. This is true even for the Jew.

# Suggested questions

◆ Why do people think they don't deserve to face God's judgement? What would your friends say?
◆ According to Paul (by the end of ch. 1), what is the terrible situation facing humankind?

## I–5 YOU, WHO THINK YOURSELVES BETTER THAN OTHERS, WILL NOT ESCAPE JUDGMENT

◆ Whom is Paul addressing at the beginning of ch. 2? Why does this person pass judgment?

◆ What is Paul's instant verdict on those who think themselves better than others?
   – What is the significance of it being the same as that in 1:20?
   – Why do these two groups of people find themselves equally condemned? (Paul gives a couple of reasons.)

◆ Summarize Paul's message to those who disapprove of sinners in God's world.

## 6–16 THE NATURE OF GOD'S FINAL JUDGMENT

◆ How does the nature of God's judgment result in everyone being condemned?
   – What is the *basis* of His judgment? Why does this condemn us? What do our deeds reveal? (Compare the vocabulary of vv. 7–8 with that of 1:21–23.)
   – How does Paul emphasize God's justice and His impartiality in judgment?

◆ In this passage, what is significantly different about God's response to sin, compared with what we read in ch. 1?

◆ People often portray heaven as sterile and boring, and hell as exciting and sociable – 'All my friends will be there.' What does Paul say?

◆ What difference does it make, having or not having the Law (vv. 12–16)? Why will the outcome be the same, either way?

◆ We have already seen that no-one will be immune from judgment because everyone has seen God's revelation in creation (1:19–20). What further evidence against 'those who haven't heard' does Paul indicate in this passage?

## 17–29 THE LAW WILL NOT SAVE THE JEWS BECAUSE OF THEIR DISOBEDIENCE

◆ What does Paul suggest is the Jews' assessment of themselves in relation to God? To what extent is it justified?

◆ What is Paul's argument against the privileged Jews? How does he apply the principle of vv. 12–13?

◆ Circumcision was the badge of membership for the Jews. What does Paul say is the implication of their disobedience?

◆ What is a true Jew, according to Paul? How do Jews in general fall short?

◆ Looking back, what is Paul's purpose in this chapter?

◆ What would Paul say to people who make claims such as the following, and who think they will escape judgement?
  – 'I'll be okay, I've never murdered anyone!'
  – 'I'm a Jew, I'm one of God's people!'
  – 'I've been baptized. I come from a Christian family. I go to church!'

◆ What would be Paul's verdict on: Gandhi, Hitler, us?

◆ What have you learned about God's judgment from this passage?

**Study 4**

# ROMANS 3:1–20

## Context

Paul is still preparing the ground for the rest of the letter by explaining the problem that faces all humankind: the wrath of God, as it is seen in the present and as it will be seen in the future. He has just explained that there are no exceptions to the rule; both Gentiles and Jews will be judged according to what they have done and thus all will be found guilty, because every individual's sins are evidence of that person's rebellion against God. Paul's application of this to the Jews, however, raises important questions about God's integrity. The whole weight of the Old Testament points to God's commitment and faithfulness to His historic people. If they are now facing His judgment, does that mean He is not keeping His promises? If so, doesn't this call into question God's righteousness? Does it mean nothing to be a Jew? Paul addresses these objections in 3:1–20.

## Structure

    **3:1–8** In condemning the Jews, God remains faithful and just
**3:9–20** Everyone, including the Jew, is guilty and is silenced before God

# Old Testament background

**God's revelation to the Jews:** Paul is still dwelling on some of the issues that appeared in ch. 2 (see OT notes for 2:1–29). One of the Jews' greatest privileges is the fact that God has revealed to them both His character and His plans. They know what God is like and also what He is doing in His world; they have been given the Law to teach them how to live as His people, and they have the words of the prophets, containing His promises for the future. All of these things set them apart from any other nation (see Deuteronomy 4:8 and Psalm 147:19–20).

**God's faithfulness and justice:** When God reveals Himself to His people, an essential element of His character is His absolute consistency: the Lord is always true to Himself. This is expressed most clearly in His absolute, unquestionable justice and in His total faithfulness to His promises (Exodus 34:6–7). When He speaks, His words are immutable; He is utterly unlike man in this regard (Numbers 23:19). This is why the question of whether God's condemnation of the Jews shows Him to be faithless is so important. His character might seem to be on the line. It is essential for Paul to show that God is still faithful.

# Text notes

### 1–8 IN CONDEMNING THE JEWS, GOD REMAINS FAITHFUL AND JUST

These verses explore the relationship between God's righteousness and Israel's unbelief. Paul demonstrated in ch. 2 that the Jews, as much as the Gentiles, are under God's condemnation. The question in v. 1 is natural enough: does this mean that there is no advantage at all in being one of God's historic, chosen people? Paul addresses this vital issue by means of a dialogue with an imaginary opponent who raises objections to his argument.

◆ **What about the advantages of being one of God's historic people? (vv. 1–2)**
In answer to this important challenge (see Context), Paul says that the Jews have the privilege of possessing the words of God.

This truth may seem self-evident, but Paul is picking up on a major issue in Israel's history (see OT notes). As Moses tells Israel in Deuteronomy 4:8, 'And what other nation is so great as to have such righteous decrees and laws as this body of laws I am setting before you today?' The Jews know about God's character and His plans and so have more incentive to respond to Him correctly. The other advantages of being a Jew that Paul has in mind are probably those he lists in 9:4–5, but here he is concerned with the Jews being the chief recipients of God's revelation.

◆ **But what about God's faithfulness to His promises? (vv. 3–4)**
The questioner asks whether having the Law is such an advantage, when some Jews don't have faith, i.e. when they don't obey the Law and end up being condemned. Doesn't this prevent God from being faithful, i.e being able to keep His promises to Israel of blessing and rescue? Again, this is a significant objection (see OT notes). Paul's answer is to point out that God's faithfulness to what He has revealed is *also* seen in judgment; He is being true to His word when He condemns, even if He ends up condemning everyone. To prove the principle, Paul points to Psalm 51, in which David confesses his guilt and acknowledges that God's judgment against him is proved right. How God manages to keep His unconditional promises of blessing made to Abraham and his descendants (Genesis 12:1–3), Paul will explain later.

◆ **Is God really just? (vv. 5–8)**
Here Paul posits the argument that God is unfair to judge rebellious Jews because He benefits from their rebellion – when He is shown to be righteous in judgment. Paul challenges this absurd and almost embarrassing 'human' reasoning with a question: if judging the sinful makes God unjust, he says, how could God judge the sinful world at all, as all Jews would have assumed He would (Malachi 4:1)? Paul goes further, though, to demonstrate just how pointless and sinful is this kind of objection, by scornfully restating it twice in vv. 7–8. Rather than vindicating God's integrity, he is condemning ours. He gives no specific answer to the question because the wretchedness of this reasoning is clear: the fact that God is glorified cannot justify falsehood or sin. When we think in this way, we merely give evidence of a depraved mind (1:28) and so justify our own condemnation.

## 9–20 EVERYONE, INCLUDING THE JEW, IS GUILTY AND IS SILENCED BEFORE GOD

With v. 9, Paul comes to the conclusion of the discussion that began in ch. 2, i.e. whether the Jews are any better off than the Gentiles, and he pulls together his argument that all humankind is captive under the power of sin (1:18–2:29). The OT quotations in vv. 10–18 are difficult to analyse neatly, but two verses (vv. 9 and 19) help us understand them.

### ◆ Everyone is under sin, according to the Law (v. 9)

The first words of v. 10, 'as it is written', tell us that the quotations are there to confirm the statement in v. 9, that all people will be judged since all are sinful. In fact, as Paul concludes his argument, he produces quotations that authenticate many of the statements he has already made. He has invented nothing. Rather, God has been saying these things for centuries in the Old Testament:

| Romans 3 | 'As it is written ...' (Old Testament) | 'We have already made the charge' (Romans 1:18–2:29) |
|----------|----------------------------------------|------------------------------------------------------|
| vv. 10–12 | Psalm 14:1–3 and 53:1–3 | The whole of mankind is unrighteous (1:18) having rejected God (1:21, 25, 28) No-one does good (1:26–32; 2:1, 23) |
| vv. 13-17 | Psalm 5:9, 140:3, 10:7, Isaiah 59:7-8 | Sins affect every area of life (1:29-31) |
| v. 18 | Psalm 36:1 | People do not fear God and His judgment (1:32, 2:3-4) |

### ◆ The Law convicts the Jew of sin ... (v. 19)

Although only one of the quotations refers specifically to Jews (vv. 15–17, from Isaiah 59), Paul's point in v. 19 is that anything the Law says, it says to Jews, and will convict them too. For the devout Jew, who has sung the psalms of David in the synagogue all his life, crying to God to punish the wicked (whether the Gentile or the faithless Israelite), it would have come as a great shock to discover that these truths in the psalms actually applied to him as well.

◆ **... so that every mouth is stopped (vv. 19–20)**
The fact that the Law convicts Jews of sin means that everyone
is silenced. 'If the Jews, the people who might seem to have reason to regard themselves as an exception, are in fact no exception, then without doubt the entire human race lies under God's
judgment' (Cranfield, p.67). Paul's concluding verses expose the
stark hopelessness of our plight: we have nothing to say in our
defence. No-one will be declared righteous at the final judgment
on account of his or her obedience to the Law because, as Paul
has shown, everyone has done evil. The only 'advantage' in
knowing the Law, which Paul will explain later on in chs 5 and
7, is that we are shown just how sinful we are.

# Key themes and application

At this point in the letter, Paul comes to the conclusion of his
argument that began at 1:18.

◆ **Absolutely everyone is under God's wrath and no objection is
possible**
The most important application of this passage, in which Paul
brings his analysis of the problem to a close, comes from the
wider context. His original thesis, that all people face God's
wrath because of their rebellion (1:18), is now proven. If even
God's people, the Jews, are convicted by the Law, then all
humanity is guilty. For the Jew, there is no comfort to be found,
even in the Law which he is privileged to possess, for no Jew can
manage to keep the Law and so be saved by it. On the contrary,
the Law testifies against him. We should not underestimate the
shock that this passage would have given the Jew, as he realized
that the Mosaic covenant, which he would have sought to
observe, results only in condemnation.

People who suppose that they can exclude themselves from
Paul's assessment of our situation find that he has eliminated all
loopholes; our position really is one of absolute helplessness.
God is angry and we need to be saved from His anger. This message is completely unpalatable to the modern world, which
assumes that we are on God's side and He is on ours. We need to

hear Paul's loud declaration of our condemnation. He has shown us that there is nothing we can do and nothing we can say in our defence. We are entirely dependent upon God's mercy if we are to avoid His wrath. This passage should leave us convicted of sin and fully aware of our need before God.

Christians should ask themselves to what extent their evangelism is faithful to this message. So often we present Christianity to people as a satisfying and fulfilling way to live and invite them to try it out for themselves. If, however, Paul's teaching is true, then we are not in the business of presenting lifestyle options. We need to wake people up to the fact that their creator is rightly angry with them for the way they treat Him and that they are powerless to save themselves. Only with such an understanding will the good news of God's rescue plan truly make sense.

◆ **God's judgment does not nullify His faithfulness or justice**

The major application of both these themes is directed towards the Jew who suggests that God has changed His mind about His promises. It reminds him that God's covenant involves not only blessing but also judgment, and that He remains just in both courses of action. This is an important issue, for if God is somehow unfair, then His righteous condemnation of us could be called into question. Yet there is no loophole here and, in fact, to appeal to His righteousness in our defence is to call His righteous judgment upon ourselves.

The same application could be made in response to the common modern objection that God will not judge us because He is a God of love. God's judgment does not mean that He is unloving: love and justice are hallmarks of His perfectly righteous character. It is symptomatic of our sinfulness that we, who are so clearly guilty ourselves, should try to justify ourselves by throwing mud at God's character.

# Unanswered questions

◆ If everyone is rightly under God's condemnation, is there any hope for us?

◆ If God is completely just and faithful, how could He righteously save anyone?

# The aim of this study

To understand the truth that there is no escaping God's righteous, wrathful judgment and to acknowledge that we have no defence.

# Suggested questions

◆ Who do we find it difficult to believe will face God's judgment? Be honest.

## 1–8 IN CONDEMNING THE JEWS, GOD REMAINS FAITHFUL AND JUST

◆ Why do the questions in vv. 1–8 matter? What aspects of God's character are at stake at the end of ch. 2?
◆ What questions does Paul raise and how does he answer them?
◆ In what way does being entrusted with the words of God give value to being Jewish?
◆ What does Paul mean by God's faithfulness (v. 3)?
  – To what is God being faithful? (See Nehemiah 9:32–33)
  – If, when you pray, you thank God for His faithfulness, what do you mean?
  – God remains faithful to His character and His promises in judgment, because that's what He said He would do. Is there any way in which His faithfulness might still be questioned?
◆ In vv. 5–8 there are two questions being put as objections. What are they?
  – Why does Paul not bother to answer the second question?
  – What do these questions reveal about the questioner? How does this compare with the diagnosis Paul gave in ch. 1?
◆ In summary, why do Paul's questions matter? What possible objections have been answered?

## 9–20 EVERYONE, INCLUDING THE JEW, IS GUILTY AND SILENCED BEFORE GOD

◆ What is Paul concluding in v. 9?

◆ What is the reason for the Old Testament quotations? How do vv. 9 and 19 help us to understand them?
  – What two or three major points do the quotations make?
  – Paul says he has 'already made the charge'. Where have we seen these points previously in Romans?
◆ What does, and what doesn't, the Law accomplish?
◆ Think back to your answer to the first question. How would Paul respond to us regarding these people?

## SUMMARY OF 1:18–3:20

◆ Paul says that everyone is guilty, and that includes us. In what ways do we demonstrate that we forget this?
  – How can we remember this truth?
◆ In explaining our guilt, where has Paul's focus been, and why? How can we remind ourselves of God's righteousness?
◆ What should our response be, at this stage in Romans? How can we encourage one another to respond in a right way?
◆ Imagine that someone at your church is planning an outreach event. He wants people to hear the gospel because he says, 'Being a Christian is the most exciting and rewarding life there is.' It is your job both to encourage and to correct him. What would you say?

# ROMANS 3:21–26

## Context

So far, Paul has explained the problem of God's wrath against humankind's rebellion and established that there are no exceptions – everybody is facing God's righteous condemnation. This leaves us wondering how God can possibly fulfil His promises of saving a people; there seems to be no hope for anyone.

The word 'But' in 3:21 is the pivotal point in Paul's line of argument, as he turns away from the problem and begins to focus on God's solution. This solution is the gospel, described by Paul as 'the power of God for the salvation of everyone who believes' (1:16). He also explains it as the revealing of 'a righteousness from God' (1:17), a state of being in a right relationship with God that only God can bring about. Although the essence of the gospel is explained in this dense passage (vv. 21–26), Paul's explanation will continue right up until the end of ch. 11, as he makes clear why he is not ashamed to preach this good news to all people.

## Structure

The pivotal point in v. 21 is emphasized by the structure of Paul's writing, before it and after it:

2:12–29   Jew and Gentile alike are condemned by what they do (works)
3:1–8   God is righteous in judgment

3:9–19  No distinction: all have sinned
  3:20  No righteousness by the Law

**BUT NOW ...**

 3:21–22a  Righteousness by faith, apart from the Law
 3:22–24  No distinction: all have sinned and all who believe are justified
 3:24–26  God is righteous in salvation, through Jesus' death
3:27–4:25  Jew and Gentile alike are justified by faith

NB: Verses 21–26 are just one sentence in the Greek. Any breakdown is somewhat arbitrary, but the text notes for this study are presented in three sections, approximately according to theme (with an overlap at v. 24), for ease of reference.

# Old Testament background

**Atonement:** This is the bringing together of two parties previously separated – dividing the English word may be helpful, 'at-one-ment' – and is a concept that appears in a couple of places in the Old Testament.

*The Day of Atonement:* Perhaps the greatest privilege of the people of Israel was to have God Himself dwelling with them in the sanctuary (Exodus 25:8). Yet it also put them in danger of being destroyed because of their rebellion (Exodus 33:3–5), so God provided the sacrificial system as a means of dealing with the problem of His wrath at their sin. At the heart of this was the Day of Atonement (see Leviticus 16), when the high priest would slaughter one goat for the sins of the people, making atonement for them. The violent spilling of blood was seen by God as the sacrifice of a life for the sake of others (Leviticus 17:11). The high priest would then place his hands on the head of another goat and confess the sins of the people. This goat would then 'carry on itself all their sins' and be sent away into the desert (Leviticus 16:20–22).

*The suffering servant:* Five hundred years later, when the shortcomings of the sacrificial system as a means of averting God's wrath had become apparent, Isaiah promised that one day there would be a better sacrifice to deal with sin. This better sacrifice would come through the suffering and death of God's rescuing servant (Isaiah 53:1–12).

**God's righteousness:** This is part of His essential character and is manifested in three important inter-related ways:

*Justice:* God tells Israel unequivocally that He will not acquit the guilty (Exodus 23:7) and that He hates those who do so (Proverbs 17:15): He has to punish sinners in order to stay true to Himself.

*Mercy:* At the same time, however, when He proclaims His name, God says His nature is also to have mercy and to show compassion and grace (Exodus 34:6–7).

*Faithfulness to His promises:* When God speaks, His word is binding, and when He makes a promise, He does not change His mind (Numbers 23:19). The question is, therefore, how can He keep His unconditional promises of blessing to Abraham's descendants (Genesis 12:2–3) and yet, at the same time, remain faithful to His word that He will punish sin (Exodus 34:7)?

## Text notes

### 21–22a RIGHTEOUSNESS BY FAITH APART FROM THE LAW
With the words 'But now ...' Paul begins his explanation of the good news.

◆ **'... a righteousness from God ...' (v. 21)**
This is the key phrase in this passage – the same Greek word-root, which gives rise to words translated as 'righteousness', 'justified', 'just' and 'justice', appears six times (see Section Notes). In this passage, as in 1:17, Paul has two meanings in mind for the word 'righteousness'. In vv. 25–26 he means God's righteous character, but in vv. 21–24 he is referring to the righteousness that God gives to people. This answers one of the key questions from 1:18–3:20: 'If everyone is under God's condemnation, what hope is there for us?' In short, says Paul, it is God Himself who makes people righteous. The importance of this cannot be overstated. Since the problem is that we are facing God's wrath *as a result* of our unrighteousness, the solution cannot come from us.

Nothing we do can change the fact that He is angry with us. We need God to step in, which is what He does.

◆ '... has been made known ...' (v. 21)
With this phrase, Paul reminds us of his 'theme sentence' in 1:17, 'For in the gospel a righteousness from God is revealed', and his assertion that he is not ashamed of God's saving gospel because it reveals His righteousness. This is vitally important in the light of 3:3–6, where Paul writes of people questioning God's righteousness. It also fulfils the expectations of the Old Testament where God promises that His rescue will reveal His righteousness (Isaiah 56:1).

◆ '... apart from the law ... through faith in Jesus Christ ...' (vv. 21–22a)
The significance of this can be better understood by referring back to v. 20: God's solution *must* be apart from the Law because no-one's good works can be sufficient to secure a right-eous verdict on judgment day. In fact, the Law only makes us conscious of our rebellion. We are told that God's righteousness is appropriated in a different way, 'by faith', which Paul will expand upon after v. 27.

◆ '... to which the Law and the Prophets testify' (v. 21)
'The Law and the Prophets' serves as shorthand for the Old Testament. Probably Paul had in mind the whole of the Old Testament, seeing it as pointing towards, and preparing the way for, New Testament fulfilment. But, as mentioned above, there are also some specific passages in which God's righteousness is declared to be bound up with the salvation He will bring. The most striking of these examples is Isaiah 59, which also reflects the helpless predicament of sinners before God steps in to res-cue. This reminds us again that the gospel is not God's new plan, but a plan that was 'promised beforehand' (1:2).

## 22–24 GOD'S RIGHTEOUSNESS IS AVAILABLE TO ALL
Paul puts the whole of humankind on a level footing when it comes to receiving righteousness from God. 'There is no differ-ence', for these reasons:

◆ **God's righteousness is given to all who believe (v. 22)**

Paul will define what it means to believe, or have faith, in ch. 4, but here his point is that the scope of the gospel is, amazingly, universal. (This has already been mentioned in 1:5 and 1:16.) Just as we may have been devastated by the fact that every single human being is facing condemnation, so now, having accepted that conclusion, we may be amazed that each and every person has the possibility of being made righteous. (NB: We know from the wider context that not everyone will be saved.)

◆ **For all have sinned and need salvation (v. 23)**

The reason why there can be no distinction as to how people are saved is because everyone has sinned and so *needs* to be saved. Paul summarizes his argument since 1:18 in the one brief sentence of v. 23: all have sinned (past tense) and continue to do so, falling short of God's glory (present tense). We are all in the same boat, facing condemnation.

◆ **But all may receive salvation (v. 24)**

Yet, though all face condemnation for their rebellion against God, Paul declares that all are able to be 'justified', to be declared righteous (v. 24). The key question now is 'How?'

## 24–26 GOD IS RIGHTEOUS IN SALVATION, THROUGH JESUS' DEATH

Paul must now explain how he can turn his argument so quickly. How can he go from proclaiming absolute, universal guilt and condemnation to announcing, suddenly, the possibility of universal righteousness? He has told us that God does it, but *how* can God do it, particularly in the light of Paul's argument that God is perfectly righteous and just (3:3–6)? If God can suddenly let us all off the hook, His justice is a sham and the gospel is a scandal. Paul explains what God has done by explaining three related concepts: justification, redemption and atonement.

◆ **'[all] … are justified …' (v. 24)**

To justify does not mean 'to let off the hook', or 'to treat as righteous'; rather it means *to declare righteous*. It is a legal term, meaning that someone is justly acquitted because the penalty for his crime has been paid. Furthermore, this verdict can be given on the spot, the moment that someone believes (v. 22).

◆ '… freely by his grace …' (v. 24)

Paul says that this verdict comes as a generous gift from God. We should understand that it has to be given, since it cannot be earned. All we deserve, according to Paul, is death (1:32). Yet, again, the previous chapters make us ask how this can be so. How can the blatantly guilty be pronounced innocent, justly?

◆ '… through the redemption that came by Christ Jesus' (v. 24)

The word 'redemption' means *a costly deliverance*. It is commonly associated with the slave market, where a slave might be purchased in order to set him free. But, for the Jews, this word would have reminded them of their deliverance from captivity in Egypt (Exodus 15:13), and in particular the night of the Passover when they were rescued from God's judgment by means of the blood of a lamb, which was used to identify their houses (see Exodus 12:1–13). Paul has said that we are all enslaved, in that we are all under the power and consequences of sin (3:9). This says, however, that we may all be redeemed through Jesus' death, and so be acquitted. We see here how our rescue comes free to us, but at great cost to God. And yet how is it that God can set us free if we are facing His wrath?

◆ 'God presented him as a sacrifice of atonement …' (v. 25)

The first half of v. 25 tells us the essence of what God has done. The word translated as 'sacrifice of atonement' is actually the word for 'propitiation', which means *the satisfaction of wrath*. This comes from the language of the temple and the Day of Atonement (see OT notes). Just as the goat was slaughtered, so that God's anger against sinful Israel could be satisfied, so Jesus is sacrificed, to satisfy God's wrath against humankind. As Isaiah had prophesied, He 'took up our infirmities … the punishment that brought us peace was upon him' (Isaiah 53:4–6). Again we are told that the benefit of this comes through faith in His blood, meaning His death (cf. v. 22). Paul emphasizes God's initiative and provision in presenting Jesus as a propitiatory sacrifice, and thus we see how God provides the solution that addresses the problem. 'Thus God himself gave himself to save us from himself' (Stott, p. 115).

NB: It is critical that propitiation be rightly understood. For further explanation and to discover the implications, read either *The Cross of Christ*, John Stott (pp. 167–203) or *The Atonement*, Leon Morris (pp. 151–76).

Why should God have put forward His Son, the promised rescuer king (1:3–4), as a sacrifice? Our conventional answer would be, 'Because of His love', but Paul says He did it in order to demonstrate His 'justice', or 'righteousness' – the big issue in Romans so far (see Section Notes on 1:18–4:25).

◆ **God shows that He was righteous in passing over former sins (v. 25)**

Paul tells us that God was resolving a problem that was as old as the Old Testament story: how did God forgive His people for their sins when He should have punished them (Exodus 34:6–7)? The answer is that God was not being 'soft' on them; He was looking forward to the cross when His wrath against them would be satisfied.

◆ **God shows that He is righteous now in justly justifying people (v. 26)**

This answers another key question from our previous study: 'If God is completely just and faithful, how can He righteously save anyone?' Again, His justice is carried out on the cross, which not only enables Him to be just in punishing evil, but also vindicates His character as the God who makes people righteous. Through Jesus' death, God demonstrates that He can 'righteously make the unrighteous righteous', or 'justly justify the unjust'. His absolute integrity is thereby upheld, even exalted, through the gospel.

# Key themes and application

A great number of issues are raised by this passage, which will be expanded upon over the next eight chapters.

◆ **The solution that God has provided**
Against the backdrop of our hopelessness and helplessness, Paul explains that God does not leave us facing His terrible wrath; He has stepped in and provided a solution. Because *He* has put for-

ward *His* Son as a sacrifice of atonement, so that *His* wrath is totally appeased, *He* is able to show us *His* grace. It is *He* who makes us righteous. This is vitally important: if we recognize that, without His action, our condemnation is certain, we will be overwhelmed by thankfulness and humbled by the fact that God has done what we could not do. Christians need to stick to this message and not move away from it. The implication for our witness to non-Christians is clear: having fully explained their need for rescue, we should tell them what God has done through Christ; the message we tell will be one of grace.

◆ **The only solution to our real problem**

God has met our greatest need. His wrath has been propitiated, with the result that we can be redeemed from the state of being under sin, and so be acquitted rather than condemned. This explains why Christians must themselves cling to the meaning of the cross of Christ, and talk about it in evangelism. Without the achievement of the cross, the gospel is robbed of its power; we cannot be rescued from our sins and condemnation is certain. Jesus' death must be understood in the same way as Paul teaches it, which is that Jesus is bearing God's wrath for our sake. Any alternative understanding, e.g. that His death is the means of taking our sin away (described as expiation), or a great example, or martyrdom, etc., still leaves us facing God's wrath at the final judgment.

◆ **The only righteous solution**

By punishing sin at the cross, God upholds His absolute righteousness when He declares people righteous. It is essential to see the cross as addressing the issue of God's justice. God did not let us off the hook, nor did He overcome His anger by means of His love: each would have been fundamentally unjust. Rather, through Jesus' death, the price has been paid.

We must be wary of our tendency to put ourselves at the centre of God's plans. Although we are great beneficiaries of His grace, He did not send His Son to die, primarily, on our account. Rather, it was for the sake of His name and His character, so that it should be proved that He is faithful and just and able to fulfil His promises (see OT notes).

◆ **The solution that comes by faith, apart from the Law**

This is great news for us in the light of Romans so far. Our attempts at good works result only in our condemnation, but now God has shown a different way of making us righteous. Thus we can stop our futile thinking and our efforts at trying to please God through doing good, and look instead to His solution. This solution is appropriated in a completely different way. Paul will go on to explain.

◆ **The worldwide solution**

Since everyone is facing condemnation and yet can also be made righteous, the door is open for world evangelization. The gospel is able to save anyone, and therefore we should not hold back from telling anyone. To say that someone does not need to be saved, or cannot be saved, is to deny the problem that Paul has shown to exist and also the solution that God has provided; it is to say that Jesus did not need to face God's wrath on the cross. But if we fully understand this good news, that everyone can be made righteous, then evangelism will be our greatest aim in all our relationships with those who do not know Christ, regardless of who they are.

## Unanswered questions

◆ What does it mean to have faith?
◆ How can one man's death deal with the sin of all people?

## The aim of this study

To grasp the wonder of the gospel, the fact that God, through Jesus' death, has righteously dealt with the problem of His wrath and that His salvation is now available to everyone.

## Suggested questions

◆ Complete this sentence in less than 20 words: 'The heart of the Christian good news is …'.
◆ In what way is 3:21 a turning point in Romans so far?

◆ In v. 21, Paul begins to write about 'a righteousness from God'. What is the significance of this phrase in Romans so far?
 – What two things can it refer to?
 – Bearing in mind that the word translated as 'justice' is the same as that translated as 'righteous', which meaning is Paul using in v. 21? And in vv. 25–26?

## 21–22a RIGHTEOUSNESS BY FAITH APART FROM THE LAW

◆ What different things does Paul tell us about this righteousness in vv. 21–22?
 – What is the significance of each?

## 22–24 GOD'S RIGHTEOUSNESS IS AVAILABLE TO ALL

◆ To whom is this righteousness available?
 – Why is this surprising in the context of Romans so far?
 – Why must Paul explain how this is possible?

## 24–26 GOD IS RIGHTEOUS IN SALVATION, THROUGH JESUS' DEATH

*(Leader: Be ready to come in with some simple and concise definitions of 'justified', 'grace', 'redemption' and 'propitiation'.)*

◆ Trace the process by which God's righteousness comes to all. *(For clarity, this could be written out stage by stage on a large sheet of paper.)*
 – What does 'justified' mean? When does this righteous verdict come to someone?
 – What does 'grace' mean? Why does the righteous verdict have to happen by God's grace?
 – Of what would 'redemption' have reminded a Jew? According to Paul, in what sense are we also helpless slaves?
 – How does God rescue us through Jesus?
 – The word translated as 'sacrifice of atonement' is the word for 'propitiation'. What does 'propitiation' mean? Of what day would 'propitiation' or 'atonement' remind the Jew? *(Leader: Briefly explain the background for the Day of Atonement – see OT notes.)*

◆ Read Leviticus 16:15–17 and 17:11. How does the Day of Atonement deal with the problem of God's wrath against Israel's sin? Explain as simply as possible.
  – How does this background help us to understand Romans 3:25?

◆ Put Paul's argument together. How does God's righteousness come to all who believe?

◆ What reason do we normally give for God having sent Jesus to die for us? How is Paul's reason different?
  – How does God demonstrate His justice with regard to the past? Why did He have to do this?
  – How does He demonstrate His justice in the present?
  – How is He just in justifying those who have faith in Jesus?

◆ Comment on the following sentences (*Leader: Most have some truth in them, but you will need to correct what is wrong*):
  – On the cross, God forgave our sins.
  – God lets Christians off the hook over their sin.
  – Jesus took our sins away.
  – 'It's just as if I'd never sinned.'
  – God overcame His justice with His love.

◆ In what ways does God's solution fit the problem we have seen in Romans so far?

◆ Look back at the sentence you completed at the beginning. How would you revise it, having studied this passage?

## Study 6

# ROMANS 3:27–4:25

## Context

In 3:21–26, Paul introduced God's solution to the problem of His wrath being upon sinful humankind – the astonishing news that God Himself is able, righteously, to make all people righteous, by faith, apart from the Law, through Jesus' death. Many of the ideas that Paul introduced in this paragraph will be developed and explained further; his argument continues until the end of ch. 11. The first issue he addresses in this passage is the way that righteousness may be appropriated, as he looks at the nature of faith (see v. 22). Paul shows how righteousness is, in fact, available to all.

## Structure

3:27–31 The One God justifies all people by faith; therefore, no boasting

4:1–25 Righteousness by faith is upheld by the Old Testament, as exemplified by Abraham ...

1–8 ... who was made righteous, but not by works

9–12 ... who was made righteous, but not by circumcision; therefore, righteousness is not restricted to the Jews

13–17a ... who was made righteous, but not by Law; therefore, righteousness is not restricted to the Jews

17b–25 ... who was made righteous by faith, as we are too

# Old Testament background

**Abraham:** Abraham is a hugely important figure in the Old Testament, for several key reasons:

*Chosen by God:* Abraham's uniqueness is established, first, by the fact that he was chosen by God to be the recipient of His blessing (Genesis 12:1–3). He is seen as the father of all God's chosen people, and so the nature of his relationship with God would have been seen as highly significant for all who were to follow.

*God's promises:* These promises, made to Abraham and his descendants (in Genesis 12 and also in Genesis 15:5) were unconditional. God promised him His blessing, a land to possess and countless descendants. The Jews had presumed that these descendants would all be *physical* descendants, but God had said, in fact, 'all peoples on earth will be blessed through you' (Genesis 12:3). These promises are important because they establish the agenda for all that God will do in the future.

*His response:* Abraham believed God's promise that he would have descendants numbered by the stars, even though he was childless, and we are told that God 'credited it to him as righteousness' (Genesis 15:2–6), i.e. he found approval in God's eyes because he trusted Him.

# Text notes

### 3:27–31 THE ONE GOD JUSTIFIES ALL PEOPLE BY FAITH; THEREFORE, NO BOASTING

This paragraph comes as an immediate reaction to vv. 21–26 and also introduces the major themes of ch. 4. We must remember that whenever Paul mentions 'being justified', he is talking about 'being made righteous'.

◆ **The principle of faith means that we cannot boast (vv. 27–28)**
The context shows that Paul is banishing pride in one's own achievements, for 'if 3:9–26 is true and we have no defence before God's judgment we cannot possibly claim any merit if God acquits us.' One could boast if one could be declared righteous by the personal achievement of observing the Law, but Paul

has told us that no-one can do this (3:20). We have just seen (vv. 21–26) that justification comes through faith in a solution that is all God's doing: *He* gives *His* righteousness; *He* presented the sacrifice to turn away *His* wrath; *He* did it to demonstrate *His* justice. It is totally incongruous for us to boast, and to do so is to demonstrate that we do not have faith in what *He* has done, but rather that we are foolishly trusting in ourselves.

◆ **The One God of all justifies all people in the same way (vv. 29–31)**

If God's way of justifying people was to require them to obey the Law, then only those under the Law (i.e. the Jews) would have had the possibility, theoretically, of being justified. But this would deny the OT claim that God is the God of all peoples, including the Gentiles, because He is the one and only God in the universe (Deuteronomy 6:4). It would also negate God's promise that His salvation would come to all nations (Isaiah 49:6). As it is, Paul stresses that the God of all saves all by faith. Undoubtedly, this would have stunned the Jews, and Paul voices their likely objection: does the principle of justification by faith undermine what the Law (probably the whole OT) was saying? He denies this emphatically: the Law supports and confirms the fact that God justifies by faith.

## 4:1–25 RIGHTEOUSNESS BY FAITH IS UPHELD BY THE OLD TESTAMENT, AS EXEMPLIFIED BY ABRAHAM …

In what way does Paul 'uphold the law' (3:31), as he presents his major theme concerning righteousness by faith alone? First, in ch. 4, he turns to consider the hero figure (in Jewish minds) of Abraham; the father of the Jews, to whom God made great promises of blessing (see OT notes). This is essential: Paul *must* show that Abraham's righteousness was by faith if his argument, that the OT taught this principle, is to stand.

◆ **…who was made righteous, but not by works (vv. 1–8)**

The example of Abraham confirms the fact that, from the beginning, God's way of relating to people was by means of their faith in Him rather than on the basis of their works. Scripture says that Abraham himself was 'credited with (granted) righteousness' not because of his works but because he believed God (v. 3 quotes Genesis 15:6).

Paul explains further by distinguishing between wages that are earned, and therefore handed over as an obligation, and something that is given as a gift. His point is that justification falls into the latter category, being given freely to those who have faith, rather than being a payment for works done. Exactly what faith is, Paul will go on to elaborate.

As if the example of Abraham were not enough, Paul adds that the greatest Jewish king, David, 'says the same thing', and quotes from Psalm 32 in which David talks of God's forgiveness of sins. There is no mention of works in this psalm: David sees himself as clearly undeserving, but he is convinced that those who trust God (Psalm 32:10) are 'righteous' (Psalm 32:11) and 'blessed' (Psalm 32:1).

This fact, that both the father figure of Israel and her greatest king knew what it was to have faith, shows that the concept of salvation by faith is firmly rooted in the Old Testament.

◆ **... who was made righteous, but not by circumcision; therefore, righteousness is not restricted to the Jews (vv. 9–12)**

The question in v. 9 is like that in 3:29. It may be that Abraham was justified by faith, but is justification only for those who have been circumcised as he was? Paul answers this question by pinpointing the moment when Abraham was declared righteous: it was *before* he was circumcised (at least thirteen years before, in fact – Genesis 15:6, cf. 17:4). Thus circumcision could not have been a condition for his justification; it was only a sign of what had already happened (v. 10). As at the end of ch. 2, Paul redefines the criterion for membership of God's people, calling Abraham the father of both uncircumcised (i.e. Gentile) believers and the Jews who follow his example by believing themselves.

◆ **... who was made righteous, but not by Law; therefore, righteousness is not restricted to the Jews (vv. 13–17a)**

The promise referred to in v. 13 is God's promise of blessing given to Abraham and his descendants (see OT notes). Paul argues thus: Abraham and his offspring did not receive the promise on account of his observation of the Law, but rather it came as a result of the righteousness that was given *to him* by faith. Furthermore, the promise can only be fulfilled *to them* if they also have faith. If the promise had been given only to those who could keep the Law, it would have been worth nothing because, as chs 1 and 2 have already shown us, no-one can keep the Law, and the result would only have been wrath and judgment; God would not have been able to keep His promise of blessing. The promise, therefore, comes by faith, so that God may indeed freely extend His blessings, both to Abraham's descendants and to all who believe as he did and thus become his children, as God had promised (Genesis 17:5).

◆ **... who was made righteous by faith, as we are too (vv. 17b–25)** Although we now know that God will declare righteous those who have faith like that of Abraham, we haven't yet been told what that faith involved. In this passage Paul explains the nature of Abraham's faith.

*Abraham's faith was in God (v. 17):* 'The nature of faith is not to be found in itself, but entirely and exclusively in its object' (Stott, p. 117), i.e. Abraham had faith *in God* 'who gives life to the dead and calls things that are not as though they were'. These aspects of God's character are clearly relevant to us, who are facing death without God's help (1:32) and who have now been declared righteous even though we are not.

*Abraham's faith meant acknowledging man's helplessness (vv. 18–19):* We may ask what Abraham knew of these truths about God. Paul tells us that his faith meant recognizing the fact that he and his wife Sarah were incapable, in and of themselves, of bringing about what God had promised, since they were childless and she was barren (see OT notes). There was no pretence, yet his trust in God did not waver. Similarly, we have no hope of life when we look at ourselves – we face only death and judgment (1:32; 2:5). Trust is our only hope.

*Abraham's faith meant trusting that God would keep His promise (vv. 20–25):* Set against his own helplessness was Abraham's firm conviction that God had the power to fulfil His promise. Despite the outward appearance of hopelessness, he trusted that God would and could do what He said He would do. We know that Abraham had anxious moments (e.g. Genesis

17:17–18), but it is significant that God did not hold them against him. The New Testament record shows that his small amount of faith was sufficient, because the key factor is God's faithfulness to His promises.

Verses 23–24 tell us explicitly that we are supposed to be learning from the case of Abraham, and that we too will receive righteousness if we believe as he did. But although Abraham is held up as an example, we have, in fact, much greater grounds for trusting that God will give life, for we know that He has raised Jesus from the dead. Nor is this merely a hopeful interpretation on our part: Paul reaffirms the reason for Jesus' death and resurrection, which is that we might be declared righteous. Thus it is through faith that Abraham is made the father of many nations, as God had promised, and it is also through faith that we are justified, becoming beneficiaries of that promise.

NB: The connection that Paul appears to make between resurrection and justification (v. 25) may be rhetorical, as the above interpretation suggests, for he would not want us to separate justification from Jesus' death, but he could be suggesting that the resurrection is essential to our trust in His death as the effective means of making us righteous.

## Key themes and application

### ◆ God has always justified by faith

By focusing on the key OT figure of Abraham, Paul demonstrates that God has made people righteous by faith from the time that He first called a people to Himself. If this were not the case, God's promises could not be fulfilled and He could not be the God of the whole world, as opposed to being only the God of the Jews.

This point has important implications for the way we read the Old Testament, which is often caricatured as being about salvation by works, with God being completely different in character from how He is seen in the New Testament. The Law and circumcision, though important in the Old Testament, do not negate the principle that justification is always by faith. Paul is assuring us that we may have great confidence in the Old

Testament because God is completely consistent in the way that He works; He doesn't go back on His promises and nor does He change His mind. We must be careful to avoid reading the Old Testament as if it contradicted the New Testament, when in fact it points towards it.

◆ **God justifies everyone in the same way**

God does not distinguish between Jew and Gentile or anyone else in the matter of salvation – all people are justified through faith. Thus we see once again how the gospel puts everyone on level ground: all will be condemned by their works, but all may be justified by faith in Jesus' death. We can therefore evangelize all people with confidence, knowing that if they come to trust in God's promise, that He will make righteous those who rely on Jesus' death, then that verdict of 'righteous' will indeed be given to them.

◆ **Faith means trusting God to keep His promise**

Faith is about putting one's confidence in the fact that God is faithful to His promises of salvation and is able to keep them. Faith is not a 'work', because it does not earn justification; in fact it is the opposite of works. Works are any activity by which some- one might hope to gain God's approval, whereas faith is trusting solely in what He has done. The example of Abraham teaches us that faith does not have to be perfect and unfaltering, but it *will* be the basic conviction that God can be trusted, and actions taken on account of this will show such faith to be genuine. Chapter 4 verse 21 is a good definition of faith which we would do well to compare with our usual understanding. In the Bible, faith is not the capacity to believe the unlikely, nor 'a leap in the dark'. Rather, it is to trust that God can fulfil His promises.

How may we recognize genuine faith? The hallmarks of faith, that indicate a clear understanding of this truth about God, will be a humble thankfulness that He justifies everyone in a way that relies upon His character rather than human ability, and also confidence, that we ourselves will be made righteous on this basis.

# Unanswered questions

◆ If we are not justified by the Law, then what about the obliga-
tions to the Law that are mentioned in the OT?
◆ What about the fact that I still sin?
◆ If I'm justified by faith, may I just keep on sinning?
◆ Is there now nothing unique about the Jews?

# The aim of this study

Firmly to believe God's promise of righteousness through Christ,
because righteousness has always been given to anyone who has
faith in God.

# Suggested questions

◆ How does this passage flow on from 3:21–26?
◆ This passage focuses on faith. What does the world think faith
is? Who does it think has faith?

### 3:27–31 THE ONE GOD JUSTIFIES ALL BY FAITH; THEREFORE, NO BOASTING

◆ What is the relationship between 3:27–31 and the passage in the
previous study?
– What conclusion/application does Paul draw?
◆ Why can there be no boasting?
– What does boasting demonstrate about our understanding of
the gospel?

### 4:1–25 RIGHTEOUSNESS BY FAITH IS UPHELD BY THE OLD TESTAMENT, AS EXEMPLIFIED BY ABRAHAM …

◆ What does Paul intend to prove, by referring to Abraham?
– Why does Paul choose Abraham as his example?
– From ch. 4, what are the main ways by which Abraham was
*not* made righteous?

## ... WHO WAS MADE RIGHTEOUS, BUT NOT BY WORKS (vv. 1–8)

◆ How does Paul show that Abraham was *not* made righteous by
works?
– How does the illustration in vv. 4–5 add to what Paul is
saying?
– How does David say the same thing?
– To summarize: What are we told in these verses about how we
are made righteous?
– Think through the implications of this for us. What should be
our attitude to our 'works'?

## ... WHO WAS MADE RIGHTEOUS, BUT NOT BY CIRCUMCISION; THEREFORE, RIGHTEOUSNESS IS NOT RESTRICTED TO THE JEWS (vv. 9–12)

◆ How does Paul show that Abraham was *not* made righteous by
being circumcised?
– What implication does Paul draw from this?
– To summarize: What are we told in these verses about how we
are made righteous?
– Think through the implications of this for us. What should be
our attitude to the whole world?

## ... ... WHO WAS MADE RIGHTEOUS, BUT NOT BY LAW; THEREFORE, RIGHTEOUSNESS IS NOT RESTRICTED TO THE JEWS (vv. 13–17a)

◆ How does Paul show that Abraham was *not* made righteous by
virtue of the Law?
– What were the promises made to Abraham? How does Paul's
argument run?
– So why does the promise have to come by faith?
– To summarize: What are we told in these verses about how we
are made righteous?
– Think through the implications of this for us. What should be
our attitude to the Old Testament?

## … WHO WAS MADE RIGHTEOUS BY FAITH, AS WE ARE TOO (vv. 17b–25)

◆ What is the nature of Abraham's faith?
  – What is it in?
  – In what circumstances did he have faith?
  – How is our faith like Abraham's? How is it different?
  – How does Paul's teaching on faith differ from the world's view? Has your understanding changed?
◆ Why are these views wrong?
  – 'Faith is a leap in the dark.'
  – 'Faith is trying to believe what you know isn't true.'
◆ For what, in this passage, can we give thanks to God as we pray?

# SECTION NOTES:
# Romans 5:1–8:39

## The big theme: explaining what it means to be justified by faith

In 1:18–4:25, Paul explained God's good news of *justification by faith* – i.e. how He can declare condemned sinners to be righteous if they trust in Jesus' death. In this section, however, he focuses on the *implications* of justification by faith – i.e. what it means to be a justified person. We see that being justified means that we are dead to sin, free from God's wrath and condemnation and sure in the hope of resurrection and eternal life.

It is often suggested that assurance is *the main point* of this section, but it would be better to say that assurance is the *goal* of the section. In other words, Paul wants his readers to be assured of their salvation, and in order to achieve this he teaches that our freedom from condemnation is made certain through our union with Christ. In this way he aims to convince us that we will be saved regardless of circumstances.

Another popular suggestion is that Paul, having taught justification, is now teaching his readers how to become more godly and obedient, i.e. sanctification. Yet Paul's emphasis throughout his letter is on what *has already happened* to us and the implications for our future, rather than on what we may be doing in the future. He *is* concerned that Christians should strive to live in obedience to God, but that is only *one* application he makes to his readers, and it is rooted in the fact that Christians have been justified.

## The flow of the argument

Chapters 5–8 of Romans contain profound and essential teaching that should transform our understanding and our Christian lives, but they are dense chapters and it is easy to get lost in detail and miss the big picture. When teaching Romans at St Helen's, the following 'realm' diagrams have been useful in helping people to see how the argument fits together. The concept of the two realms, Adam's and Christ's, is referred to specifically in 5:12–21, but it could also be seen to underlie Paul's argument right until the end of ch. 8. In particular, we recommend using the diagrams when teaching these passages: 5:12–21, 6:1–14 and 7:7–25.

1 **Paul's thesis (5:1–11)**
   Paul says that if we have been justified through faith, we will definitely be saved in the future.
2 **The realm of Adam (5:12–14)**
   (NB: As he starts to prove his thesis, Paul begins by describing two realms, one established by Adam, the other by Christ.)
   Paul says that since the time when Adam sinned, everyone has lived in a realm that is characterized by sin and death. We can represent this realm in a diagram, as follows:

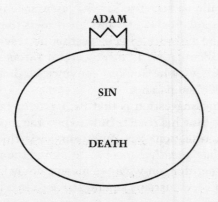

3  **Christ establishes a new realm (5:15–21)**
   Through His death, Jesus has established a new realm that is
   characterized by life, grace and righteousness. (For the time
   being, however, the old realm of Adam continues to exist.)

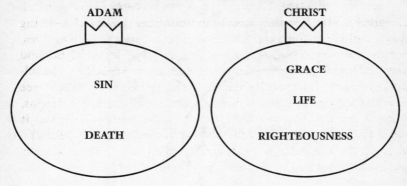

4  **Christians are brought into the new realm of Christ (6:1–7:6)**
   As a result of our union with Jesus in His death – which makes
   certain our future resurrection – Christians have been transferred to Jesus' realm. Consequently, they are freed from the
   dominion of sin, Law and death, and should therefore live as
   those who belong to this new realm.

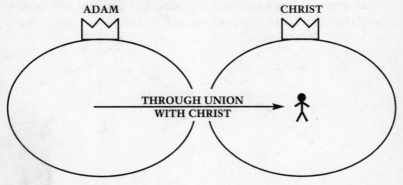

5  **Christians currently live in the 'overlap' of the realms
   (7:7–8:17)**
   The reason why Christians needed to be freed from the Law is
   not because the Law itself is bad. In fact, the Law is good, but it

condemned us because we broke it. In the present, Christians still sin, even though, deep down, they do not want to do so. This is because we live in an overlap of the realms, which will continue until we are fully freed from Adam's realm by being physically resurrected (8:11). They are, however, no longer condemned for their sin because they have been freed from the Law (8:1–4).

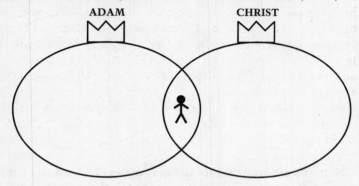

## 6 The final triumph of Christ's realm (8:18–30)

Until we are fully freed from Adam's realm, Christians will still suffer in this fallen world. But this suffering doesn't begin to compare with the wonderful experience that will be ours, when God brings Adam's realm of suffering and death to an end and completes His plan to glorify us with Christ.

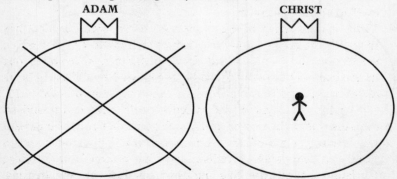

## 7 Conclusion (18:31–39)

Paul proves his thesis in 5:1–11 by giving Christians full assurance that the final completion of God's plan of salvation is unstoppable.

# Key themes

◆ **Jesus has established a new realm**

Most of the section chs 5–8 is about the justification of individuals, but in order to explain the implications of this, Paul needs to show how Jesus has changed the whole of history. He does this by describing two realms which are ruled by certain principles, or powers. His contention is that before Jesus died on the cross, everyone lived in the realm of Adam, where sin and death rule. In this realm everyone is dominated by rebellion against God and, as a consequence, faces death and condemnation. But through His death, Jesus inaugurated a realm of grace, and those who are transferred to this realm receive righteousness and eternal life. Paul teaches about these realms explicitly in 5:12–21, but this teaching is implicit in much of what follows.

◆ **Christians have been united with Jesus**

In 1:18–4:25, Paul talks about Jesus dying *for us* as a sacrifice of atonement (or propitiation). In chs 5–8, however, and specifically in 6:1–14, he says that Christians are *united with Jesus* in His death and resurrection. By using the words *union with Christ*, Paul helps us to understand how Christians have been transferred to the new realm: Jesus takes them with Him to live in a new realm where He is.

◆ **What does it mean to be united with Christ *now*? We live in the overlap of the two realms**

There is an overlap between the two realms because God has not yet brought the realm of Adam to an end. Until He does so, we live in the overlap. Paul draws a distinction between our 'inner being' (7:22) which has been captured by Christ, who is alive for eternity in the new realm, and our 'mortal body' (6:12; 8:11) which has yet to be raised to this new realm and so remains under the power of sin and death. We must be careful not to suggest a dualism which sees a total division between mind and body; such a dualism says that matter (and therefore the body) is inherently bad and cannot endure for ever. Instead, the division, and therefore the tension, that Paul describes (e.g. in 7:25) are only temporary. For when the realm of Adam comes to an end, our mortal bodies will be raised and will also live in the new realm for ever.

When he demonstrates that Christians are ruled by Christ in their inner being, Paul is showing us that, at the most fundamental level, God has put right what was most wrong with us, i.e. our rebellion against Him. This originated in our inner being, where we deliberately chose to suppress the knowledge about God, but now at the deepest level we want to please Him (7:22).

NB: We need to understand correctly the labels that Paul uses to describe these different aspects of the Christian. When Paul refers to 'our mortal body' he means both our physical body and our sinful thinking and attitudes. Yet Paul also uses the word 'mind' to refer to the Christian's inner being which is under the rule of Christ (e.g. 7:25). Another key word is 'flesh', which the NIV unhelpfully translates as 'sinful nature'. Paul uses the word 'flesh' to refer to the body while it remains in the realm of Adam. As such 'flesh' always carries negative connotations since the mortal body, while it is in this realm, continues to sin (7:17–18). David Seccombe comments helpfully:

What this all adds up to is two conflicting principles or laws at work in the Christian believer. The first is wholehearted inward commitment to love the law of God and to do God's will. The second is that sinful power which runs riot in our 'members', turning the Christian's life into a civil war (7:21–23) ... It would be a mistake to press Paul's language here too hard in the interests of some sort of analysis of the human person. The 'members' that are affected by sin include not just physical limbs, but moral, intellectual and emotional structures too ... The point to be grasped is that Christians, at their deepest and truest, love God and hate evil. Enmeshed though they are in sin, it is alien to them, and one day they will throw it off altogether.(pp. 125–6)

## Paul's application

As he teaches what it means to be justified by faith, Paul draws implications for his readers.

### ◆ We should not sin

Since we live in the overlap of the two realms, it sounds as though we are doomed to keep on sinning while we are in this world and that we might as well give up. But Paul says we do have a responsibility to fight against sin. The essence of being a Christian is to be a citizen of a new realm where there is no sin. As citizens of that realm (though we live in a time of overlap with the realm of Adam), Paul says that we should battle, now, for the values of that realm. We should note that he does not promise that we *will* not sin, because as long as we are in our mortal bodies we are still in the realm of Adam, where sin reigns. But, in the light of our death with Christ and our future resurrection, we should strive not to sin.

### ◆ Our hope

As we live in the overlap of the two realms, we long for the future day when we will live fully in the realm where we will no longer sin (8:23). Then we will be fully revealed as God's children (8:19), we will share in Jesus' inheritance (8:17), and we will be conformed fully to Jesus' likeness (8:29).

### ◆ Assurance

Paul assures us that this hope will certainly be realized because we have been united with Christ and no-one can separate us from Him (8:35–39). We know that God is on our side (8:31) and that no-one can stop Him from completing His plan to make us like Christ.

## Structure

**5:1–11**      **Paul's Thesis**
We have been justified by faith in Jesus' death and will be saved from God's wrath

**5:12–21**      **The realm of Adam and the realm of Christ**
Christ in His death and resurrection has established a new realm of grace and life

**6:1–7:6**   **Christians are brought into the new realm of Christ**

6:1–14   We must fight sin now, because God has united us with Jesus' death and resurrection in order to transfer us to this new realm where there is no sin

6:15–23   If we do persist in sinning wilfully, we show that we do not belong to the new realm. This means that, because we are still serving sin, we will die condemned

7:1–6   By dying with Christ we have been set free from the Law which used to arouse sin in us and sentence us to death

**7:7–8:17**   **Christians currently live in the 'overlap' of the realms**

7:7–13   But the Law itself is not sinful. It exposes sin and is itself good

7:14–25   My current situation: I do not do what I want to do – though I want to serve God I find that I don't. In my inner being I now want to serve God, but the problem lies with my flesh, which still wants to serve sin

8:1–17   It is on account of this – 'Therefore' – that Christians are not condemned; the fact that they want to serve God shows they have the Holy Spirit within them. If they have the Spirit, then their mortal bodies will be raised to life as well, they are children of God and they will share in Christ's inheritance. If, by virtue of having the Spirit within us, we belong to the new realm, we will have our minds set on what the Spirit desires and so we will fight against sin

**8:18–39**   **The final triumph of Christ's realm and Paul's conclusion**

8:18–27   Christians now have a great hope of future glory despite the fact that they suffer in this present world.

8:28–39   God is on our side, therefore nothing can stop Him now from fulfilling His plan to glorify us with Christ

# ROMANS 5:1–11

## Context

Paul has explained the essence of God's good news for condemned sinners, the fact that He now makes people righteous through faith in Christ Jesus. In this passage Paul spells out the consequences of the justified believer's new status, relating how justification by faith is the solution to the problem of God's wrath (both His present anger and His future condemnation of us), as was set out in chs 1–3. Chapter 5:1–11 celebrates the Christian's certain hope of future salvation, in spite of present suffering.

The word 'rejoice', which appears three times in this passage, comes from the same Greek word as that translated 'boast' in 3:27. Boasting in *oneself* is excluded by the gospel (3:27), but boasting in what *God* has done is presented in these verses as the natural response.

## Structure

5:1–2a  Our new status: peace with God
5:2b–4  We now have a great hope in which to rejoice, even in suffering
5:5–11  Our hope is certain …
      6–8 … since it is based on God's love
      9–10 … since it is based on the fact that we have been justified and reconciled
      11 … and so we rejoice in God who has done all this

# Old Testament background

**The hope of God's glory:** Although Israel had been sent into exile in Babylon on account of her disobedience, she had been given many promises that God would rescue her. And so the expectation of these promises being fulfilled became a constant theme in the Old Testament. A key element of this fulfilment was the fact that God Himself would be glorified (Isaiah 40:5); it is for the sake of His own honour that He rescues Israel (Ezekiel 36:22–23), although *she would share in His glory*. At the time of Israel's return from exile, however, in 539 BC, these promises were far from being realized. The Jews were still awaiting their fulfilment when Jesus came.

# Text notes

### 1–2a OUR NEW STATUS: PEACE WITH GOD
Summarizing his argument so far – 'Therefore, since we have been justified through faith ...' – Paul turns to the implications of this statement and describes the benefits that the justified sinner now enjoys.

◆ **We have peace with God ... (v. 1)**
  The message of Romans so far enables us to understand how remarkable this statement is. Previously, our relationship with God could only be described in terms of extreme enmity. This was due not only to our wilful rebellion against Him – we were His enemies (v. 10) – but also, more significantly, to His righteous response to us – we were objects of His wrath, facing certain condemnation. Yet now, because God's wrath is dealt with by Jesus' wrath-bearing sacrifice (3:25), our relationship with Him has been restored; we have been reconciled to Him. This achievement of the cross is to be seen, in the context of the whole Bible, as the solution to the problem of humankind's sin against God that dates back to the Fall, the solution that was promised to Israel but never fully enjoyed by her (see OT notes). In v. 2 Paul describes our peace with God in another way. Whereas we used to be 'under sin' and 'under the Law', a

situation in which we could only face condemnation, Jesus has now enabled us to stand in 'grace', i.e. we are now standing in God's favour.

◆ **... through faith in Christ (vv. 1–2)**
At the heart of these two verses stands the agent of our reconciliation to God, 'our Lord Jesus Christ', who is also the subject of God's gospel (1:2). Twice we are told that it is 'through Him' that our relationship with God has been transformed, and twice we are reminded that we benefit from His work 'through faith' (cf. 3:25). Peace with God comes through trusting the atoning work of Christ.

## 2b–4 WE NOW HAVE A GREAT HOPE IN WHICH TO REJOICE, EVEN IN SUFFERING

Paul moves on to describe the believer's perspective on the future that God has promised for His people, and shows how present sufferings do not detract from it.

◆ **A great hope ... (v. 2b)**
One of the clearest hallmarks of the justified believer is his or her perspective on the future. When we lived under God's condemnation, the future held only wrath and anger, trouble and distress (2:8–9). Now, however, we can look forward and rejoice (or 'boast', see Context) in the hope of the glory of God. To understand this phrase better we should look at its OT context, which is Israel looking forward to sharing in God's glory as He fulfils His promises of rescue (see OT notes); in addition, we shall have Paul's further explanation in ch. 8. We do not see God's glory now, but we look forward with expectation.

◆ **... even in suffering (vv. 3–4)**
It is a great surprise, in this passage, to find that Paul's attitude towards present sufferings is the same as that regarding future glory – 'we rejoice'. Reading ahead, we know that these 'sufferings' relate to all the pain, hostility, frustration and suffering that come from living in a fallen world (8:18–27). We might expect suffering to undermine our confidence in the future hope, but Paul takes the opposite point of view, arguing by means of a chain of cause and effect, as follows: suffering produces both the

opportunity and the need for endurance which, in turn, produces character – the Greek word used here describes the 'provenness' of a character that has stood up under examination – and finally, a character thus proven will have stronger confidence in the future. Sufferings are therefore important because they strengthen our hope, for 'hope, like a muscle, will not be strong if it goes unused' (Moo, p. 303).

## 5–11 OUR HOPE IS CERTAIN ...

Verse 5 is the pivot upon which this passage turns. Paul has told us that we can rejoice in the future and that we can even rejoice in the sufferings of the present, because they lead to an increase in our confidence about what God will do; but how do we know that this confidence is well founded? Paul gives the Christian two clear reasons:

### ◆ ...since it is based on God's love (vv. 5–8)

Paul states that our hope does not disappoint us (or, literally, 'will not put us to shame', i.e. on the last day), and adds, by way of explanation, that 'God has poured out his love into our hearts by the Holy Spirit, whom he has given us'. This phrase needs close attention. Paul is saying that our hope of receiving God's promise about the future is absolutely certain, because God makes us beneficiaries of His love when He brings us into a right relationship with Himself. This happens through the Holy Spirit, who changes our hearts such that we believe in, and so benefit from, Christ's atoning death. Paul is not saying that we experience intense feelings of love for God, although that may well be true. Rather, he means that the Spirit converts us and therefore convinces us of God's love expressed in the gospel. This is what guarantees that we are justified and therefore will be saved.

The proof of God's love is seen when we look back to what God did for us in Christ's death on the cross. Paul makes his point by considering what we were like when God put forward Jesus as a sacrifice: we were ungodly (1:18), and powerless to do anything about it. Even the greatest imaginable human love, Paul suggests, would only, under very unusual circumstances, prompt the giving of one's life for someone else, and even then, it would only be for the very best of humanity. So how much greater is God's love, in that Christ died for us while we were still wilful rebels in His world.

◆ **...since it is based on the fact that we have been justified and reconciled (vv. 9–10)**

The final link in the chain of Paul's argument is that what God has done for us in the past proves that He will not neglect us in the future. If we have been declared righteous by Jesus' death, then how much more certain it is that we will be saved on the day of God's righteous judgment. If God's wrath against us has been turned away by Jesus taking our place then we will not have to face it ourselves. Paul restates the case using the language of reconciliation (restored relationships) – i.e. our being at peace with God – and suggests that since God has already done the 'hard work' of reconciling His enemies to Himself, there is no question but that He will do the comparatively easy job of saving us at the end, now that we are His friends.

Having established that we have peace with God through Christ (v. 1), Paul's line of argument is as follows:

– We rejoice in our hope ...

– ... even when we suffer, since suffering, ultimately, increases our hope.

– We rejoice because our hope is certain.

– Our hope is certain because it is based on God's love, and we benefit from this love as God gives us the Holy Spirit, who enables us to trust in Christ's atoning death.

– God's love is proven by God sending Jesus to die for us while we were sinners.

– Our hope is also certain because God justified us while we were still His enemies. Since we are now His friends, we can wait confidently for judgment day, secure in the expectation that He will save us from His wrath and give us the promised hope.

◆ **And so we 'boast' in God who has done all this (v. 11)**

Having proved that our hope for the future has a sure foundation, Paul exults in the fact that all this has been achieved by God Himself. *He* has reconciled us to Himself, and *He* has done it all *through Christ*.

# Key themes and application

◆ **We have peace with God**

Because God has made us righteous through faith, our relationship with Him is one in which hostilities are over. We need to understand that 'peace with God' is a state of affairs, rather than a state of mind. As the previous chapters will have taught us, God's wrath against us was the critical problem, and so we saw that His propitiation is the most important benefit of His rescue plan. Our peace with God, therefore, comes from the *fact* of what He has done; it is not a *feeling* of peace that we might or might not have. Of course, what God has done should give us peace of mind, as we consider where we stand before Him, but this feeling is not the foundation of our relationship with God. Moreover, we should not expect to have constant peace within, for, as Paul is about to tell us, the Christian life is in fact a battle and a struggle.

◆ **God's love for us**

God's love is proved by the fact that Jesus died for us while we were living in open hostility to God. This ties in closely with the issue of assurance, an area that often presents problems. The question, 'How do I know that God loves me?' is one that every Christian will ask at some time, and here a wrong perspective will cause much doubt. If we look at ourselves, we may see ourselves as 'lovable' because, wrongly, we think of ourselves as worthy in God's eyes. On the other hand, Christians convicted of their sin are likely to see themselves as completely unlovable. Paul, however, teaches us to look instead to the cross, where God's love has been demonstrated beyond doubt. In the light of this, we should be amazed and overwhelmed with thankfulness. This is a powerful message to present to the world which, though preoccupied with the pursuit of love, sees love as conditional and ephemeral. God's love, on the other hand, has been shown to be entirely unconditional. And it will never diminish.

◆ **We can be sure that we will be saved**

In the present, we can be fully confident that we will be saved on judgment day because God has enabled us, by his Spirit, to receive His love personally, and to benefit from it. God's love is certain – it has been demonstrated by Jesus' death on behalf of sinners like us. And since, through His death, we have been made righteous, we will definitely be saved. This assurance, the central theme of the passage, is a wonderful truth on which we should meditate.

Paul is presenting, here, an essential aspect of the Christian life. We are people who have a certain hope for the future, a hope that is guaranteed by what God has already done in the past. The implication is that this always remains true, regardless of present circumstances. No matter what troubles we may be facing, our righteous status has been established by Jesus' death and so our resultant salvation, on the last day, is guaranteed. We need to remember this, because our tendency will always be to focus on our present experience in order to gauge our spiritual welfare. Yet the fact that, as we are told, this life *will* bring suffering, means that to focus on our circumstances will cause our assurance to be undermined. Christians need constantly to remind one another to look to the cross in order to be certain of our standing before God and our future with Him.

## Unanswered questions

◆ Is Jesus' death sufficient for the whole of humanity?
◆ If I know I'll be saved in the future, can I just keep on sinning now?
◆ Does the fact that I still sin now mean I may not be saved in the end?

## The aim of this study

To exult in the certainty of our future salvation, which is guaranteed by God's proven love for us and by our justification through Christ.

## Suggested questions

◆ What is the best thing about being a Christian? When you are with your friends, what do you enthuse about regarding your faith?

## 1–2a OUR NEW STATUS: PEACE WITH GOD

◆ We have reached the point in Romans where Paul begins to write about the benefits of being a Christian (i.e. what it means to be justified). What does Paul say are the benefits of being a Christian?

– The world doesn't think peace with God is anything to shout about. Why not?

– What would most people think 'peace with God' is? What does Paul mean by the phrase?

– In the context of Romans, why is it remarkable that Paul can say that we have peace with God and that we stand in 'grace'? What is our natural relationship with God like?

– How has this incredible change in the state of affairs between ourselves and God come about? Someone summarize.

## 2b–4 WE NOW HAVE A GREAT HOPE IN WHICH TO REJOICE, EVEN IN SUFFERING

◆ The word translated as 'rejoice' in this passage is the same word as that translated as 'boast' in 3:27–31. Why is boasting permitted now, when it was excluded before?

◆ How does the believer's perspective on the future change?

◆ What about the present? How does it affect our perspective on the future? Is this surprising? How does Paul's argument flow?

– How does this challenge our reaction to the suffering that we encounter (e.g. hostility from non-Christians)?

## 5–11 OUR HOPE IS CERTAIN

◆ How has God demonstrated His love (vv. 6–8)?

– How does Paul emphasize the depths of God's love?

– Being honest, where do we normally look to gauge God's view of us day to day? Where should we look?

– How does someone benefit personally from God's love (v. 5)?

– 'How do I know God loves me?'

◆ How does our knowledge about what God has done in the past give us confidence for the future (vv. 9–11)?

– Put v. 9 into your own words.

– How does Paul put it differently in v. 10?

◆ Put the argument together. How can Christians be sure that they will be saved on judgment day?

– Are you sure you will be saved from God's anger? What is necessary for you to be sure? How can we help one another to be certain of our salvation?

– Why is it important that Christians should be sure they are going to heaven?

◆ Imagine that tragedy strikes in the life of a Christian friend. He starts to doubt that God loves him and then worries that he is not a real Christian because if he were, God wouldn't have let this happen. How would you begin to answer him?

◆ How might this study change the way you pray this week?

**Study 8**

# ROMANS 5:12–21

## Context

Paul has been explaining the consequences, for believers, of justification by faith. First of all he has established the amazing fact that our standing before God is now transformed: instead of being His enemies we are now at peace with God and able to enjoy the certain hope of future salvation, hope that is rooted in what God has already achieved, in the past, through Christ.

This passage is linked to the one preceding it by the word 'therefore'. There are two apparent connections:

◆ Paul is crystallizing, and drawing out, the implications of what he has said in 1:18–4:25, that all humankind faces death because of sin, but that life and righteousness come through Christ, and that this represents a cosmic change in human history.

◆ Also, Paul continues to show how believers may have confidence in God's salvation through the gospel. Beginning at 5:1, he has explained Christ's achievements, making it clear that these alone form the basis for their confidence.

We also see, here, the introduction of the idea that the whole of humanity lives in one of two realms: the realm of sin and death, inaugurated by Adam, or the realm of grace and life, inaugurated by Jesus. A recognition of these two realms will be important as we read chs 6–8 (see Section Notes on chs 5–8).

# Structure

**5:12–14** Adam's universal and disastrous influence
**5:15–17** The differences between Adam and Christ
**5:18–19** The similarity between Adam and Christ: one man's action affects everyone
**5:20–21** The Law magnifies the reign of grace inaugurated by Christ

NB: In v. 12 Paul begins a comparison between Adam and Christ that he will complete in v. 18.

# Old Testament background

**Adam:** The Fall is a cosmic event in human history. Originally, in the garden of Eden, Adam and Eve's life was established perfectly by God: they were to live under God's rule and enjoy His blessings. They chose, however, to sin (see Genesis 3), rejecting God's authority over them and disobeying the one command He had given them. We should note that although it is Eve who sins first, it is Adam, to whom the command had been given (Genesis 2:17), who is held accountable by God (Genesis 3:9–11, 22). Their sin inaugurates a new era for humankind: from this point onwards, all people will sin and all, as a result, will face the certainty of death (Genesis 3:22–26).

# Text notes

## 12–14 ADAM'S UNIVERSAL AND DISASTROUS INFLUENCE

With the words 'just as', Paul begins a comparison that will not be completed until v. 18. We might be surprised that he should compare Christ with Adam, but in terms of human history they are both inaugurators: Adam inaugurated an era (of sin and death) that affects all humankind, and Christ, in the same way, inaugurated an era (of grace) that will affect all humankind and which will endure for all eternity. Christ and Adam stand 'as the respective heads of two aeons' (Nygren, p. 210). This is why Paul sees Adam as a pattern, or 'type', of Christ, 'the one to come' (v. 14).

◆ **Death came to all through one man's sin (v. 12)**

Though he doesn't go into detail, Paul is here implying original sin. Adam was not just the first of many sinners; the sense is, rather, that on account of his sin all people became sinners and therefore suffer the consequence, which is death (see OT notes). The phrase 'because all sinned' may be thought to suggest the sin of individuals also, but the continuation of the comparison in vv. 18–19 makes this unlikely, and in any case Paul has already demonstrated, in 1:18–3:20, that everyone is individually guilty. Either way, the end point is the same: Adam's sin resulted in everyone sinning (rebelling against God) and consequently dying. We cannot, however, blame Adam for our sinfulness, since v. 12 strongly suggests that Adam's sin was the sin of all people, i.e. in sinning he was our representative, and we, who sin repeatedly, are guilty as he was. (On this interpretation, which has a very strong tradition in the church, see Moo, pp. 323–8.)

◆ **All were affected by the consequence of Adam's sin, even before the Law was given (vv. 13–14)**

Although these are difficult verses, the overall point is clear. In the time between Adam and the Mosaic Law being given, all people suffered death as a result of Adam's sin – and the Law did not change that fact. Before the Law was given, sin was 'not taken into account', in the sense that it was not explicitly identified, and yet people died ('death reigned' over them), not because they had broken the Law that had yet to be given, but because they had become sinners due to Adam's sin. The evidence of humankind's rebellion in this period is clear, e.g. in Genesis 6:5.

## 15–17 THE DIFFERENCES BETWEEN ADAM AND CHRIST

Having begun to show the similarity between Adam and Christ, Paul now sets out the clear differences between them with regard to their achievement. These differences are crucially significant. Using the 'how much more' formula to point out the contrasts (cf. 5:9–10), Paul continues to build the believer's confidence in what God has done.

◆ **The difference in consequences (vv. 15–16)**
Whereas Adam brought death and condemnation, Christ reverses all of this and brings grace and justification (the gift of God). This is what Paul has been explaining from the beginning of his letter.

◆ **The difference in character (v. 15)**
At first glance, the gift *does* appear to be like the trespass in v. 15, in that the act of one man is seen as affecting many people, the point that Paul makes in vv. 12 and 18–19. Here, however, he is emphasizing the difference of 'character' between the two things. The trespass brings death as a matter of principle: every sin deserves and will receive the punishment of death (1:32 and 6:23). The gift that Christ brings, on the other hand, is undeserved and is a matter of grace (mentioned twice) that overflows to the many. So, whereas the former is a simple matter of justice, the latter is a picture of God's abundant generosity.

◆ **The difference in starting points (v. 16)**
The verdict of condemnation that affected humankind came after only one sin, but God's gift of salvation came after an unimaginable number of sins committed by all people. The vastness of God's grace shows clearly against the backdrop of so much wickedness.

◆ **Summary of differences (v. 17)**
Paul now draws together the threads of vv. 15 and 16. Whereas Adam's trespass has brought death, God has brought, through Jesus, abundant grace, life and righteousness. The striking difference here is that whereas death 'reigned' through Adam, it is not life that reigns, as we might expect, but people – those who receive God's grace – who will reign. Before, we were subjects of the rule of death, but now it is we who will triumph for ever, through Christ. Once again, Paul gives the believer reason to be certain of future glory (5:2).

## 18–19 THE SIMILARITY BETWEEN ADAM AND CHRIST: ONE MAN'S ACTION AFFECTS EVERYONE

Paul now picks up the comparison he began in v. 12, the parallels being indicated by the words 'just as … so also'. And yet he also takes into account the significant differences he has just spelt out. Bearing these in mind, how is Christ like Adam?

◆ **The similarity in effect: one man's action affects all (vv. 18–19)**
The point of comparison is that what each man did had implications for the whole of humanity. Verses 18 and 19 run in close
parallel emphasizing that Jesus' righteousness and obedience
have had just as much effect upon human history as did Adam's
trespass and disobedience.

The words 'all men' at the end of v. 18 have raised the question of whether Paul is teaching 'universalism', the idea that all
people will be saved at the final judgment. The argument of the
letter so far makes it crystal clear that Paul cannot possibly
believe this: he has been asserting that all humankind are facing
God's final wrathful judgment unless they have faith in what
God has provided, i.e. in Christ's propitiating sacrifice.
Moreover, in the previous verse (v. 17) he has just said that life
comes to those 'who receive' God's grace. The reason for 'all
men', here, is that in this passage Paul is arguing that 'Christ
affects those who are his just as certainly as Adam does those
who are his' (Moo, p. 343; for fuller discussion see pp. 342–4).
Paul is no more suggesting, in v. 18, that all will be saved than
he is suggesting, in v. 19, that only 'many' (but not all) were
made sinners.

## 20–21 THE LAW INCREASES THE REIGN OF GRACE INAUGURATED BY CHRIST

Paul has just divided humankind into two camps: all people must
be seen as standing, now, either under Adam or under Christ. But
before he concludes this part of his letter, he explains an important point about the Law; although, when it was introduced, it did
not change man's standing under sin and death, it did have a role
to play.

◆ **The Law increases sin and thereby increases grace also (v. 20)**
Verse 20 explains the flip side of v. 13b. The Law makes sin
increase in three senses. First, by defining what is right and
wrong, the Law identifies more activities and attitudes as sinful
than we would know without it. Second, because the Law
asserts that sin is wrong, it makes the breaking of Law all the
more wilful and wicked. Third, the Law 'provokes sin', as Paul

will explain in 7:8–11. Yet, Paul argues, this only makes grace increase all the more, for it shows God's gifts of righteousness and eternal life to be even more generous. Indeed, he says that this was the purpose for which God 'added' the Law, to magnify the effect of sin and thus magnify His saving grace even more.

◆ **The two eras, of sin and of grace (v.21)**
Finally, Paul sets the two eras side by side. He implies that they are similar, and yet v. 20 must mean that the era of grace is greater. Earlier in the passage, Paul had stated that death reigned (v. 14), but now he says that sin reigned, in the sense that it condemns everyone to death. Yet whereas all humankind were once subjects in this realm, now some have been transferred to a realm where God's grace reigns instead and the future holds eternal life. So now every individual believer can see his or her place in God's entire plan of salvation for humankind.

# Key themes and application

Paul's focus in this passage is the similarity between Adam and Christ, both of them being responsible for a new era in human history. What happens in these two eras, however, and the means by which these eras are opened are completely different.

◆ **Jesus has inaugurated a new realm**
In this passage, Paul means us to see the cosmic significance of what God has done in Christ. The whole history of humankind has been changed by the death of His Son on the cross. God has established a totally new realm of existence, in which it is possible for all people to be declared righteous and to be given eternal life. This realm will be fully established in the future.

This teaching should challenge our generally personal or parochial views of what God is doing in the world. Jesus' death is not just a private event that benefits me and small groups of believers. God has changed the world; He will, one day, consummate this change and everybody will be affected by it. Everyone who has ever lived is either in or out of the new realm that He has established. We should gain huge confidence from this, being assured that we are not living in a make-believe world, but rather we are living in the greatest reality. Conversely, our friends who do not believe are not enjoying real life; they are ignoring the way that God has changed history and how that change will affect their eternal destiny.

◆ **The content of the new realm**

The contrast between the two realms could not be greater. Previously everyone was subject to sin and death, facing no alternative, but now through Christ all may be declared righteous and may be given eternal life. Moreover, those who belong to Christ will reign; they will no longer be dominated by death, but they will rule in and with Christ for ever. It should be noted that the promise concerning this, in v. 17, is to be fulfilled in the future. This should give the Christian great assurance, in that no matter how hard the present may appear, the problem of sin and death has been resolved for ever, by God. And if we have received His grace, by faith (v. 17), then justification and eternal life are ours.

We may be inclined to think of our conversion as a small thing, a change that brings modest reform to some areas of our lives, but according to Paul the difference between the two realms is infinitely great. This being so, our transfer from one realm to the other should affect the whole of our lives, as Paul explains in ch. 6 and, more especially, from ch. 12 onwards.

◆ **How it happens**

Paul's careful use of words makes it plain that whereas the realm of sin and death was the result of man's rebellion, the realm of grace exists only through God's work. It is His gift, coming out of His grace and demonstrating His abundant generosity. We can take no credit; our part is only to praise Him for His love and mercy. This teaching reinforces our need to rely fully on God, and also warns us against the futility of trying to add to what He has done.

# Unanswered questions

◆ Has God simply deemed sin irrelevant, now that all can be justified and saved regardless of their sin?

◆ 'Shall we go on sinning, so that grace may increase?' (6:1)

# The aim of this study

To see the cosmic significance and effect of Jesus' death, so that we gain both a true perspective on the magnitude of what God has achieved and, for ourselves, a sure confidence in the future.

# Suggested questions

*(Warning to Leader: Do not allow this study to be hijacked by the issue of original sin!)*

◆ 'Christianity is an old-fashioned, irrelevant way of life and does not have a place in the twenty-first century.' How would you respond?

◆ Divide this passage into parts and give each part a heading.

## 12–14 ADAM'S UNIVERSAL AND DISASTROUS INFLUENCE

◆ Paul seems to begin a comparison in v. 12 and then breaks off. Where does he continue?

◆ Meanwhile, he teaches about the influence of Adam.
  – What do we learn about Adam?
  – Who is affected by Adam's sin? In what way?

◆ 'Apart from a few notable exceptions, humankind is comprised of essentially good and worthy individuals.' How should we respond?

## 15–17 THE DIFFERENCES BETWEEN ADAM AND CHRIST

◆ What are the differences between the influences of Adam and Christ?
  – In what ways are they different?
  – How does v. 17 summarize the differences?

## 18–19 THE SIMILARITY BETWEEN ADAM AND CHRIST: ONE MAN'S ACTION AFFECTS EVERYONE

◆ What is the similarity between Adam and Christ?

◆ How do we know that Paul is not teaching that every person will be saved? Why do you think Paul uses this language here?

◆ How do vv. 15–19 increase our confidence that we will be saved?

## 20–21 THE LAW MAGNIFIES THE REIGN OF GRACE INAUGURATED BY CHRIST

◆ How do these verses continue Paul's argument in vv. 13–14?

◆ Throughout, Paul speaks of two different eras or realms. What are they?
  – What are the features of each realm?

◆ Return to the first question. How might we respond now? Who is living in the past? To what extent do we live as if we were part of the greatest reality?

◆ It is easy to think that being a Christian is a relatively small and personal matter. How should this passage change our thinking?

# Romans 6:1–14

## Context

In ch. 5, Paul explained how the gospel of justification by faith in Jesus Christ has not only brought benefits to the individual who believes, but has also changed the course of human history. Without Christ, human existence was and is lived under the tyranny of sin and death (5:12–14), in an era determined by Adam's original rebellion. Our only prospect was and is condemnation. With Christ, however, a new era has begun, in which we can be made righteous and be given eternal life (5:17). These two distinct eras provide the context for chs 6–8, and it is essential that we keep them in mind if we are going to understand what Paul is saying in the difficult two chapters that come next. If we don't, we will end up with false expectations about the Christian life in the present.

Paul tells us – and this is very significant – that the Christian relates to both eras. For although we belong to the new realm, with Christ as our ever-present Lord, we are not yet free from the realm of Adam while we live in this world: 'we suffer from living in the overlap of the ages' (Peterson, p. 96). Through His death and resurrection, Jesus has brought us into the new era, but the old era is not yet over: God has not finally brought the realm of Adam to a close. We can see this in the fact that sin and death (the distinctives of Adam's realm) continue in this world and afflict all Christians.

In this passage, the issue of whether the gospel promotes sin comes to the fore. To answer this Paul teaches that, since

Christians have been united with the living Lord Jesus who has paid the penalty for sin, they have an obligation to battle against sin. Paul wants us to realize what we have become through being united with Christ, and so to live accordingly.

## Structure

6:1  Question: 'Shall we go on sinning, so that grace may increase?'

6:2  Answer: No! We died to sin, so how can we go on sinning?

6:3–5  We have been united with Christ in His death and will be united with Him in His resurrection

6:6–11  As those who are united with Christ, we are dead to sin and alive to God

6:12–14  Therefore those who are united with Christ should serve God, their new master

## Old Testament background

**A changed heart:** The Old Testament makes it clear that sin is abhorrent to God and always has been (Genesis 6:5–6). Moreover, it had always been part of God's rescue plan that His people should turn away from their rebellion against Him and, instead, serve Him. Following Israel's failure to obey Him, God promises that He will enable His people to turn away from sin by giving them new hearts, so that they *will* follow His laws (Ezekiel 36:24–27 and Jeremiah 31:33).

## Text notes

### 1 OBJECTION: 'SHALL WE GO ON SINNING, SO THAT GRACE MAY INCREASE?'

This objection springs most immediately from Paul's assertion, in 5:20, that the Law increases sin, with the result that God's gift of righteousness and life is seen to be even more generous. Naturally the question arises, 'Does not the "reign of grace" simply encourage sinning?' In short, does the gospel promote sin?

Yet the objection also comes from the context of the previous five chapters, in which Paul has shown a complete solution to the problem of how God can, justly, make rebellious people righteous. But this solution is founded on God's grace, and it involves Christ taking upon Himself all our sinful deeds. So does it mean that we can now sin with impunity, since Christ will always bear our sins? Such an idea flies in the face of the Old Testament's teaching that God hates sin and intends to rescue us from it (see OT notes). Paul, therefore, must answer the objector who suggests that the gospel promotes sin.

## 2 SUMMARY ANSWER: NO! WE DIED TO SIN, SO HOW CAN WE GO ON SINNING?

Paul instantly dismisses the objection, exposing its folly by pointing to one of God's actions in the gospel – in Christ believers have 'died to sin'. Paul then explains God's intention behind this action – His intention is that we should no longer 'live in sin'.

NB: In vv. 2–10 Paul establishes an important teaching pattern: first, he teaches about *God's action* (both in the past and in the future), then he points to *God's intention* behind that action, i.e. that we should not sin. This intention is for the way we live now, although Paul gives no indication that it will be completely fulfilled in the present. On the contrary, his commands in vv. 11–14 presuppose an ongoing battle against sin. Much confusion will be caused if we misread Paul as telling us that we *will not* sin in this world. Furthermore, we should hold back the specific application of the passage until we see the application that Paul himself gives in vv. 11–14.

## 3–5 WE HAVE BEEN UNITED WITH CHRIST IN HIS DEATH AND WILL BE UNITED WITH HIM IN HIS RESURRECTION, SO THAT WE MAY LIVE NEW LIVES

Paul follows up his summary answer in v. 2 by appealing to what he expects the Romans to know already, that when they were baptized into Christ, they died with Him. (By baptism Paul is referring to their initial regeneration at conversion, i.e. when they were born again. Baptism is the outward sign of this regeneration.) Also, since they have died with Christ, they will certainly be raised as He was. We should carefully observe the tenses that Paul uses in these verses, for they express an important tension in this part of Romans. Although we have already been fully united with Jesus in His death, we have not yet been fully united with Him in His resurrection.

◆ **God's action: We died with Christ and will be raised like Him (vv. 4a and 5)**
Paul is teaching here not only that Jesus died as our substitute (i.e. instead of us), but also that we were united with Him in His death, so that when we became Christians we died, in a sense, with Him (4a). Furthermore, v. 5 (linked to v. 4 by 'for' in the Greek) tells us that the fact that we have already been united with Jesus in His death means that our future resurrection is certain. As He was raised by God, so we too will be raised.

◆ **God's intention: We should live a new life (v. 4b)**
Jesus was raised up to new life and God's intention, in making us alive with Christ, is that we too should live new lives, rather than continue in our old sinful ways. We should (literally) 'walk in newness of life'. Furthermore, through being united with Jesus we have a hope of future resurrection and this also shows what God desires for us. 'We are to live in the present as those expecting to share the ultimate renewal of all things with Him' (Peterson, p. 98).

## 6–11 AS THOSE WHO ARE UNITED WITH CHRIST, WE ARE DEAD TO SIN AND ALIVE TO GOD

Here Paul goes through the same argument in more detail, enabling us to see the principle, that we shouldn't keep serving sin, within the context of our union with Christ in His crucifixion and in His resurrection life. At each stage, Paul appeals to what we know, hinting at what he later calls the 'renewal of our minds' (12:2).

◆ **God's action: Our old self was crucified with Him (v. 6)**
'Our old self' is 'not a part of us called our old nature, but the whole of us as we were in our pre-conversion state' (Stott, p. 176): it is the description of the person who lives in the old realm, who is given up to sin now, and who is facing condemnation in the future. Through our union with Christ, however, that person has been put to death.

◆ **God's intention: We should not serve sin (vv. 6–7)**
Again, Paul expresses the purpose behind this union. It was that
the 'body of sin', i.e. the person who lives under the power of sin,
'might be done away with'. This is not a promise of deliverance
from the present influence of sin. Rather, it is the implication
which flows from the fact of our crucifixion with Christ. In other
words, as Paul adds in v. 6b, we should no longer serve our old
master, continuing to live in rebellion against God. The principle
laid out in v. 7 explains why: those who have died have been
freed from sin. Note, however, that the word translated as 'freed'
is the same as the word that is also translated as 'justified'. Paul
is saying that through our union with Christ in His death, we
are freed from the *penalty* of sin. This should remind us of
the lessons of ch. 5: by dying with Him, we have been freed from
the old realm, where sin reigned (5:21) and condemnation was a
certainty (5:18), and have been transferred to the realm of grace.

◆ **God's action: We know that we will also live with Him (vv.
8–10)**
Having established the implications of our union with Jesus in
His death, Paul now goes on to consider the new life which
comes to us through His resurrection.
*For Jesus died to sin once for all time ... (vv. 9–10a):* In this
paragraph Paul gives us confidence in our future new life by
focusing on the sufficiency of Jesus' death and the permanence
of His resurrection. He 'cannot die again', unlike, say, Lazarus,
because the resurrection proves that the penalty for sin has been
fully paid.
*... and He now lives to God (v. 10b):* Since His death, Jesus lives
and reigns in the new realm of grace which He established; He
now lives to God, i.e. to glorify God.

◆ **God's intention: So see yourselves in Christ Jesus as dead to sin
but alive to God (v. 11)**
This instruction pulls together the argument that began in v. 6.
Paul tells us to consider ourselves in the light of what has
already happened to us, in the past, and also of what will certainly happen to us in the future. Knowing that we have been
united with Christ's death to sin and that therefore the penalty
has been paid, and knowing also that we will be raised, as He

was raised, to live for God, we should regard ourselves, in as much as we are in Christ Jesus – i.e. Christians – as being dead to sin and alive to God in the present. We are to recognize the fact that we have already been transferred from the realm of sin to the realm of grace, and that this will have consequences for the way we live, as Paul now starts to spell out.

## 12–14 THEREFORE, SERVE GOD, YOUR NEW MASTER

Paul applies the principles he has been teaching so far by telling believers to live in accordance with their union with Christ. By being united with Him we are dead to sin's penalty and thus, in Christ, we are free from sin's grasp; we will one day be raised to be free from the power and presence of sin, in the same way that Jesus has been raised. Knowing these things, it is utterly incongruous that we should persist in sin. Such a rebellious lifestyle would show scant understanding of what is true for us in Christ. We have been moved from one realm to another, so Paul instructs us to live our lives in service to our new master. He describes a conscious effort on our part, a constant battle that must be waged while we wait for our mortal bodies to be raised (8:11–13).

◆ **Do not let sin reign (12–13a)**
When we lived in the realm of sin and death inaugurated by Adam, we were wilful rebels in God's world, given over by Him to more and more sinful acts (1:21–32). We were under God's wrath and condemnation and had no hope of eventual release. Yet now we have been transferred to a new realm; we have died to sin and we will be raised. Therefore, we should no longer allow the master of the realm from which we have been released to dictate our lifestyle; we should not give our bodies in his service. Paul is not saying that we are entirely free from sin now (see Context), but that in Christ we are free to fight sin.

◆ **Offer yourselves to God (13b–14)**
We now have a new master, who has brought us from death to life, and so we should give ourselves to our saviour God and use our bodies and minds to serve Him.

Paul ends this part of his letter in strong terms, pressing home God's intention that our old master, sin, should not reign over us, for the reason that we, by God's action through the gospel, 'are not under Law but under grace'. To be under the Law is to be under the condemnation that the Law brings (5:20 and 3:20), to be in the realm of sin and death, but the believer lives in the realm of grace and looks forward to eternal life. So, Paul exhorts, sin should not be 'the lord of those who have been captured by God's grace through the gospel' (Peterson, p. 101). Later on, in 7:1–6, he will explain how it is that we are not under the Law.

# Key themes and application

The teaching in this passage is founded upon the fact that we are united with Christ. If we have faith in Jesus, His death is our death and His life, our life. Paul brings out two aspects of this union:

## ◆ We died to sin

'... union with Christ is the way we identify with Him in His epoch-changing death and draw on its benefits' (Peterson, p. 97). The rebellious person that the Christian used to be has died with Christ, the penalty for his sin has been paid and he has been transferred to the realm of grace and life. It is critical that we should not see being 'dead to sin' as being free from sin in our lives in this world, as this passage has often been taken to mean. To suppose that we can be sinless now is a cruel burden to place on one another, producing either great discouragement or self-deception. What it fails to recognize is the very real tension of our current position; we are waiting for the death and resurrection of our bodies, for the time when the realm of Adam will finally be brought to an end. The correct application of this passage is that we must fight against sin.

## ◆ We will be raised

Although it has yet to happen, our bodily resurrection is a future certainty. Just as Christ was raised, so we will be raised and then we will finally be free from sin for ever. It is vital that Christians teach and encourage one another about the certainties of heaven, for we need clear convictions about what God will do in the future if we are to survive in the present struggle against sin, and if we are to avoid raising false expectations for this life.

### ◆ The fight against sin

Paul suggests that understanding our union with Christ will actually motivate us to fight in the present. On the one hand, we know we have died to sin. We are therefore freed from sin's penalty and its ultimate power, i.e. death. God's purpose in uniting us with Christ in His death is that we should be what we have become and live a new life. On the other hand, we also know that in the future we will live to God like the risen Christ, and that the certainty of this destination should also encourage our present obedience to God. The gospel does not promote licentiousness! Quite the opposite: we are to acknowledge what *has* happened to us and what *will* happen to us, and live accordingly.

We need to see ourselves as we actually are – people who have died to the old realm of sin and death and who have been raised to the realm of life. Yet, until our resurrection is complete, we are caught in the tension of living in the overlap of these two eras/realms. Meanwhile, we have an obligation to battle against sin – it is God's will that we should do so. This presents us with a constant challenge, to avoid putting our bodies, faculties and gifts at the disposal of sin, but instead to use them all in the service of the God who has saved us. For example, our speech could be used to puff ourselves up or to deceive others, but instead it should be employed to build up believers and to point others towards Christ. The Christian's life should be characterized by a conscious resistance to sin and by a desire to serve God instead. If these two things are not present in someone's life, we would question that person's understanding of the gospel. (NB: Paul will expand his application in ch. 12.)

Throughout this passage, Paul appeals to what we know. The problem of our rebellion originated in our minds (1:21) and the solution to the problem results in a changed mind. This is not to say that our thinking will now be free from sin, but that we now know differently about ourselves in the light of the gospel.

## Unanswered questions

◆ Why do I constantly fail if I have died to sin?

◆ If the Law no longer condemns me, can I get away with sin anyway (6:15)?

# The aim of this study

To recognize that in Christ we have died to sin and will be raised to new righteous life. We are therefore alive in Christ, in the present. We should be what we have become and do battle with sin.

# Suggested questions

◆ All Christians know they should not sin. Why then do we find it so hard to obey God?

**1 OBJECTION: 'SHALL WE GO ON SINNING, SO THAT GRACE MAY INCREASE?'**

◆ Why does the question in 6:1 arise? Can you put it in your own words?

**2 SUMMARY ANSWER: NO! WE DIED TO SIN, SO HOW CAN WE GO ON SINNING?**

◆ What is Paul's immediate answer? What questions does his answer raise for us?

**3–5 WE HAVE BEEN UNITED WITH CHRIST IN HIS DEATH AND WILL BE UNITED WITH HIM IN HIS RESURRECTION, SO THAT WE MAY LIVE NEW LIVES**

◆ What has taken place, in the past, in the lives of Christians (i.e. those who have been baptized into Christ Jesus)? What will happen to Christians in the future?
◆ What, therefore, is God's intention for His people?
◆ Why shouldn't we go on sinning?

**6–11 AS THOSE WHO ARE UNITED WITH CHRIST, WE ARE DEAD TO SIN AND ALIVE TO GOD**

◆ What does Paul mean when he says that our 'old self was crucified with him'? (Think back to 5:12–21.)

◆ What was God's *intention* in doing this? When Paul says 'we should no longer serve sin' what can he *not* mean? What does he mean?
◆ NB: The word translated as 'freed' in v. 7 could also be translated as 'justified'. How are we 'justified from sin'?
◆ How does Jesus' resurrection give us confidence that we have truly 'died to sin' and that we will definitely be raised?
◆ How are we to view ourselves? And why?
◆ Again, why shouldn't we go on sinning?

## 12–14 THEREFORE, SERVE GOD, YOUR NEW MASTER
◆ In the light of vv. 1–11, how do these instructions make sense?
  – How do vv. 1–11 encourage us to fight against sin?
◆ For the following two questions, consider the two areas of speech and how we use our gifts. Try to think as practically and specifically as possible.
  – In what sense can we offer the parts of our body to sin?
  – In what sense should we offer ourselves to God?

# ROMANS 6:15–7:6

## Context

Paul is continuing to address the issue of sin in the life of the believer. In 1:18–5:21, the gospel is shown to offer a solution to the problem of God's *wrath* against our rebellion, but might that mean that present acts of rebellion no longer matter? The first half of ch. 6 started to answer that question: Paul has told us that we were united with Christ in His death in order that we should live a new life (6:4), and that we will one day be resurrected, as Jesus was (6:5), to live for God, totally free from sin and death (6:10). Both our past experience and our future expectation, therefore, show us that God's intention for us is that we should not sin; being aware of this should motivate us in our battle, in the present, against sin.

In 6:14, Paul said that we are not under Law, and later on, in 7:1–6, he explains how this can be so. But first, in 6:15–23, he deals with the suggestion that Christians may sin with impunity, because they know that the gospel proclaims forgiveness for believers. 'Not at all!' says Paul. Wilful persistence in sin, such that a person was unwilling to repent in a given area of his life, would clearly demonstrate that that person was serving sin rather than God and therefore will not be saved. The larger context of chs 6–8, however, reminds us of sin's present reality; despite our clear obligation to resist it (6:12, 19), sin will nevertheless continue to be a feature of our lives (lived in mortal bodies, 7:14–23) until our bodies are themselves raised (8:11).

# Structure

**6:15** Question: 'Shall we sin because we are not under Law but under grace?'

**6:16** Answer: You must not sin! You are slaves to the master you obey – either sin or righteousness

**6:17–19** Through obedience to the gospel, you have become slaves to righteousness, so obey your new master

**6:20–23** The consequences of being a slave to sin or to righteousness

**7:1–6** You are not under Law, since you died with Christ

# Old Testament background

**The Law:** The Law had been given to the Jews by God. It was given for their benefit, that they might know how to live as His people, and they would have assumed that, since it came from God, the Law was good. Many parts of the Old Testament give the impression that it will be binding for ever (e.g. Psalm 119:89–91). Furthermore, the Jews had been told that the consequences of disobedience to the Law would be their own destruction (Deuteronomy 30:15–18). Thus, to the vast majority of Jews the idea of living as one of God's people without the Law would have been preposterous.

# Text notes

### 15 QUESTION:'SHALL WE SIN BECAUSE WE ARE NOT UNDER LAW BUT UNDER GRACE?'

We need to see whether this question is different from that in 6:1 and if so, in what way. There, the objection was that we might be able to justify sinning if it increased God's grace. Paul's answer was that to continue to sin is incongruous, in the light of God's purpose in uniting us with Christ (see Context). This, however, still leaves a question: it may be God's intention that we should not sin, but are we free to sin anyway, since we are not under Law but under grace and will not face the consequences of our rebellion? This possibility may have caused great concern among the Jews, who would have seen the removal of the Law and its commands as giving people licence to sin freely (see OT notes). Yet, as Paul goes on to show, this betrays a misunderstanding of the role of the Law.

## 16 ANSWER: YOU MUST NOT SIN! YOU ARE SLAVES TO THE MASTER YOU OBEY – EITHER SIN OR RIGHTEOUSNESS

The concept of offering oneself to someone as his slave was not alien to Rome in the first century, when some slaves, having been released, would give up their freedom in order to become a slave to the master of their choice. Paul's point here is simple enough: the way you behave shows the master to whom you belong. Two possible masters are available: 'sin', leading to death, or 'obedience', leading to righteousness. We should note that at this point 'obedience' cannot be obedience to the Law, since Paul has told us we are not under the Law. In the next verses Paul explains what he does mean.

## 17–19 THROUGH OBEDIENCE TO THE GOSPEL, YOU HAVE BECOME SLAVES TO RIGHTEOUSNESS, SO OBEY YOUR NEW MASTER

Paul's illustration is imperfect, as he concedes in v. 19, for we do not choose our master in the first place; we are all slaves to sin unless rescued by God. So Paul is not presenting the Romans with a choice, and nor is he teaching salvation by works. Rather, he explains here that a change of loyalty has occurred and that this has implications.

♦ **By trusting the gospel, you have been given a new master (vv. 17–18)**

Paul praises God for the fact that the Roman Christians have been set free from slavery to sin and have become slaves to righteousness. This happened when they wholeheartedly obeyed – literally, became 'obedient from the heart to' – the gospel. Or, in the language of ch. 5, Paul tells them that by receiving 'God's abundant provision of grace' (5:17) they have been transferred from the realm of sin and death to the realm of grace and righteousness (5:21). Sin no longer reigns over them.

### ✦ Serve your new master with your body (v. 19)

Despite this change of master, Christians still live in the 'overlap' of the two realms (see Context to 6:1–14 in the previous study): while, on the one hand, we have become slaves to righteousness, on the other hand our bodies have yet to be redeemed from the realm of sin and death (8:23). And so we still struggle with sin. Nevertheless, we still have an obligation. We are to give our bodies in the service of our new master. 'Be what you have become, not what you were' is the thrust of Paul's argument here. In the past we gave ourselves to the rebellion and ever-increasing lawlessness described in 1:18–32, but now that we have been moved into a new realm, we should give ourselves – our faculties, our time, our effort – to righteousness which leads to holiness. 'Holiness', here, is 'the alternative to the condition of uncleanness and lawlessness from which we were rescued' (Peterson, p. 103).

Going back to the principle laid down in v. 16, we see that it is by striving to give our bodies in obedient service to God that we demonstrate that He is our master. If we don't do so, we show that He isn't.

## 20–23 THE CONSEQUENCES OF BEING A SLAVE TO SIN OR TO RIGHTEOUSNESS

Having given the command to obey, Paul presents the motivation that is necessary if we are to do so. It comes from a clear-eyed examination of the realities of the two realms.

As slaves to sin, we were unable to live in a way that acknowledged God's rule. Looking back, we can see that we enjoyed no benefits at the time; our lives were dominated by the sins outlined in ch. 1, which eventually result in condemnation (2:9). However, now that we are slaves to righteousness, we know that we are seen as holy by God and that we can look forward to eternal life. When the two alternatives are laid alongside each other like this, in stark contrast, the command to give our bodies in obedience to God makes perfect sense. Verse 23 clarifies the matter even further: the life that is lived in obedience to sin rightly earns death, but to those who, by grace, live with Christ as Lord, God gives eternal life. The contrast might be laid out as follows:

| When? | Relation to sin | Relation to righteousness | Fruit | Result |
|-------|-----------------|---------------------------|-------|--------|
| Previously | slave | free | shameful things* | death |
| But now ... | set free | slave | holiness** | eternal life |

*Notes on the NIV translation*
\* Verse 21a may just as easily be translated: 'What benefit did you reap ("what fruit") at the time? The things you are now ashamed of.'
\*\* Verse 22b could also be translated: '... and the return you get is sanctification/holiness' (same word in the Greek).

## 7:1–6 YOU ARE NOT UNDER LAW, SINCE YOU DIED WITH CHRIST

The whole of this passage so far has rested on Paul's assertion that believers are no longer under Law (v. 15). This teaching, if misunderstood, is the only reason why anyone might have thought he could sin with impunity, but Paul has shown how such thinking is fatally flawed. He now returns to his earlier line of argument and explains how it is that we are not under the Law.

◆ **Death releases someone from the Law (vv. 1–3)**
Paul uses the Law on marriage to illustrate the point that a contract binding two people in relationship will no longer stand if one party dies. The wife will not be called an adulteress if she remarries after her husband's death (v. 3).

◆ **You have been released from the Law to belong to God (v. 4)**
The principle is true for us, too. We used to relate to God by the Law He had set up to bind us to Himself, but our disobedience meant that we faced death – the Law said so (see OT notes). Now, however, we have died with Christ, so that the Law can no longer condemn us to death. Instead, we have been raised with Christ to eternal life, to belong to Him by grace.

At this point Paul explains how different is our relationship to sin, now that we have been transferred from the realm of sin to the new realm of grace. He describes our previous experience as, literally, 'when we were in the flesh'. This refers to our entire pre-Christian existence: we were controlled by our rebellious hearts, in accordance with the principles of the realm of sin and death, and we were dominated by sin, the Law and death, with death having the final say over us. With Christ, though, we have died to the power of these things and been released from the Law to serve God in the new way of the Spirit. In both realms we are servants, but there is all the difference in the world between serving evil and serving the Lord Jesus (v. 4). In the rest of ch. 7 and in ch. 8, Paul goes on to elaborate upon how the Law arouses sinful passions, and also to describe the nature of this new life in the Spirit (v. 6).

# Key themes and application

✦ **Despite being saved by grace, we still need to fight against sin**
Once again, in this passage, Paul presents the great news of the gospel, that through God's grace we may be set free from the tyranny of sin in order to serve God instead. Living with God as our master, we have an obvious obligation to serve Him. So, although we know that we will still sin, we are to offer the whole of ourselves, our minds, our bodies and our gifts, in the service of God, doing so consciously and in as much as we are able. We do so, not because it will earn God's favour, but in response to His goodness in releasing us from the mastery of sin. Paul's command in v. 19 calls for careful reflection: to what extent do we put our gifts, our plans and our time at God's disposal? And in what areas is radical change needed?

This passage has much to teach us about freedom. The world tells us that freedom means being able to do what you want, to please yourself, but Paul says that this is impossible, since all who are not in Christ are in fact slaves to sin, the Law and death. Furthermore, we are not released from these things in order to be our own master, but in order to serve the God who has saved us. This service is *true* freedom, producing holiness and guaranteeing eternal life. The extent to which we may still think of freedom as serving ourselves shows the extent to which the world's thinking still infects our minds.

◆ **To sin wilfully and unrepentantly shows that we are not saved**
The objection in v. 15, that life under grace might allow us to sin with impunity, is thoroughly refuted; we should heed the severity of tone in Paul's warning. To suggest that it no longer matters if we sin, because God will forgive us anyway, is to demonstrate that our allegiance is to rebellion – we show that ultimately we want to serve ourselves. Also, such an attitude shows our ignorance of the results of wilful, unrepentant sin. If we continue to sin in this deliberate manner, we will deserve the wage that we are paid, i.e. death. This passage, and also the one in the previous study, should teach us that God does not in any way take sinning lightly; we should be wary of the temptation ever to think that it doesn't matter.

◆ **We have been set free from the Law by Jesus' death**
If Christ had not died, we would still be bound to the Law and therefore to death. Having died with Him, though, we are free to serve Him. Having died to the Law, totally, we should beware of slipping back into legalism, i.e. thinking we have to *do good or religious things* in order to earn God's favour – according to Paul, this is an impossibility in any case (3:20). Once again, it is only God's work through Christ that saves us, a fact that we should hold on to with ever-deepening gratitude.

## Unanswered questions

◆ How does the Law arouse sinful passions (7:5)?
◆ What does it mean to 'serve in the new way of the Spirit' (7:6)?
◆ What about my constant failure to live up to the obligation to fight sin?
◆ If the Law arouses sinfulness, is the Law itself sinful? (7:7)

## The aim of this study

To see how our freedom, from sin and from the Law, brings with it a greater obligation to obey God.

# Suggested questions

◆ Summarize Paul's answer, in 6:1–14, as to why the Christian shouldn't go on sinning.

## 15 QUESTION: 'SHALL WE SIN BECAUSE WE ARE NOT UNDER LAW BUT UNDER GRACE?'

◆ Why might the fact that we are 'under grace' lead someone to think that he could go on sinning? Put Paul's question in your own words.

## 16 ANSWER: YOU MUST NOT SIN! YOU ARE SLAVES TO THE MASTER YOU OBEY – EITHER SIN OR RIGHTEOUSNESS

◆ Explain Paul's illustration in v. 16.
◆ If we persist in sinning wilfully, what does that say about us?
◆ 'I don't want to be a Christian, because I want to be free to do what I want.' How would Paul respond?

## 17–19 THROUGH OBEDIENCE TO THE GOSPEL, YOU HAVE BECOME SLAVES TO RIGHTEOUSNESS, SO OBEY YOUR NEW MASTER

◆ What has happened to the Christian? How?
◆ What are we now obliged to do? Why? Give examples of what that would involve.

## 20–23 THE CONSEQUENCES OF BEING A SLAVE TO SIN OR TO RIGHTEOUSNESS

◆ Paul draws a contrast between two ways of life – what are they? What is each one like? To what does each one lead?
◆ How does this contrast motivate us to obey God?

## 7:1–6 YOU ARE NOT UNDER LAW, SINCE YOU DIED WITH CHRIST

(NB: Paul is now coming back to explain how it is that Christians are no longer under the Law (6:15).)

◆ What is the point of Paul's illustration from marriage?
◆ How have we been released from the authority of the Law?
◆ Contrast the life lived under the Law with the life that belongs to Christ.

## SUMMARY

◆ 'It doesn't matter if I sin, because God will forgive me anyway.'
Use Paul's arguments in this passage to answer this statement.

# ROMANS 7:7–25

## Context

At this point in his letter, Paul needs to address two important issues that have been raised by his argument so far.

The first concerns the Law. Paul has been showing how the Law has a very close relationship with sin: the Law makes us conscious of sin (3:20) and it makes sin increase (5:20). There is also the connection, that Paul points out, between the Christian's death to (or freedom from) sin and his or her death to (or freedom from) the Law (6:22; 7:6); the former is even caused by the latter (6:14). The Jews would have understood the Law to be essentially good (see OT notes), but it could be inferred that Paul is saying that the Law and sin are practically synonymous. He must clarify.

The second issue is that of sin in the life of the Christian. Paul has stressed our obligation not to sin, on the basis, first, of our union with Christ in His death and resurrection (6:11–14) and, second, because God is our new master. Yet the Christian is still faced with the fact that he or she nevertheless continues to sin. Why is this so? In dealing with both issues, Paul sharpens his teaching by speaking from his own experience.

NB: This section of Romans, 7:14–25, has been an exegetical battleground for hundreds of years. The central question concerns Paul's experience: is he talking about himself in his pre-Christian state, or himself as a Christian, or is he perhaps viewing the former through the eyes of the latter? The question is raised because the struggle within himself that he describes is deemed to be unusual in the life of a Christian, let alone that of an apostle.

Both Stott and Moo find a contradiction between this passage and 6:6, where Paul told us that Christians are no longer slaves to sin. Stott's solution is to suggest that Paul is imagining he were an Old Testament believer who is regenerate, but who does not yet know anything of the indwelling Spirit and so struggles as he tries and fails to live according to the Law (Stott, pp. 205–10). Moo concludes that Paul is looking back, with his Christian understanding, upon his own plight and that of the Jews, all of them living under the Law (Moo, pp. 443–51). Neither commentator, however, takes account of the tension that exists between the inner being and the flesh, as will be discussed in the Text Notes.

Here we will take the view that Paul is describing the normal experience of a Christian believer. The main reasons for following this interpretation are as follows:

1 The apparent plain meaning of the text. Paul writes in the present tense, whereas he has used the past tense in vv. 7–13.
2 The wider context. Throughout chs 5–8, the subject is what it means to be justified, i.e. Christian (see Context).
3 Verse 25 describes, undeniably, Paul's present experience.

For commentators supporting this position, see Cranfield, pp. 164–5, Peterson, pp. 106–9, Seccombe, pp. 122–7 and, especially, Nygren, p. 284 ff.

## Structure

**7:7–13** The Law shows sin to be sin, but the Law itself is good
**7:14–25** Christian experience: slavery to two masters

## Old Testament background

**The Law ...**
   ... *was given by God:* As such it was dominant in the life of the people of Israel.

... *is good:* The Law appeared to be built upon God's character, and to reflect it. Furthermore, He consistently called His people back to follow it. There seems to be no escaping its goodness.

... *is life-giving:* The Law was given to the people of Israel with the promise that if they obeyed it, they would live (see Leviticus 18:5). To break it, however, meant death (see Deuteronomy 30:15–20).

... *drives people to seek mercy:* God always knew that Israel would fail (see Deuteronomy 31:16–21), and so the Law's main purpose is, actually, to reveal sin. It drives people to seek God's mercy (Psalm 51) and so, ultimately, to seek Jesus (Galatians 3:23–24). The Jews in the New Testament, however, did not see this part of the Law's purpose.

# Text notes

### 7–13 THE LAW SHOWS SIN TO BE SIN, BUT THE LAW ITSELF IS GOOD

As before, Paul raises a question in order to advance his argument; it is important that we should know what lies behind the question.

◆ **Question: Is the Law sinful? (v. 7a)**
Although this may not be a question that naturally comes to our minds, it is one that demands an answer because of the connection Paul has been making between the Law and sin (see Context). If the Law exposes sin and causes it to increase, is it in fact sinful itself? And if it is sinful, how does this square with the Old Testament (see OT notes)?

◆ **No! The Law defines sin (v. 7b)**
Paul stresses that although the Law has a close relationship with sin, the two things are different. The Law defines sin by telling us what is right or wrong; for example, coveting is shown to be outlawed.

◆ **Sin uses the Law to provoke evil (v. 8)**
Although the Law and sin are different things, sin makes use of the Law. But apart from the Law, sin is powerless; Paul even describes it as dead. When sin is confronted with God's Law,

however, it revives. It now knows which laws to break, which lines to cross, and so produces every kind of rebellious inclination in the individual. For example, as soon as we are told, 'Do not covet' we immediately start thinking of things we do covet.

NB: In this passage, we need to think carefully about what Paul means by 'sin'. In chs 1–3, sin was defined as people's personal rebellion against God. In chs 6–8, however, Paul personifies sin as a master that holds people under its power and which, though it is no longer the Christians' master, still influences their mortal bodies.

◆ **Sin uses the Law to sentence people to death (vv. 9–11)**
Although Paul speaks from his own experience, we cannot be sure of the time to which he is referring. He may be identifying himself with Adam, who did live apart from any law before he was commanded not to eat the fruit (see 5:12–14), or he could be referring to the experience of the people of Israel when they received the Mosaic Law. More likely, he is thinking back to the time before *he* knew the Law. His point, however, is that when, in his own life, he was confronted with God's Law, sin seized its moment and caused him to rebel against the Law – which was supposed to give life – with the result that he ended up condemned to death as a Law-breaker (see OT notes).

◆ **Therefore the Law is good and sin is seen to be sinful (vv. 12–13)**
Throughout this description of the relationship between sin and the Law, Paul demonstrates that it is sin that is active, causing us to rebel and die, whereas the God-given Law is only intended to give life. It is therefore sin, and not the Law, that causes us to disobey. The Law is itself untainted and Paul describes it in the highest possible terms: it is holy, righteous and good.

The goodness of the Law, as described here, seems so much at odds with the ruin experienced by the individual under the Law that Paul is prompted to ask again whether something so perfect could have been responsible for his death. Again, his denial is emphatic, but this time he gives more insight into God's purpose. Sin is allowed to separate someone from God, by means of His perfect Law, in order that sin itself might be exposed in all its wretchedness. In its wilful corruption of God's life-giving Law, the depravity of sin is laid bare.

## 14–25 CHRISTIAN EXPERIENCE: SLAVERY TO TWO MASTERS

Verse 14 is connected to v. 13, in the Greek, by the word 'for', so clearly Paul is continuing to explain his relationship with God's Law. But here he switches to the present tense – speaking specifically of his ongoing battle, as a believer, with sin. Although this is an interpretation that some reject (see Context), it is the key to understanding a vitally important passage on authentic Christian experience.

In v. 14 Paul identifies a problem. Although the Law is spiritual, he himself is 'unspiritual, sold as a slave to sin'. We might ask how it is possible for him to say this, in the light of 6:7, 18 and 22, where we were assured that Christians have been set free from sin. He goes on to explain.

◆ **The experience** (vv. 14–20)
Although, from the debate that this passage has aroused, we might not expect it, Paul does in fact describe his experience with stark clarity. In brief, he finds that there is a tension between his intentions and his actions. He has the desire to do what is good, but finds he cannot carry it out (v. 18b); despite good desires and intentions, he does evil instead (v. 19).

◆ **The implication** (vv. 16–20)
Paul draws an implication from his contradictory experience: his good intention demonstrates that, despite his inability to obey consistently, he does agree with God's good Law. He concludes that ultimately, as a Christian, it is not he who is responsible for doing wrong, but sin inside him (v. 17) which, again, is shown to be utterly rebellious. Paul runs through the logic again in vv. 18–20, this time identifying his sinful nature (better translated as 'flesh') as the culprit.

◆ **The explanation** (vv. 21–23)
The explanation is that there is a conflict between Paul's inner being, regenerated by the Spirit, and his flesh. As a justified believer, he knows that his inner being has been captured by God, and that at his very heart he has been set free from sin. Now he is a slave to God (6:22) and to His Law (7:25), which means that his will agrees with, and delights in, God's Law, wanting to obey it and therefore hating his constant rebellion. (See Section Notes for comments on Paul's use of the word 'mind', e.g. in v. 25.)

Waging war against the Christian's inner being is his flesh, referred to variously as his 'members' (v. 23) and his 'body of death' (v. 24). This aspect of the Christian remains 'a slave to sin', belonging still to the realm of sin and death (vv. 14, 25) and so, despite the protestations of the inner being, continuing to do what is wrong and rebelling against God's Law. This phenomenon, also referred to in Galatians 5:17, is different from the rebellion that was being described earlier in Romans, in 1:18–32. There, there was no battle, because our inner being was set, fundamentally, against God's rule. Only the Christian will experience this battle. Although many unbelievers want to live better lives than they do, fundamentally they do not want to glorify God. In the language of ch. 5, the struggle that Paul writes about here is the consequence of living in the overlap of two realms. The Christian's inner being is under the influence of the realm of grace and life (5:21) but, while living in this world, his or her sinful nature remains in the realm, and under the mastery, of sin and death (5:14).

◆ **The future rescue (vv. 24–25)**
This constant battle is a certain reality in the life of the Christian. But Paul's cry for relief in v. 24, though desperate, is not hopeless. He goes on to answer his own question in v. 25, praising God because the rescue that is accomplished through Christ will bring relief from our struggle with the flesh. In ch. 8, Paul tells us that the fulfilment of this rescue will happen when our bodies are resurrected, as Jesus' body was (8:11).

# Key themes and application

◆ **God's Law is good: sin is evil**
Paul clarifies the relationship between the Law and sin, showing that the Law should not be identified as sinful, and explaining how sin uses the Law to bring sin and death to mankind. This is an important reassurance for the Jew (see Context), who will realize that the gospel does not contradict God's Law but, rather, sees it as holy, righteous and good. It means that we may have full confidence in the utter goodness of all God's plans, and of His standards, and so avoid the danger of questioning His motives or character. The Law is good and is upheld by

the gospel. Understanding this, we should also acknowledge the absolute depravity of sin.

◆ **The normal Christian experience of struggling against sin**
In the Christian life there is a struggle between what we want to do and what, in fact, we do, while sin continues to assault our mortal, unresurrected bodies. But we know that our cry for relief from this battle *will* be answered; our future rescue is certain.

To interpret this passage as being a description of Paul's pre-Christian life is a serious mistake; it would mean that the Christian who may be struggling with sin would be denied one of the Bible's most reassuring passages. If we are weary from the ongoing temptations to sin and from our constant failure to obey, even after many previous stumbles, then Paul's affirmation, that we need not pretend we are unscathed by such battles, is a great relief. Paul describes this conflict as a normal experience for the believer, which encourages us to join with him in the desperate cry of v. 24 and to hold on to the certain answer of v. 25. Only the Christian will be bothered by sin in this way because only the Christian, to whom God has brought new life, will genuinely want to obey Him. Unbelievers may want to do good, but not in submission to God's authority.

Taking it that this passage does refer to the Christian, there is a challenge for us here if we do not experience this battle, for Paul sees it as proof that someone is regenerate.

It has been suggested that this experience of struggle is the experience of Christians who are not trusting the Holy Spirit to help them. A classic statement of this position is as follows: 'If we live in the Spirit, if we walk by faith in the risen Christ, we can truly "stand aside" while the Spirit gains new victories over the flesh every day' (Watchman Nee, *The Normal Christian Life*, p.120, Kingsway, 1962). Yet this kind of teaching, about the possibility of living lives that are constantly victorious against sin – teaching that is still common today – stems from a wrong interpretation of Romans 7. This matters because it places an unnecessary burden upon genuine Christians, who continue to struggle with sin while they wait for the redemption of their bodies (8:23).

Paul does not say that we will not resist sin at all – indeed we must, as Paul taught us in 6:15–23 – but it is important that we face the reality of our sin while we live in this world.

## Unanswered questions

◆ How will God rescue me from this body of death?
◆ How do I keep on fighting? When will the struggle end?

## The aim of this study

The main aim is to acknowledge that a constant battle with sin is a hallmark of the normal Christian life; relief will come in the future. Other aims: to have confidence in the goodness of the Law and to see the rebelliousness of sin.

## Suggested questions

◆ What are our normal reactions to ongoing sin in our lives?

### 7–13 THE LAW SHOWS SIN TO BE SIN, BUT THE LAW ITSELF IS GOOD

◆ The question in 7:7, 'Is the Law sin?', seems unexpected. Why might it arise from Paul's teaching so far? (Look at 5:20; 6:14; 6:22; 7:6.) Why does the question matter? And why must Paul refute it?
◆ How does Paul describe the relationship between the Law and sin?
    – In what sense is Paul using the word 'sin'?
◆ What effect does the Law have on sin?
    – Paul is here giving a personal testimony: to what period is he referring? Describe what happened to him. Think of another example apart from coveting.
    – What conclusions does Paul draw from his experience? And why?
◆ So, is the Law sin? Summarize Paul's answer.

## 14–25 CHRISTIAN EXPERIENCE: SLAVERY TO TWO MASTERS

◆ Why do you think v. 14 has caused so much trouble for Christians over the years? What questions does it force us to ask, in the light of Paul's teaching so far?

– Earlier on, Paul said that Christians have been freed from sin (6:7, 18 and 22), but now he says he is 'sold as a slave to sin' (7:14). How is this possible, according to Paul?

◆ How does Paul describe his present experience as a Christian?

– Is our experience anything like his? Put his experience into your own words.

– What *implications* does Paul draw from his experience? Where does the problem lie?

– What are Paul's observations in vv. 21–23?

– What is his reaction?

– Is his cry in v. 24 a hopeless cry? Why/why not?

– What is his conclusion?

◆ What should be our expectations, regarding sin in our Christian lives?

– Many Christian writers describe the way we may live lives that are constantly victorious over sin. How does this contrast with Paul's experience? How would he react to such teaching?

– A young Christian writes to you in distress: 'I thought I was a Christian, but I'm not sure any more. Over the weekend I saw some old friends and before I knew it, I was back into all my old habits. Someone has told me that my faith was obviously not real. I don't know what to think. Please help!' How would you reply?

# Romans 8:1–17

## Context

Since 5:12, Paul has been describing the Christian as someone who has been released from the joint tyranny of sin and the Law. Both caused us to be separated from God: sin led to death (6:21) and the Law caused us to be condemned for our sin (7:5). Now, however, Paul says we have been set free from both sin (6:22) and the Law (7:6) by dying with Christ, as a result of which we can and should live to serve God as our new master. This week's passage, 8:1–17, concludes the arguments of these chapters, announcing that Christians no longer face condemnation for sin and that they *will* be raised from the dead.

Paul's aim in these verses is to reassure Christians, and this he does by telling them that (1) Jesus has died for them, (2) they have the Spirit, (3) they will be raised from the dead, and (4) they are members of God's family.

## Structure

8:1–4 Christians are free from condemnation

8:5–11 Christians have new minds now and, in the future, will have new bodies too

8:12–17 Christians, if genuine, have a certain glorious future

# Old Testament background

**Ezekiel 36 and Jeremiah 31:** When the LORD told Israel that He would rescue her from exile (into which she had been thrown for her rebellion against Him), He promised that He would put His Spirit in His people (Ezekiel 36:26–27), giving them new hearts and moving them to obey Him (Jeremiah 31:33). Both passages will have their ultimate fulfilment in heaven, but in Romans 8 we see the Spirit beginning this work, as He causes us to battle with sin.

# Text notes

## 1–4 CHRISTIANS ARE FREE FROM CONDEMNATION …

Paul brings his argument to a climax with a momentous statement about believers: 'those who are in Christ Jesus' are not condemned. But why does he introduce this great truth about their status with the word 'therefore'? There are three possibilities. First, he may have had in mind the early part of Romans, where he demonstrated how Jesus' death provides the solution to the condemnation that is faced by the whole of mankind, on account of its rebellion against God (see 3:21–26). Second, he could be continuing the line of thought at the end of ch. 7, aiming to show how the Christian who finds himself battling with sin is not condemned – this certainly becomes the theme of vv. 12–17. Paul's main intention, however, must be the third possibility, which is to pull together all the threads of his argument in chs 6 and 7. In these chapters he has established that Christians are free from the mastery of sin and the Law. 'Therefore,' he concludes, 'there is no condemnation for those who are in Christ Jesus.' As for the reasons for this, he will now explain.

◆ **… because the Spirit of life has set us free from sin and death (v. 2)**
Not for the first time, Paul describes the Christian as having been freed, but now he begins to explain how this has happened, presenting the Holy Spirit in His role of liberator. Paul's use of the word 'law', here, is ambiguous. The 'law of the Spirit of life' seems to refer to a 'power' or 'authority' (as in 7:21, 23) that overcomes the 'law' or 'power' of sin and death. His point, however,

is that although we used to be under the constant rule of sin, which made use of the Law in order to condemn us to death for our disobedience (7:9), the Spirit has set us free and given us life. But what does this mean in the light of the fact that we still sin, as Paul described in 7:14–25?

◆ ... because God fulfilled the Law's righteous demands through Jesus' death (vv. 3–4)

The Law that God gave to the Jews was given so that they might have life (see OT notes for 7:7–25), but it was unable to give life because the flesh, dominated by sin, was trapped in rebellion. But God stepped in, achieving what the Law could not do by sending Jesus. Verses 3b–4a may be taken as a summary of 3:21–26, since they describe the achievements of the cross:

1  Jesus came as a sacrifice when He died as 'a sin offering'.
2  He died as our substitute, 'in the likeness of sinful man (flesh)'. Stott explains this phrase carefully: 'neither "in the likeness of flesh", only seeming to be human ... for His humanity was real; nor "in sinful flesh", assuming a fallen nature, for His humanity was sinless, but "in the likeness of sinful flesh", because His humanity was both real and sinless simultaneously'.
3  God did this to execute His judgment upon sin, so that His righteous Law, which required that our sin be justly punished, was satisfied. (NB: In the light of the Christian's struggle with sin in 7:14–25, 'the righteous requirements of the Law' must refer to God's judgment on sin rather than to our obedience to the Law.)

This is not true for everyone, but only for those who have been justified by trusting in what God has done. Paul describes such people as those who live (or 'walk') according to the Spirit rather than the flesh. Living according to the Spirit means living as a justified person. *It does not refer to a means by which the Spirit gives us extra power to do God's will.* (See Key Themes and Application on 'The empowering presence'.)

## 5–11 CHRISTIANS HAVE NEW MINDS NOW AND, IN THE FUTURE, WILL HAVE NEW BODIES TOO

◆ **The distinction between Christian and non-Christian is a difference of mind (vv. 5–8)**

Paul here defines what it means to live according to the Spirit or according to the flesh. He insists that the minds of the Christian and the non-Christian, at their cores, have desires that are essentially different. The non-Christian wants what the flesh wants, i.e. to live in rebellion against God, and this is a mindset that results in death. Although the Christian does still sin, as Paul established in 7:15–23, ultimately he or she wants what the Spirit (i.e. God) wants (7:25); with this mindset comes the experience of the life and peace given by God's grace. (NB: The Greek word used for 'mind' here is different from that used in 7:25, but the two are practically synonymous.)

Verses 7–8 put it more starkly, reminding us that the essence of sin is found in the mind, as we saw back in 1:18–32; it is the wilful suppressing of the truth about God. The non-Christian cannot and will not obey God and, in fact, is incapable of pleasing Him.

◆ **All Christians are controlled by the Spirit within them and will therefore one day be given new bodies (vv. 9–11)**

Despite the fact that Christians continue to battle with the flesh (7:23), the contrast with the non-Christian could not be greater, because the Christian is controlled by the Holy Spirit. Paul now explains the implications of having or not having the Holy Spirit. Those who don't have the Spirit are simply not Christians. But those who do have the Spirit can be certain that their bodies of death (cf. 7:24) will, in the future, be raised to life.

We should note that the Holy Spirit is described as both the Spirit of Christ and as the Spirit of God: there is no division in their nature or their work.

## 12–17 CHRISTIANS, IF GENUINE, HAVE A CERTAIN GLORIOUS FUTURE

As in 6:1–14, Paul follows his words of assurance about God's saving work in Christ with words of exhortation. If we belong to Christ, through His Spirit living in us, then we should live appropriately, i.e. as those who show that their minds are set on what the Spirit desires by battling with sin. Conversely, if we don't battle, we show that we don't have the Spirit and are not saved. There is then a tight logic to Paul's argument, as he goes on to explain the link between a Christian's battle and his or her attaining life and glory.

◆ **Our new obligation to be ridding ourselves of sin (vv. 12–13)**
Paul calls us, literally, 'debtors' – those who have an obligation to someone. We are no longer in debt to the flesh, but (he implies, despite not finishing his sentence) to the Spirit. Again, we are reminded of the solemn warning of 6:20–23, that if we go on living (the tense here is present continuous) according to the flesh, as stated in 8:5, we will die with no hope of resurrection, for we will be demonstrating that we are set on rebellion against God (vv. 5a, 6a, 7–8).

Instead of living according to the sinful nature, we are to go to war against sin in our lives. The attitude that Paul describes is not one of token resistance, but of absolute ruthlessness; we are to go on putting to death (again, the present continuous tense) everything that the flesh desires. This is a great responsibility for every Christian; it means conscious ongoing effort on our part, but 'not apart from, not distinct from the activity of God's Spirit, who subdues the flesh as we mortify it in his power, and as we set our minds upon the things of the Spirit' (Peterson, p. 113). We must be careful not to read salvation-by-works into Paul's instruction: this battle, which results in life (v. 13b), comes about because the Christian now has a renewed mind, one that is set on what the Spirit desires (v. 5b). This is the mind of the person who is already justified by God.

◆ **If we are battling, we are sons (vv. 14–16)**
Anyone who is seriously struggling to put to death the sin in his life is clearly being led by the Spirit (v. 13, cf. v. 5b), and those who are led by the Spirit are sons of God (v. 14). How is this so? Paul points to the nature of the Spirit whom we have received: He does not produce a fear of God's judgment – such fear might well threaten to undermine the Christian who hates his inability to obey God consistently – but, as Paul tells us, He is the Spirit of sonship (the Greek word means 'adoption'), who

assures us that we are God's children and causes us to cry out to our Father. Only a true child will do this. The cry of 'Abba' is neither ecstatic praise nor cosy sentimentality, but rather it is a cry of agony in the heat of battle (7:24), the same as the cry that Jesus made at Gethsemane (Mark 14:36) – a cry of trust in seemingly overwhelming circumstances.

◆ **If sons, then heirs of glory (v. 17)**
In Roman society, adopted children enjoyed exactly the same privileges as the natural children of the family. Paul here gives us the remarkable assurance that the same will be true in God's family: if we are adopted by God then we will share in Christ's inheritance in heaven. The only condition for our sharing in Christ's glory, in the future, is that we should be God's children – and the hallmark of His children is a willingness to share in Christ's suffering now. We have already seen how we are to be putting to death, in our bodies (v. 13), the sin that He condemned through His death (v. 3) and the constant anguish within that this struggle will produce (7:23–24). There is, however, further suffering that assaults the believer from without, as Paul will describe later on (8:18–27).

# Key themes and application

◆ **No condemnation now for those who are in Christ**
This passage should give Christians great assurance about their salvation. Assurance stems principally from the conclusion that Paul reached at the end of chs 6 and 7: although the Law and sin used to lead us to certain death, on account of our disobedience, we can now be sure that we are not condemned, because of God's solution in Christ. When we look to Jesus' death, we should be completely confident about this verdict, knowing that He has done what we could not do.

If this is true, then we should not seek assurance anywhere else. It is pointless to look for assurance in, for example, the doing of good works, for we know that we shall only be condemned for our failure. Instead, we should seek to have a better grasp of God's gospel about Jesus, and to help one another stay focused on the cross, with great thankfulness for it.

◆ **The difference between the Christian mind and the non-Christian mind**

Christians and non-Christians have fundamentally different mindsets. The former, having minds controlled by the Holy Spirit, want to obey God – though they do not always manage to do so – but the latter instinctively reject Him as their ruler. The very fact of our own battle with sin teaches us that the new mind, given by the Spirit, has to come first, i.e. before we can obey God – indeed, the implication of our having minds that are controlled by the Spirit is that we *will* battle.

There are lessons here for us as we speak to non-Christians. There is no point in trying to change the behaviour of unbelievers, for their rebellion, as we saw in ch. 1, originates in their minds. But here we are shown that the gospel provides a solution to this problem – it is possible to be given a new mind. Our responsibility, therefore, is not to moralize, but to tell them the gospel.

We should not underestimate Paul's hard words on the state of unbelievers. We tend to think that God looks favourably on the things that we appreciate in unbelievers, but Paul is unequivocal: they cannot please God. We struggle with this because we tend to divorce the concept of sin from the concept of rebellion against God Himself. Being good, or living to please Him, involves submitting to Him as God by obeying the gospel, not simply being nice people. We easily forget the lessons of 1:18–3:20.

◆ **A guaranteed future inheritance if, by the Spirit, we are battling with sin**

According to Paul, if we are battling to do what pleases God, we are led by the Spirit; if we have the Spirit, we are children of God; if we are children of God, we are heirs and will share in Jesus' inheritance. Christians are often shaken in their faith by their inability to get rid of sinfulness, yet, far from calling our status into question, Paul demonstrates that a struggle against sin is the evidence of our membership of God's family; it guarantees our future place in heaven. This should be a tremendous reassurance for the Christian who is struggling with sin. And we should look to encourage one another in the battle.

With this encouragement comes the serious responsibility to aim, consciously, at ridding ourselves of sin. Although we know that we will not be free from sin until we are raised (v. 11), we are not to be satisfied with a half-hearted effort. Understanding that we are justified, we are to be ruthless with ourselves, doing all we can to prevent sin from taking a hold on us. This will involve wisdom about the circumstances in which we put ourselves – avoiding circumstances in which we know we will be easily tempted – and also a constant dependence upon God.

### ◆ The Holy Spirit

This is one of the most important passages in the Bible on the Holy Spirit and, in an age when so much is taught about Him, we should pay close attention to what the Bible itself tells us. We have already learnt from Romans that the Spirit liberates us from sin and death by uniting us with Christ, that He controls our minds (our inmost being rather than our thinking, which is still corrupted), and that He will raise us from the dead. We see also that Paul takes the following for granted:

*All Christians have the Holy Spirit*: It is sometimes taught that we are not given the Spirit straight away, when we become Christians, or else that He comes in greater measure to the especially spiritual. Paul, however, tells us that it is not possible to be a Christian without the Spirit (v. 9). Therefore it is not necessary – or, indeed, possible in this world – to be sinless in order to receive the Spirit. This means that all Christians, without exception, have the Holy Spirit.

*The Holy Spirit is the Spirit of Christ and the Spirit of God:* We cannot separate the person and work of the Holy Spirit from the person and work of the Father or of Jesus. To have the Holy Spirit within you is to have Christ and God dwelling in you.

*The empowering presence:* Many have taken living 'according to the Spirit' (v. 4) as describing the way in which the Holy Spirit gives Christians the power not to sin – the Spirit providing a magical enabling to help us obey God's will. Of course the Spirit does equip and enable us to battle with sin (v. 14), but He does this by convincing us of the great work of Christ on the cross. It is He who causes us to believe in, and thereby benefit from, Christ's death. Our 'obligation' (v. 12) to fight sin is therefore rooted in the understanding that in Christ we are no longer condemned.

# Unanswered questions

◆ Is the suffering that we endure worth it?
◆ Can we be sure that we will survive all this suffering?

# The aim of this study

To be fully confident that if we desire what the Spirit desires, we are not condemned.

# Suggested questions

◆ Think of the nicest person you know who is not a Christian. What are the qualities of this person? Think of a non-Christian who, from the way he lives, is clearly not a Christian. What is this person like?

### 1–4 CHRISTIANS ARE FREE FROM CONDEMNATION

◆ The 'therefore' in v. 1 suggests that Paul has reached a conclusion. What is he concluding?
◆ Verses 1 and 2 tell us that we are not condemned because we have been set free – how have we been set free?
◆ What different things can we thank Jesus for in these verses?

### 5–11 CHRISTIANS HAVE NEW MINDS NOW AND, IN THE FUTURE, WILL HAVE NEW BODIES TOO

◆ What are the hallmarks of those who 'live according to the flesh'?
  – What is their mindset? What is their relationship to God?
  – What are the implications of this teaching for our non-Christian friends? For those who are 'nice' and also for those who have openly sinful lifestyles? What should/shouldn't we say to them? How does God see them? How will this affect our prayers for them?
◆ What are the hallmarks of those who 'live according to the spirit'?
  – What is their mindset? What is their relationship to God?
◆ What does this passage teach us about the Holy Spirit?

– Who is He? Do we think of Him in this way?
– What does He do?
– Who has the Spirit and who does not?

## 12–17 CHRISTIANS, IF GENUINE, HAVE A CERTAIN GLORIOUS FUTURE

◆ What are the implications, for the believer, of having the Spirit? *(See also the previous group of questions.)*

– Why is v. 11 such good news? (Remember 7:14–24.)

– What obligation is there for those who have the Spirit? What is involved in 'going on putting to death the misdeeds of the body'? Is this our attitude to the sin in our lives? What needs to change? How can we help one another?

– List the amazing privileges that are ours when we have the Spirit.

◆ How does this passage give assurance to the Christian who is struggling against sin?

◆ How does this passage teach us to:
– encourage one another?
– warn one another?
– praise God?

# ROMANS 8:17–30

## Context

Chapter 8 of Paul's letter to the Romans begins with his proclamation of our freedom from condemnation; this is the conclusion of his line of argument that began in ch. 6. He asserts that we have been released from the total tyranny of sin and also from the just verdict of the Law – all of which is achieved through the sacrificial death of Jesus (vv. 3–4). He goes on to describe the Christian way of life, explaining, in particular, how it is that Christians who battle against sin show clear evidence of the Holy Spirit within them; they can be sure, therefore, that they are God's children who will share in Jesus' inheritance.

In v. 17, however, Paul says that our sharing in Jesus' inheritance is connected with our sharing in His sufferings. This is the starting point for an important passage in which he contrasts our present experience with our future glory. He explains what life is like while we wait for our mortal bodies to be resurrected – it involves suffering. Paul puts our sufferings within the context of a decaying world, and yet, he says, both for us and for the world there is the certain hope of future glory. Finally, he gives us the great assurance that, even though we suffer, no trials in the present can hinder God's purposes for us.

## Structure

**8:17–18** God's suffering children have an incomparably glorious future

**8:19–30** Present suffering leads to future glory

19–22 Creation groans, waiting for its future liberation from decay

23–25 Christians also groan, in hope, until the future redemption of our bodies

26–30 Now we have the Spirit to intercede for us, in accordance with God's will to glorify us in the future

## Old Testament background

**Creation and new creation:** When sin entered the world through man's disobedience, the perfect created order that God had established was turned on its head by God's judgment. This meant that enmity arose among people and that the world was tainted by pain, suffering and death. One particular consequence was that God cursed the ground, making man's habitat a frustrating and decaying environment (Genesis 3:16–24).

Yet in the writings of the prophets, alongside the promises of redemption for Israel and the nations, there are promises that the whole of creation will one day be renewed – not just made slightly better; there will be 'new heavens and a new earth' (see Isaiah 11:6–9; 65:17–25). When we look at these chapters, we see, in the place of enmity, the restoration of perfect peace and harmony among people and also between man and his environment. All of these promises are shown, in the book of Revelation, to have been fulfilled by God (Revelation 21:1–5); they will be fulfilled at the end of time, not before.

**Hope:** The story of the Bible tells how God fulfils His promises to save rebellious mankind. A key experience for God's people, therefore, is that of waiting for the fulfilment of these promises. One example, from the Old Testament, is the expectation of the people of Israel, in the wilderness, as they headed towards the promised land; another is the hope of return from exile, after God had promised to rescue His people out of Babylon. God's faithful character means that God's people may always look forward, confidently, to the fulfilment of His promises.

# Text notes

## 17–18 GOD'S SUFFERING CHILDREN HAVE AN INCOMPARABLY GLORIOUS FUTURE

Verse 17 serves both as a conclusion to the last passage and as an introduction to this. In a rapid sequence of logical steps, Paul has demonstrated that the Christian's struggle against sin demonstrates the indwelling presence of the Holy Spirit, and that it is He, the Spirit of Christ who is God's Son, who testifies to the Christian that he too is a child of God. Adoption into God's family is no small matter. Contrary to popular opinion, none of us is naturally a child of God, yet through the gospel not only are we adopted, but also we are given a share in Jesus' inheritance. That inheritance, however, lies in the future: the present is very different.

◆ **Present suffering (v. 17)**
Paul says that those who hope to share in Jesus' glory will be prepared to share, also, in His suffering (v. 17). He then goes on to give us the reason for this, and also to describe the sufferings he has in mind. He has already depicted the constant struggle with sin that believers suffer, as a result of their mortal unregenerate bodies still being slaves to sin (7:25), and how this involves a lifelong frustration, expressed in 7:24, as we wait for our bodies to be redeemed (8:23). Now Paul focuses on the context of our suffering, the marred and fallen world (v. 21, see OT notes), in which we will inevitably face hardship, not merely on account of our environment but also from those who still live in rebellion against God (v. 35). It seems that Paul has in mind both the ordinary suffering of humanity and Christian suffering.

◆ **An infinitely greater future (v. 18)**
Though our sufferings in this world may be real and often very painful, Paul reckons that when they are set against our future glory, there is simply no comparison. This must be true, for to share in Christ's inheritance will mean that we experience the fulfilment of all God's promises – a perfectly restored

relationship with Him and a new creation in which there is no suffering (see Revelation 21). Being aware of such a future should give us a proper perspective on the hardships of the present.

## 19–22 CREATION GROANS, WAITING FOR ITS FUTURE LIBERATION FROM DECAY

This tension between the 'now' and the 'not yet' is felt not just by believers, but also by creation as a whole:

◆ **Present frustration and decay (vv. 19–22)**

When we are glorified, it will be clear for all to see who God's true children are (unlike now), and Paul portrays the creation as eagerly anticipating this event. Why is this so? The world itself was caught up in the consequences of the Fall and, owing to God's curse, it has been marked ever since by decay and futility (see OT notes). Yet God has promised that He will bring about a new heaven and a new earth, and the signal for this to happen will be our revelation as God's children when we are raised (see Revelation 20:1–21:1)

Until its renewal, creation is 'groaning as in the pains of child-birth'. This description, though odd, perfectly conveys Paul's point, which is about eager anticipation of the future, or 'hope' (v. 20). Birth pangs do bring pain in the present but, more significantly, they also point to imminent new life and great joy.

◆ **Future liberation (v. 21)**

Although we are to expect frustration and pain in this world, Paul gives us the great assurance that our decaying world has a glorious future; it *will* be liberated from frustration and decay, as the prophets promised (see OT notes), and a time will come when all death and suffering and enmity will be finished. Just as the world suffered with mankind at the Fall, so the world will be renewed when our salvation is complete: indeed, 'Creation itself must be redeemed so that redeemed humanity may have a fitting environment in which to live' (Peterson, p. 117).

## 23–25 CHRISTIANS ALSO GROAN, IN HOPE, UNTIL THE FUTURE REDEMPTION OF THEIR BODIES

Here Paul expands on his assertion in v. 18.

### ◆ Present suffering (vv. 23–25)

In this world, we groan with creation as we live out our lives in mortal unregenerate bodies. This groaning must include the groaning that Paul articulated in 7:24, but just as Paul was not hopeless in that case, so, in this wider context, we are not hopeless either. We understand the focus on the future that characterizes the Christian life and, like Abraham (see 4:18–25), we realize that what God is promising is for the future, not for the present. If God's promises were fulfilled now, there would be no need for us to hope. Since we do need to hope, Paul encourages us by emphasizing the confident and patient expectation that should be ours as we wait for the fulfilment of God's promises. This expectation is another of the convictions that the Holy Spirit, dwelling within, gives us. By His presence we have the first fruits of what God has in store for us in the future and, at the same time, He makes us long for that future. 'Having the foretaste, we long for the feast! But the foretaste is in itself the guarantee that the feast is going to follow' (Olyott, p. 78).

### ◆ Future redemption of our bodies (v. 23)

Here Paul assures us that Christians can look forward to being liberated, finally, from their mortal bodies. This is exactly what we need, for it is our 'flesh' that causes us to keep on sinning, contrary to our deepest desires (7:15–23), and also, since our mortal bodies are unregenerate, they are subject to the frailty and decay that belong to our whole world. Furthermore, when we are raised, everything will be clear for us to see: our membership of God's family will be fully revealed (v. 19) and we will enjoy a new creation, unspoilt by suffering or death (v. 21).

### 26–30 NOW WE HAVE THE SPIRIT TO INTERCEDE FOR US, IN ACCORDANCE WITH GOD'S WILL TO GLORIFY US IN THE FUTURE

God does not leave us to cope alone with the sufferings mentioned above. In the present He helps us and, for the future, gives us guarantees.

### ◆ Present help while we wait (vv. 26–27)

Apart from waiting patiently for the future, how does Paul picture our present experience? He sees it as a state of weakness: we need help because often we don't know what we ought to pray for. From our own experience of prayer we know that sometimes our motives may be entangled by sin, and that often we are not able to think rationally, finding ourselves distracted because we are hurting so much. But these verses give us the comforting assurance that, in our needy state, the Spirit helps us. He, too, is described as groaning, but His groans are the prayers that we find ourselves unable to articulate. The logic of v. 27 is hard to follow, but several points are clear: as we struggle to pray, the Spirit intercedes for us; He prays according to God's will; and His mind is known by God. When we put these things together they make a line of perfect communication: the Spirit prays perfectly for us in our suffering and God answers those prayers, because they are in line with His will.

### ◆ Future prospect: God will one day glorify us with Christ (vv. 28–30)

Verses 28–30 carry straight on from v. 27b, explaining what the will of God is.

'... *in all things God works* ...' *(v. 28):* Verse 28 is well known and well loved by many Christians, but rarely understood in its context. It is a precious truth for Christians who, as Paul describes in vv. 18–27, are enduring all the sufferings that go with living in a fallen world in a mortal body. As we long for our future resurrection and the renewal of all things, it is vital we recognize that God's sovereignty is complete: He is active in all circumstances – no matter how bad they may look to us – for our eventual future benefit.

*... to make us like Jesus, 'that he might be the firstborn among many brothers.' (vv. 28–29):* Our 'good' is not our personal happiness or fulfilment now, in this world, but our future joy in heaven when we will be glorified and conformed to Jesus' likeness (vv. 28–29). When that happens, we shall be like Him in that we will be sinless, we will have resurrected bodies, and we will rule (5:17). Yet this is not all; God's purpose is deeper still. Paul reminds us, as he does so often in this letter, that God's

plans are not centred around us but around Jesus: Paul is writing about God's gospel 'regarding his Son' (1:3). This explains why life is as it is now, i.e. a struggle and often painful: God's overall plan is to provide Jesus with a family of believers who conform to His likeness, a family in which He is pre-eminent as the firstborn. This, the hope into which we were saved (v. 24), is God's will, and it is in accordance with this that the Spirit prays for us (v. 27).

# Key themes and application

◆ **Understanding the present and the future**

Throughout this passage, Paul helps us to distinguish between the 'now' and the 'not yet'. Christians feel a tension between what they experience in the present and what they are looking forward to in the 'not yet', and the whole of creation shares in this phenomenon.

*For Christians – suffering in this world but glory in eternity:* Although we are God's children, we are currently caught up in a fallen world and so will have to endure all the hardship that comes with our hostile and decaying environment. Christians are not immune from disease or disaster or suffering of any kind. Although God has certainly promised that we will be released from suffering, the fulfilment of this promise lies firmly in the future. On that day, freedom from suffering will be certain, for we will have resurrected bodies and the world itself will be made new. The same goes for suffering which is distinctively Christian, i.e. our struggle with sin and having to face persecution. Romans, and indeed the rest of the New Testament, presents these things as normal experience for the Christian. Yet, in contrast with the realities of present suffering, we are told that the future will be immeasurably wonderful (see Revelation 21), for then we will be glorified, having been conformed to the likeness of Christ.

We should also remember that we are not left to fend for ourselves while we wait for glory. The Holy Spirit helps us in our weakness and prays for us according to God's will, which is that we should be made into the likeness of Christ and so give Him a family of glorified believers.

There is authoritative teaching, here, about the work of the Holy Spirit in all believers. He is not given to us to enable us to fulfil our potential or our desires, but rather He works according to God's agenda, which is to get us to heaven and to glorify His Son.

*For Creation – decay now but liberation in eternity:* Paul is clear that we live in a world that is in bondage to decay and that it will continue to be so until resurrection day, the day when Jesus returns. Indeed, creation itself is not looking to be renewed now, but rather it is looking, first, for God's children to be identified. It is therefore wrong to think that mankind's ultimate responsibility is to 'save the world'; Utopia will never be achieved in this world. Although we do have a serious God-given obligation to be good stewards of God's creation, we know that nothing will save it from decay and destruction until God Himself brings about a new heaven and a new earth.

Heaven (and eternal life too) is often portrayed as an ethereal, intangible realm and so, not surprisingly, it has been rejected by many as being insubstantial and dull. This passage, however, assures us that creation will be made new, and that therefore the future will in fact be physical and infinitely better than the world we now enjoy. It follows from this that the Bible does not teach Platonic dualism, i.e. the idea that matter or material things are bad, compared with the spiritual, which is good. Rather, the physical world is to be recognized as fallen. But it *will* be made perfect and it *will* be a feature of eternity. Furthermore, we too will have physical bodies when we are raised.

### ◆ A right perspective on both the present and the future

Besides giving us an understanding of the present and of what to expect in the future, Paul also teaches us how to live in the meanwhile. First, we should have right expectations about the present and, therefore, not be surprised by the hardship we endure in this world. Many Christians find suffering to be a potential stumbling-block for their faith, but often this happens because we have blurred the distinction that the Bible makes between the future, when God's promises of freedom from suffering will be fulfilled, and the present, the time in which we wait. Paul is clear that the present does involve groaning. Those who teach that God will preserve us from suffering are misrepresenting God's word and causing His suffering people unnecessary extra concern.

Our perspective on the future is to be characterized by a great longing for that which will be immeasurably glorious. Here Paul shows us that *hope* should be an essential Christian experience. This is not the vague desire that the world calls 'hope' but a confident hope for the future (like that shown by Abraham; see 4:18). Patiently, but eagerly, we are to desire God's fulfilment of His promises, and cry out to Him, assured that the Spirit prays for us as we struggle. As Christians living in a society that is completely focused on present fulfilment, we need to encourage one another as we wait for what God has promised, regularly reminding ourselves and one another of the glorious future that awaits us. Only a clear understanding of our future glory will enable us to persevere, in hope, through all suffering in the present.

Paul shows us that we should not worry about whether we are going to survive our sufferings in this world. To suffer here is to follow the path that Jesus Himself walked, a path that leads to certain glory (v. 17). Also, none of the sufferings we face can stop us from being glorified, for we are told that God works 'in all things' to achieve His will. This does not mean that everything will work out well in this world (see above); rather, it means that God is using every situation – *however it may appear to us* – to bring us to glory, such is His power and sovereignty. The effect of this passage should be to lift our eyes from our present circumstances, which may often discourage us, and instead to focus our attention both on the future that God has promised and on God Himself, who helps us now and who is at work, through all circumstances, to bring us to that future.

*(NB: The certainty of God's plan being fulfilled will be covered in the next passage.)*

# Unanswered questions

✦ Can we be absolutely sure that God will get us there (to heaven)?

# The aim of this study

That we should look forward to God's certain, glorious future in heaven and, at the same time, be realistic about the suffering and frustration of the present.

# Suggested questions

As we go through this study, bear in mind these three characters:

> *Colin the conservationist* sees that God's world is in a mess and thinks that Christians should be giving much of their time to preserving it.
> *Harry the healer* says that God loves us and wants the best for us, and that therefore we can ask Him to heal us today, in the confident expectation that He will do so.
> *Demoralized Deborah* is a Christian going through the mill. Her job is really stressful and her sister has been unwell for a long time. She is also aware that she keeps letting God down because, although she genuinely tries not to sin, she keeps giving in to temptation.

✦ What encouragement could you give Deborah, from what we have seen in 8:1–17? What could you tell her about the future? How about the present?

## 17–18 GOD'S SUFFERING CHILDREN HAVE AN INCOMPARABLY GLORIOUS FUTURE

✦ What is Paul's perspective on the present, and on the future, for Christians?
  – What kind of suffering is Paul likely to have in mind, from this context? And from the context of chs 6–8?

## 19–22 CREATION GROANS, WAITING FOR ITS FUTURE LIBERATION FROM DECAY

◆ According to Paul, what will life in this world entail? And why?
◆ How could you use these verses to speak to Colin? Should we devote ourselves to conservation?
  – Is there, then, no hope for our world?
  – Why does Paul use the image of childbirth? How does it make his point?

## 23–25 CHRISTIANS ALSO GROAN, IN HOPE, UNTIL THE FUTURE REDEMPTION OF THEIR BODIES

◆ How does the experience of Christians relate to the experience of creation?
◆ What does Paul teach us about our present and our future?
  – In the light of these things, what should be our present perspective?
◆ How could you use these verses to speak to Harry? What does Harry not understand?
  – How should Paul's teaching here help Deborah? And us?

## 26–30 WE HAVE THE SPIRIT TO INTERCEDE FOR US, IN ACCORDANCE WITH GOD'S WILL TO GLORIFY US IN THE FUTURE

◆ How does God help us in the present? Why do we not know, sometimes, what to pray for?
  – From these verses, what exactly does the Holy Spirit do in our lives?
◆ Colin, Harry and Deborah all leap on v. 28. Colin says that God will work to enable him to preserve endangered species. Harry says that this verse means that, no matter what we go through, God will make things right very soon. Deborah, though, is discouraged because nothing seems to be working for her good at the moment. Where are our three friends going wrong?
  – What does Paul mean by our 'good', in v. 28? What can he not mean? Why not? How does the rest of v. 28 help?
  – What is God's 'purpose' (or His will, v. 27)? What do vv. 29–30 tell us? *(Leader: In our next study we will look more closely at the detail of v. 30. Don't get caught up with it now!)*

– In what way do we see, again, that Jesus is at the centre of God's plans? How does this further encourage us in our sufferings?

◆ What do vv. 28–30 tell us about the sufferings that we face in the present? How is our usual perspective different from Paul's?
– What sufferings are we, in this study group, facing at the moment? How can we pray about them in the light of this passage?

## Study 14

# Romans 8:28–39

## Context

In this passage Paul continues with what has been the dominant issue since v. 18, expressing his confidence that none of our present sufferings, as we live out our lives in mortal bodies within a decaying world, can hinder God's plan to glorify us, together with Jesus, in the future (v. 29). These verses correspond closely to 5:1–11, having the same central theme, i.e. the assurance of future salvation and of the eventual completion of God's work, regardless of what may be happening in the present. These verses also bring chs 5–8 to a conclusion.

The end of ch. 8 (from v. 18 onwards), however, also serves to conclude the argument that began at 6:1. Paul has established that we have been released from the total ruling power of sin (ch. 6), that we are free from the power of the Law to condemn us to death (ch. 7), and that if we are Christians – as evidenced by having new minds that want to serve God – then our sinful mortal bodies will also be redeemed, through the same Spirit who makes us children of God and co-heirs with Christ (8:1–17). It is on these foundations that Paul builds his assurance that God will complete His work of glorifying us.

It is also possible to see that Paul's conclusions here cover the consequences of justification by faith, and so may be taken as summarizing all that he has written since 3:21. People who have been declared to be right with God, through their trust in the substitutionary death of Christ, now know that, through Christ, God is for them rather than against them. Therefore, they may have full assurance that they will be saved on the day of judgment.

## Structure

(NB: This study overlaps the previous study at vv. 28–30. See Text Notes.)

**8:29–30** God's plan to glorify us and Jesus is unstoppable
**8:31–39** Our confidence in God: no-one can oppose Him

## Old Testament background

**Psalm 44:** This psalm expresses the anguish of God's people at a time when they were enduring great suffering. They remember His mighty victories in the past (vv. 1–3) and call out to Him to rescue them again (v. 26). Usually, in the Old Testament, it is because of her sin that Israel suffers (as God had promised – Leviticus 26:14–39), but here, it is a faithful people who are 'crushed' (vv. 17–19) and, significantly, they recognize that God has been acting sovereignly through their misery (vv. 9–19).

## Text notes

### 28–30 GOD'S PLAN TO GLORIFY US AND JESUS IS UNSTOPPABLE
NB: God's plan is not mentioned here because it was included in the last study, in explanation of 'God's will' in v. 27. Briefly, God's plan (also 'His purpose' and our 'good', v. 28) is that Christians should be made into the likeness of Christ, so that He will be glorified in a large family (see previous study).

If God's plan were described only in this way, we might wonder how it could possibly be realized. Far from seeing its fulfilment now, we are confronted with the manifold sufferings that are part of our life in a fallen world. But Paul also explains that God's plan is an inexorable process. In these verses the four statements, linked to each other, tell us that God's purpose *will* be achieved: each one asserts that if one thing is true the next thing must surely follow, and together they form an unbreakable chain of fulfilment.

'Foreknew' means more than that God simply 'foresaw' who would respond freely to the gospel. This would mean that, ultimately, our salvation was in our own hands, but Paul has consistently shown that we are powerless to obtain our own salvation (1:18–3:20; 5:6). The sense of the word is much stronger; Paul is here using an Hebraic term which describes an intimate relationship initiated by God (see Jeremiah 1:5). This is how the argument goes: if God initiated such a relationship with us before the creation, He also predestined us to gain the full extent of His promises in heaven, when we are made into Jesus' likeness. Those He has thus predestined, He therefore summons to Himself, declaring them to be righteous on the basis of Jesus' death, and He will certainly go on to glorify them. The past tense of the verb, 'glorified', only strengthens this certainty, indicating that the action is as good as done. The point is that Christians cannot, ultimately, lose their salvation on account of the sufferings of this world. Their future glorification is part of the plan that God initiated before history began, which He is working out through history, and which He will complete in eternity.

*(NB: Predestination is difficult to comprehend, but this is no reason to reject what the Bible teaches. God is completely sovereign over His universe and yet, at the same time, we are held responsible, both for our culpable rebellion (3:19–20) and for our willingness to believe in God's promise of salvation (4:24). The Bible asserts both God's sovereignty and our responsibility, and we should hold on to both concepts. Chapter 9 will tell us more.)*

## 31–39 OUR CONFIDENCE IN GOD: NO-ONE CAN OPPOSE HIM
Having laid out the fullness of God's plan and purposes, Paul steps back and considers the response of God's people who suffer in the present. His conclusions show his total conviction that God will complete what He has begun and that nothing can stop Him.

### ◆ God is for us: who can oppose Him? (vv. 31b–34)
A superficial answer to Paul's question, in v. 31b, would be that many are against us. Many will oppose God's people, for many reasons and in a variety of ways, in this world, but Paul's point is that no-one can keep us from glory because 'God is for us'

(v. 31b). In the context of chs 1–3 and, indeed, of the whole Bible, this is a remarkable statement, for mankind's rebellion warrants only God's anger and punishment. Indeed, 'perhaps the most terrible words which human ears would ever hear are those which God uttered many times in the Old Testament: "I am against you" (e.g. Jeremiah 50:31; Ezekiel 13:8)' (Stott, p. 254). But the amazing news of the gospel is that God is now on the side of those He has chosen. Paul goes on to give three explanations to convince us that God is on our side and that He will complete His work.

◆ **God's commitment is seen at the cross (v. 32)**

As in ch. 5, Paul points us to the cross for proof that God is on our side (5:6–8) and sees there, also, the guarantee of our future hope. The fact that God did not spare His own Son, but willingly gave Him up for us, can leave us in no doubt that He will give us 'all things'. These things are not the worldly desires of our hearts, but the things that God intends for us, namely, glory (v. 30) and a share in Jesus' inheritance (v. 17).

◆ **God justifies us: who can accuse us? (v. 33)**

Paul has already taught us that the greatest potential danger facing mankind is God's wrath on the last day (2:5). Here he adopts judicial language and asks whether *anyone* could make a charge against us on judgment day. Even the question seems feeble, however, for we are 'those whom God has chosen' and we have already seen that His decision cannot be thwarted (vv. 29–30). Paul's reply reminds us that it is God Himself who has given our righteous verdict. Though we were guilty, God has declared us righteous, and so no charge can stand against us.

◆ **Jesus is interceding for us: who can condemn us? (v. 34)**

If no-one can even accuse us, then certainly no-one can condemn us. Paul now points to Jesus, who is pleading our case. How confident we can be that His intercessions are accepted, when His death and resurrection have assured our justification (4:25) and He is now at God's right hand! When God and His Son are both standing for us, there is no opposition that could possibly threaten us.

◆ **Conclusion: neither anyone nor anything can separate us from Jesus' love (vv. 35–39)**
In Christ, then, our justification and salvation are secure. Could any enemy, though, break the bond between Him and us? Here, Paul names some of the things which, through the ages, have threatened many believers and caused them to wonder whether their faith would survive – indeed, most of these things were experienced by the apostle himself (see 2 Corinthians 11:26–27). The list does include hardships that are shared by all people living in a fallen world, such as famine, and yet, in the light of the psalm that Paul quotes in v. 36, the emphasis is likely to be on experiences met by Christians, on suffering that comes as a result of believing in Christ.

Trials and persecution are not exclusive to New Testament believers; godly people have endured suffering throughout history. In Psalm 44 (quoted in v. 36) we find God's people suffering, not because of their disobedience, but rather 'for your sake' (see OT notes). Although they have not broken the covenant (Psalm 44:17) they are scorned and opposed (Psalm 44:13–16). And yet there is the confident cry for God's help, because they know that He is in control and that victory comes from Him (Psalm 44:7, 26). Paul's own response is emphatic: not only shall we survive, but we will triumph over all these threats, through Jesus, who has demonstrated His love for us.

◆ **For I am convinced ... (v. 38)**
Here is the climax of Paul's argument, his personal conviction about the Christian's security in Christ. He considers all the possible threats that could come from any conceivable direction and his conclusion is clear: nothing at all, now or in the future, within or without our world, can divide us from our saviour in whom, above all, we see God's love. Paul's cast-iron assurance is a fitting conclusion to this section of his letter and a priceless truth for all believers at all times.

# Key themes and applications

## ◆ God's unstoppable plan

In our last two studies we have looked at the future that God has in store for His children. We will share in Christ's inheritance (8:17), we will be freed from all suffering (8:21), and our bodies will be redeemed (8:23) as we wait to be conformed to the image of Christ (8:29). In this study we see Paul assuring the Roman Christians that God's plan to glorify them in this way will be achieved, no matter what they may be facing in the present. For the work that He is doing in them (and us) is the work that He started before the beginning of time and that He will definitely complete in eternity. This is one of the Bible's greatest passages on the sovereignty of God, reminding us that He really does rule over His world and that our lives really are in His hands. This is a particular comfort for Christians who are suffering in the present and who may find many reasons to doubt their security.

The fact of God's absolute sovereignty is a truth of which we need to be reminded today. Our age has domesticated God and reduced Him to our level, to that of a loyal friend. Such a diminutive figure cannot cope with the complexities that life will invariably throw at us and cannot bear the weight of our faith. The God of the Bible, however, is working out His purposes through history and cannot be thwarted. Therefore we should confidently urge one another to trust Him in all circumstances. It is ironic that predestination should cause many Christians so much anxiety, when it is taught in order to reassure us and to give us confidence in a God whose plans for us will not be altered.

## ◆ Christian assurance

At the heart of this passage is the wonderful truth that Christians may be fully confident of all the good that God intends for us, the good that culminates in our glorification in heaven. Paul teaches the point from two essential standpoints. First, we can be sure because of God's sovereignty (see above). Also we can be confident because God is for us. Although we have done nothing to deserve His favour, Christians can say that God is on their side. He has declared us righteous through the death and resurrection of Jesus Christ and, in case we should ever have any doubt that this work is sufficient for our justification, Paul tells us that Jesus is now in heaven pleading our case in the light of His death.

It is in looking to God, and to God alone, that we gain our assurance. It is He who enables us to look any hardship in the face and say, with Paul's conviction, that it is incapable of severing us from the lifeline that we have in Christ. All Christians will feel a lack of assurance at some time in their lives, but this always arises through the loss of a correct perspective. We tend, naturally, to look at ourselves and our experience, both of which are bound to discourage us: Paul has already told us that in ourselves we will find ongoing sin, because of our mortal bodies that have yet to be redeemed (7:21–25), and also that life in this world will always be hallmarked by 'present sufferings' (8:18). And so, instead, Paul urges us to look to the future that God has in store for us (8:28–30) and, above all, to the God who has saved us, because His power and His commitment to us are both perfect.

## Unanswered questions

◆ If nothing can separate us from God's love, why do most of God's historic people (the Jews) appear to have been separated from Him?

## The aim of this study

To have full assurance of all that God has promised us, assurance founded on the conviction that His plan cannot be stopped, that nothing can stop the God who loves us from saving us through Jesus.

## Suggested questions

◆ What different things make us doubt God's promise to take us to heaven?

♦ Looking back at our last study (8:17–30), what does Paul say should be the Christian's expectations concerning the present? What is God's plan for the future?

♦ The issue in this study is: how we can know for certain that the future God has promised will actually materialize?
  – What encouragement does v. 28 give us?

## 28–30 GOD'S PLAN TO GLORIFY US AND JESUS IS UNSTOPPABLE

♦ How do we know that God's plan, to glorify us eventually, will succeed?
  *(Leader: Be ready to explain the meaning of 'foreknew'. See Text Notes.)*
  – How does Paul show that God's plan is unstoppable?
  – What different things in vv. 29–30 emphasize this certainty?
  – Where are we in the chain of events? How does this encourage us?
  – Why is it ironic that predestination causes Christians so much anxiety?

♦ How does this description of God differ from how we may imagine Him to be when we are suffering?

## 31–39 OUR CONFIDENCE IN GOD: NO-ONE CAN OPPOSE HIM

♦ 'If God is for us, who can be against us?' (v. 31)
  – How do we know that God is for us?

♦ What kind of opposition does Paul suggest, in vv. 33–34, we may fear? Why does he adopt the language of accusation and condemnation?
  – What is the basis for Paul's confidence that we can be neither accused nor condemned? Do we have this confidence? How can we help one another in this area?

♦ Why does the question in v. 35 arise?
  – Paul names some potential enemies. Which ones are real for us now and how do they manifest themselves? How do we suspect they may manifest themselves in the future?
  – Is Paul saying that we will not face any enemies?
  – Look up Psalm 44, from which Paul quotes. Why does he quote from this psalm?

– How can we learn from the attitude of God's people in this psalm?

– How does Paul himself answer the question in v. 35?

– How do vv. 38–39 summarize the last four chapters?

◆ What does Paul teach us about having a correct perspective in the face of suffering?

– What will happen if we look at ourselves and at our present circumstances?

– What will happen if we look to God and to the future?

◆ Think back to the first question. Explain why each of these things is unable to prevent us from getting to heaven.

# SECTION NOTES:
## Romans 9:1–11:36

Chapters 9 to 11 are primarily concerned with why God does not seem to be saving the nation of Israel, when in the Old Testament He had singled them out for so many privileges. Paul explains why it is that so few Jews believe the gospel, and comes to the conclusion is that God *is* saving those to whom the promises were made, but that this group of people does not include all ethnic Jews.

## The place of chapters 9–11 in Romans

These chapters are often treated as though they stood alone, but they are important as an integral part of Paul's letter, for two central reasons.

### ◆ Christian assurance

Paul ends ch. 8 proclaiming his absolute confidence in God's future salvation of His people, and stressing that nothing can stop God from fulfilling His promises to save and glorify us with Christ. The position of the nation of Israel, however, could be seen to cast doubt on the reliability of God's character. If God has gone back on His promises to the Jews, then He cannot be trusted to keep His promises to us. So Paul tackles the question very strenuously, demonstrating that God *has* been faithful to what He actually promised in the Old Testament, and that therefore we may be sure of His faithfulness towards us. Thus we see that chs 9–11 form a critically important part of Paul's line of argument concerning the gospel, which started in 1:16 and continues until 11:36. It is important that we should remember this, since these chapters are often ignored, or else taught as if they were not connected with what Paul has written in earlier chapters.

◆ **Tension between Jews and Gentiles in the Roman church**
Another theme that emerges in various parts of the letter is that Jews and Gentiles within the church in Rome were not fully accepting one another, but were boasting over one another. But Paul stresses, in 1:16, that the gospel is powerful to save both Jews and Gentiles. God's plan to save both Jews and Gentiles becomes the focus of ch. 11, where Paul explains God's working throughout history. Paul does this so that the Gentiles will think rightly, both of themselves and of the Jews.

# Structure

The three chapters are quite detailed, but the structure of the argument is as follows.

9:1–29    **A defence of God's character: God's word has not failed**
The nation of Israel is not the same thing as God's chosen people, i.e. those to whom the promises were made
God has always had mercy on whom He chooses, so ancestry is irrelevant for salvation
Scripture testifies that God's people would comprise relatively few Jews and many Gentiles – i.e. the situation we see is exactly what God said would happen

9:30–10:21    **Where the Jews went wrong: i.e. the reason they are not being saved**
The Jews made the mistake of trying to earn righteousness by good works, instead of trusting God for salvation
Although Israel heard and understood God's message of salvation, they did not receive salvation because they were stubborn and disobedient

**11:1–36    God's future for the Jews**

God has preserved a remnant of the Jews, saved by grace

Other Jews have been hardened, in order that salvation might go to the Gentiles

Through the salvation of the Gentiles, more Jews will become envious and will seek salvation

Thus God will save the complete number of Jews and Gentiles that He intends to save

# ROMANS 9:1–29

## Context

Chapter 8 ended with a wonderful assurance for all those who are trusting in God's promise of salvation through Jesus' death. Nothing can stop God's plan to glorify His people eventually with Christ (8:28–30), no-one can oppose Him (8:31–34), and nothing at all can separate us from the God who will give us all that He intends (8:35–39).

Paul now goes on to address a major question about the nation of Israel. In ch. 1, we saw that the gospel was God's powerful way of saving everyone who believes, 'first for the Jew, then for the Gentile' (1:16). At this point in his letter it is now essential that Paul should address the issue of Israel's unbelief. In the Old Testament God seems to have made so many promises of salvation to Israel, and yet, as the apostle looks around him, most Jews seem hardened to the gospel. Two connected difficulties arise from this. First, it might seem that God's character could be called into question, for if God's plans for His historic people, Israel, have not come to fruition, it might be that His word is not reliable. Leading on from this, there is the second problem that Israel's spiritual state could shake the Christian's assurance. For if His promises to them have not been kept, how can we be sure that nothing will separate us from God's love, as Paul has proclaimed (8:38–39)? The apostle must show that the gospel God has given us does not contradict His word in the past, and that therefore His character is completely trustworthy.

# Structure

9:1–5   Paul's anguish at Israel's unbelief
9:6–13  God's word has not failed: not all of the nation of Israel are His true chosen people
9:14–18 God's character has always been to have mercy on whom He wishes
9:19–24 God is not answerable to man in His sovereign purposes
9:25–29 God has always said that His people would comprise many Gentiles and a remnant of Israel

# Old Testament background

**Israel:** The privileges of the nation of Israel cannot be overstated. Israel was the nation to whom God had revealed Himself, with whom He had made the covenants, through Abraham, Moses and David, the people He had rescued from slavery and set apart to be His own people (Exodus 6:7) and the people He had called His own son (Exodus 4:22). The people of Israel were the recipients of the Law (Deuteronomy 4:8; Psalm 147:19–20), by which they knew how they were to live, and they were also given the sacrificial system – the priesthood and the sacrifices – in order that they, though sinful, might be able to remain in relationship with God. For all these reasons and more, Israel stood alone among the nations of the earth.

**Isaac:** God had promised Abraham a son in his old age (Genesis 15:4), but when his wife continued to be barren, they decided that he should father a child by Sarah's maid, Hagar (Genesis 16:1–4). The child, Ishmael, was a circumcised, physical son of Abraham. God then promised Abraham a son by Sarah (Genesis 17:15–22; 18:10, 14) and made a covenant only with Sarah's son, Isaac (Genesis 21:12). Ishmael's descendants became another nation (Genesis 21:13).

**Jacob and Esau:** Isaac's wife, Rebekah, had twin sons. Before they were born, God told her that He had chosen the younger rather than the elder (Genesis 25:23). Subsequently, the younger twin, Jacob, tricked Esau out of his birthright (Genesis 25:24–34). God made His covenant with Jacob (Genesis 28:13–15) and renamed him Israel (Genesis 32:28). Esau became the father of the Gentile nation of Edom (Genesis 36:1). Malachi, writing after some Jews returned from the exile in Babylon, applies Jacob's story to unbelieving Jews. Judah as a whole has broken faith (Malachi 2:10), but God's love has not failed; in the Old Testament as well as the New He has always said that He loved some, but not all, of the physical descendants of Abraham (Malachi 1:2).

# Text notes

## 1–5 PAUL'S ANGUISH AT ISRAEL'S UNBELIEF

### ◆ The apostle's agony (vv. 1–3)

The impact of 9:1–3 should not be lost on us. Having assured us that nothing in all creation can separate us from the love of Christ (8:39), Paul now says that he is so desperate for the Jews to be saved that he would ask God to cut him off from Christ if that would bring their salvation. Though he is the apostle to the Gentiles, he remains a Jew; not only is he distressed at their unbelief, he even wishes himself to be condemned for their sake, thus emulating Moses' desire in Exodus 32:32 and, ultimately, Christ's substitutionary sacrifice (Isaiah 53:8). We should note that Paul's understanding of God's absolute sovereignty (8:28–39) leads not to the complacency or apathy that so often paralyse us, but to a deep concern for those who are lost.

### ◆ The privileged people of Israel (vv. 4–5)

The reason for Paul's distress is that the Jews – the current generation of Israel – seem to have lost the privileges that God had given His people (see OT notes). The first two listed in v. 4 are particularly striking, reminding us of the blessings of adoption into God's family and the hope of glory which Paul says are guaranteed to those in Christ. But the list covers all the unique privileges that God had conferred upon Israel: His covenants with them, the promises of blessing, His words in the Law and the sacrificial system to deal with sin. In addition, they are related to Abraham, Isaac and Jacob, belonging to the same race as Christ Himself. When set against this background of blessings, the Jews' unbelief and exclusion from the blessings of the gospel are seen to be overwhelmingly tragic.

## 6–13 GOD'S WORD HAS NOT FAILED: NOT ALL OF THE NATION OF ISRAEL ARE HIS TRUE CHOSEN PEOPLE

Concerned as he is for his own people, Paul needs to tackle a broader question raised by the unbelief of the Jews concerning the reliability, or faithfulness, of God's word. Has God gone back on the promises that He made to Israel? (See Context.) Paul immediately denies this suggestion and goes on to explain the reason why it is not true. His thesis, essentially, is that there is, and has always been, a difference between the physically descended nation of Israel and God's true people. God's promises of salvation are for His true people who will be Gentiles as well as Jews. In other words, God remains faithful to those who are His true people.

♦ **The true Israel come not through ancestry, but through promise (vv. 6b–9)**

Paul reminds us of the story of Isaac (see OT notes) which demonstrates that being a physical descendant of the patriarchs is not the membership badge of God's people (as seen in ch. 4). If it were, we would have expected that God would give His promises of blessing to Abraham's elder son, Ishmael, and yet it is to Isaac that He does so (Genesis 21:12). Isaac was a descendant, as Ishmael was, but the significant fact about him is that he was born to Abraham and Sarah in their old age *as a result of God's promise*. So Paul makes his point, in v. 8, that the promises given to Abraham's children apply only to the promised children. God's initiative, emphasized in v. 9, is more important than mere family relationship. In this way Paul shows that physical descent does not equate with being chosen by God.

♦ **The true Israel comes not by man's works but by God's choice (vv. 10–13)**

The story of Jacob (see OT notes) plainly emphasizes God's initiative in His choice of Jacob over Esau. Because the choice was made before their birth, it could not possibly have been based upon their works. Instead, as we are explicitly told, the timing of this choice was to show God's purpose in *election*: He chose the younger twin. This teaches us that God's people have always been defined by God's choice, not by physical descent. The importance of God's choice is seen again at the end of the Old

Testament, in Malachi 1:2 (see OT notes). The prophet applies the story of Jacob and Esau to the nations of Judah and Edom that were descended from them. God's choice of Jacob over Esau means that, although both nations have been unfaithful, God will only restore Judah (Malachi 1:4, cf. Malachi 3:4).

*(NB: Although this is undeniably hard teaching, we should not misunderstand the language of 'love' and 'hate' (v. 13). These are not emotions felt by God, but actions carried out by Him. 'Love' in this sense is synonymous with election, God's action of stepping in to rescue people and call them to Himself. 'Hate' is the opposite, i.e. not intervening but leaving us to our own destructive devices.)*

## 14–18 GOD'S CHARACTER HAS ALWAYS BEEN TO HAVE MERCY ON WHOM HE WISHES

The teaching that salvation is a matter of God's choice raises the objection that He is unfair. Why should only some of Abraham's descendants be blessed? Surely God does not show favouritism (2:11)?

Paul answers the objection by showing that 'justice' is not the issue. We have already seen that justice would bring about the condemnation of all, but here Paul looks to God's character and purposes in the history of Israel and shows that it is part of God's essential nature to have mercy on whom He wishes.

First (in v. 15) he quotes from Exodus, where God proclaims His character to Moses (Exodus 33:19). In the context, Israel has just rebelled against God and He threatens to abandon them because of their sin. If God had been *just*, He would have destroyed them, but instead He relents and then proclaims His very nature to Moses. His justice, we discover, has been mixed with compassion and He therefore has mercy on whom He wishes. Verse 16 reiterates the point made in vv. 10–13: election has nothing to do with us or our worthiness, it is God's choice. No-one can say that God has been unjust to the people of Israel, the Jews, if so few of them believe.

Also, see v. 17, God may choose not to have mercy if that serves His purposes. This is the lesson to be learnt from the case of Pharaoh (Exodus 9:15–16). As Pharaoh continually refuses to let the Israelites go, God says that He could have destroyed him and all of Egypt instantly, but instead He has raised up Pharaoh so that He may show His power and proclaim His name to the whole world, as indeed He does, through the plagues and His destruction of Pharaoh's army at the Exodus. Paul concludes, simply, in v. 18: God will be God and He will choose whether or not to have mercy on individual Jews.

*(NB: In Exodus, we are told both that God hardens Pharaoh's heart (Exodus 4:21; 7:3; 9:12) and that Pharaoh hardens his own heart (Exodus 8:15; 8:32; 9:34). So even when God uses Pharaoh to display His power and majesty, Pharaoh is culpable. In the next study we shall see that Israel too are fully culpable. They are not excused by the fact of God's sovereign choice.)*

## 19–24 GOD IS NOT ANSWERABLE TO MAN IN HIS SOVEREIGN PURPOSES

Paul anticipates the natural human reaction in v. 19: if God sovereignly hardens the heart of some Jews, how can He blame them for not repenting?

◆ **We are in no position to answer back to our maker (vv. 19–21)**
Paul rebuts our challenge with a warning that God once gave Israel, beginning 'Woe to him who quarrels with his Maker' (Isaiah 45:9). For us to question our maker is as preposterous as the pot talking back to the potter. The Jews are in no position to put the creator of heaven and earth in the dock. He is God and He has the right to do with us as He wishes. All mankind is made of the same sinful clay and it is God's prerogative to choose to bless some but not others, with no comeback from His creatures.

◆ **God can use those who don't receive mercy in order to extend His purposes of mercy towards others – even us (vv. 22–24)**
Having told us that God can act as He wishes, Paul now helps us understand what He is doing. God chooses to hold back His wrath from those who will eventually be destroyed, such as Pharaoh, in order to reveal His glory to those whom He will eventually save (e.g. Israel, especially Moses in Exodus 33:18–34:7). But Paul's main point is that God has worked in this way to extend His mercy, not only to Jews but also, now, *to*

*Gentiles*, and that in the case of the Gentiles He has treated unsaved Israel as He did Pharaoh. We who are Christians should understand that God has patiently put up with those destined for judgment, so that we might know the great extent of His mercy and blessing towards us.

## 25–29 GOD ALWAYS SAID HIS PEOPLE WOULD COMPRISE MANY GENTILES AND A REMNANT OF ISRAEL

Paul quotes from the Old Testament to show how it had been promised that God would show the riches of His glory and mercy to the Gentiles, as he states in v. 24b. These quotations also contain predictions about the unbelief of the majority of Israel. By using these quotations Paul is able to show, once again, the consistency of God's character throughout history.

◆ **'as he says in Hosea:' (vv. 25–26)**
On a first reading, this quotation clearly promises that outsiders will be brought into God's people. The difficulty here, though, is that Paul is using a message given originally to Israel, and is applying it now to the salvation of Gentiles; the explanation, however, lies in the story. Owing to Israel's unfaithfulness, the people were sent by God into an exile from which they never returned. As a symbol of this judgment, God told Hosea to call his two sons, by his adulterous wife, 'Not-loved' and 'Not-my-people' (Hosea 1:2–9), names which describe the status of Gentiles. God also promised, however, that He would one day restore these 'Gentiles' to Himself (Hosea 2:23). On that day, there would be a vast number of them, united with Judah (Hosea 1:10–11), and called sons of God (Hosea 1:10). Paul says that this prophecy is now being fulfilled through the gospel (v. 24).

◆ **Isaiah cries out (vv. 27–29)**
Isaiah prophesied to the southern kingdom of Judah, warning them of exile on account of their complacency and hypocrisy. He promises that a few Jews will be saved (Isaiah 10:22–23); only a very small number will be preserved from God's destruction. The second quotation, from Isaiah 1:9, reinforces Paul's point, that it is God's action alone that prevents total destruction, as at Sodom and Gomorrah (Genesis 18:16–19:29).

The Old Testament tells us, therefore, that we should not be surprised to see comparatively few from the nation of Israel included in God's people, for this is what God has promised.

# Key themes and application

◆ **The definition of the true Israel**

Paul rebuts the suggestion that God may have gone back on His promises to Israel by defining the true Israel. Not all in the nation of Israel are God's true people. On the contrary, it has always been the case that God's people are identified not by their physical ancestry, or indeed by their own goodness or effort, but by virtue of His initiative and His sovereign choice. This helps us to understand some of the Old Testament and indeed the New Testament – especially the gospels – when it appears that Israel are losing their status as God's people. God's true people comprise some of the nation of Israel, but the greater number will be Gentiles. The fact that His promises applied to the true Israel, as defined in this way, may be seen at key stages in the Old Testament, and so we may be fully confident that God has not changed and that His character is reliable. Paul's readers should not be surprised that the vast majority of believers are Gentiles rather than Jews. The believer's assurance and confidence in God, that Paul expressed at the end of ch. 8, should remain unshaken.

This chapter also gives us a proper perspective on Israel today. The re-establishment of the state of Israel in 1948 has been proclaimed by many Christian writers as being confirmation of God's continuing concern for the Jews. Paul tells us, however, that the physical nation of Israel is not the same as the group of people whom God has elected. *He chooses* those on whom He will have mercy.

◆ **Let God be God**

Paul paints an awesome picture of God in this passage, showing how it is His choice alone that determines who will be included among His people. Paul also demonstrates that this is how He has been working, consistently, throughout history. It is part of God's very character that He can choose to save whom He wants and, similarly, that He can harden the hearts of others. Our response should be one of trust with regard to His word and confidence that His nature does not change.

Alongside this, however, there should be an awe and submission in our actions and in our thinking. We have no right to turn to God and question His character or His purposes. If we wish to take issue with Him, we have fundamentally misunderstood our position in relation to Him. He is our maker and He can do with us as He wishes. This is an important message for our age. Modern man's greatest folly is to think he knows better than God Himself, but we should know our place. This point needs also to be made to Christians when we struggle to understand what God is doing in His world. It is easy to become frustrated when those for whom we care do not seem to come to faith, but while our concern is fitting – and indeed we *should* take our concerns and prayers to God – we are in no position to demand answers from Him or to dictate how He should choose to work. This passage should provoke a deep humility before Him.

The other great truth about God that emerges from this passage is that He is a God of mercy. This was proclaimed clearly to Moses, in Exodus, but we have the greater revelation of God's character as demonstrated in the cross of Christ. Our God is awesome in His majesty and authority, yet we can praise Him that He is a God who loves to have compassion on sinful mankind, and that He has provided the means by which He may declare us righteous and so save us for an eternal relationship with Himself.

## Unanswered questions

◆ Why have the Jews missed out on salvation if they were pursuing righteousness by God's good Law?

## The aim of this study

To see that not all the nation of Israel are God's chosen people and to accept that God has the right to have mercy on whom He will.

# Suggested questions

◆ Why do some people believe in Jesus and others not? When might we ask this question, and why?

## 1–5 PAUL'S ANGUISH AT ISRAEL'S UNBELIEF

◆ In your own words, how would you describe Paul's condition in vv. 1–3? How does he emphasize his anguish? He says that he could wish himself 'cut off'. Why is this significant, in the light of ch. 8?

◆ Why is he in such anguish?
– What makes the situation of these Jews so tragic? Explain one or two of the privileges of Israel that Paul lists.

## 6–13 GOD'S WORD HAS NOT FAILED: NOT ALL OF THE NATION OF ISRAEL ARE HIS TRUE CHOSEN PEOPLE

◆ Why might it appear that God's word 'had failed'?
– Why must Paul show that God has kept His word? Why does this matter to us?

◆ Why does Paul say that God's word has not failed? (Leader: Note that the examples in vv. 7–13 will explain what v. 6b means.)

◆ How does Paul show that God's word hasn't failed? (Leader: Be ready with summaries of the Old Testament stories. See OT notes.)
– What is the background to the story of Isaac? What is the point of the story? What is emphasized? How does it show that 'not all who are descended from Israel are Israel'?
– What is the background to the story of Esau and Jacob? What is the point of the story? What is emphasized? How does it show that 'not all who are descended from Israel are Israel'? How does the quotation from Malachi prove the point?
– In summary: what defines those who are God's people? What does not define them? So why do so few of the nation of Israel believe?

## 14–18 GOD'S CHARACTER HAS ALWAYS BEEN TO HAVE MERCY ON WHOM HE WISHES

◆ Why does Paul ask the question in v. 14? Is this a question you would ask? *(Leader: Be ready to explain the context of God's words to Moses in v. 15.)*
  – What would have happened if God had been 'just'?
  – What do God's words to Moses teach us?
◆ How does the example of Pharaoh add to this answer?
◆ A friend hears that the Bible teaches that God predestines only some people to salvation, and complains that it isn't fair. How would you answer in the light of vv. 14–18?

## 19–24 GOD IS NOT ANSWERABLE TO MAN IN HIS SOVEREIGN PURPOSES

◆ Why does the question arise in v. 19? Do you identify with the questioner?
◆ What is our position before God? How should that influence our relationship with Him?
◆ What is God's purpose in choosing some and not others?
  – How is this being seen in Paul's present situation?

## 25–29 GOD ALWAYS SAID HIS PEOPLE WOULD COMPRISE MANY GENTILES AND A REMNANT OF ISRAEL

◆ How do the quotations from Hosea and Isaiah confirm God's purpose?
  – What does Hosea say about the Gentiles?
  – What does Isaiah say about Israel?
  – How do these quotations explain what Paul sees around him?

## SUMMARY

◆ What reasons does Paul give as to why so few from the nation of Israel believe?
◆ What does this passage teach us about God?
  – What answers does this passage give as to why some people believe while others do not?
  – How does our thinking about Him and about ourselves need to change?

**Study 16**

# ROMANS 9:30–10:21

## Context

Why do the majority of Jews not believe, when God seemed to have chosen the nation of Israel? This is the question that Paul addresses in chs 9–11 and, in doing so, he tackles the important implications regarding God's character and faithfulness. In an earlier part of ch. 9 he has already answered this question by defining the true people of God and showing that they are different from the nation of Israel (9:6). Pointing us to the Old Testament, he has shown that God never chose people on the basis of human ancestry, but that rather it was always a matter of His promise (9:6–9) and His choice (9:10–13). The sobering truth is that His choice has nothing to do with man's descent, merit, desire or goodness, but is rooted in His character: it is His nature to have mercy and He has mercy on whom He wishes (9:14–18). This, we were told, is entirely His prerogative; we, being His creatures, are in no position to question His purposes – He works for His own glory (9:19–23). Finally we were shown that His choice, to rescue many Gentiles and a remnant of Israel, was promised in scripture itself (9:25–29) and that therefore God has remained faithful.

Chapter 9:6–29, then, can be seen as answering the question from God's side. This passage (9:30–10:21) explains what has happened from the human perspective, as Paul examines how Israel have distorted God's word and rejected the message of salvation, which clearly pointed to faith in Christ. This salvation is available to all people, but Israel's rejection of the offer of salvation is the reason they remain, largely, under judgment.

Paul backs up his argument with many quotations from the Old Testament, showing that both the message of salvation by faith and Israel's rejection of that message have always been there. It is noteworthy that Paul has no difficulty, here, in laying human responsibility alongside God's sovereignty (the main theme of the previous study).

## Structure

**9:30–10:4** Unlike the Gentiles, the Jews have not obtained right-eousness because they tried to do so through obedience to the Law instead of through faith

**10:5–13** The Old Testament teaches that righteousness is by faith, not the Law

**10:14–17** Faith comes from accepting the preached word about Jesus. But Israel would not accept it

**10:18–21** Israel heard and was able to understand, but they continued to reject God, so He turned to save Gentiles instead

## Old Testament background

**Obedience demanded in the Law:** The covenant that God made with Israel through Moses stated that blessing was conditional on obedience to the Law and, conversely, that disobedience would result in curse (Deuteronomy 28). Yet the Law itself indicated that Israel would never receive the promised blessings through obedience, because of their sin. Instead, it would have to be through God's action.

**Rebellion predicted in the Law:** Even as the covenant is made, God predicts that Israel will break it by rebelling against Him and turning to other gods. He tells them they will consequently face disaster as He curses them (Deuteronomy 31:14–18). Moses is told to teach Israel a song, predicting their rebellion and judgment, which will be a witness against them (Deuteronomy 31:19–32:43).

**Future hope seen in the Law:** Yet God also talks of the future when He will bring them back to Himself and circumcise their hearts, so that they will obey Him and love Him (Deuteronomy

30:4–8). These promises are developed in the writings of the prophets (e.g. Isaiah 28, 53).

## Text notes

### 9:30–10:4 UNLIKE THE GENTILES, THE JEWS HAVE NOT OBTAINED RIGHTEOUSNESS BECAUSE THEY TRIED TO DO SO THROUGH OBEDIENCE TO THE LAW INSTEAD OF THROUGH FAITH

Having shown that God had always promised that He would choose many Gentiles and only a remnant of Israel, Paul now looks at the human side of the equation. The Gentiles seem to have found salvation and righteousness (i.e. a right standing before God), having previously had no regard for God and His ways. Yet the Israelites have missed out on righteousness, when they were at least trying to follow God's righteous Law (7:12), and could have hoped to claim the life and blessing that the Law offered (see OT notes). Why has most of Israel missed out?

◆ **Israel pursued righteousness, not by faith, but by works (v. 32a)**
 Their error was to try to obtain righteousness by their own effort and to ignore the offer of rescue from God. As Paul has already been at pains to point out, it is not possible to become righteous by following the Law, because we are incapable of perfect obedience (3:20). Yet, for Israel, trying to be right with God by their obedience had become their focus and goal: they did not trust God and His promises that He would save them Himself (e.g. Isaiah 59:16).

◆ **They stumbled over the stumbling-stone (vv. 32b–33)**
 When Paul refers to a stone he is using a metaphor that appears in two passages in Isaiah. In Isaiah 8, God announces judgment on Israel for their blatant refusal to fear and trust Him (Isaiah 8: 12–15). Though He will be a sanctuary for some, God says that Israel will stumble and fall over Him, as over a stone (Isaiah 8:14). In v. 33, however, Paul is also alluding to Isaiah 28, where Israel are once again under judgment for not trusting God (a central theme in Isaiah; see 7:9). But here the stone, that God lays, is a precious 'cornerstone' and anyone who puts his trust in it will not be put to shame.

The way that Paul uses these two quotations suggests that he sees the two stones as one – they both represent Jesus, the Messiah. The 'cornerstone' that could have been the salvation of Israel has become, instead, the 'stumbling-stone', the cause of their downfall, because instead of trusting God they are trying to please Him through good works. The stone is a metaphor for Jesus, who is both saviour and judge.

◆ **Israel are zealous, but they have rejected Christ who is the end of the Law (10:1–4)**
Again we see Paul's deep concern for his own race (cf. 9:1–3), but here he homes in on the heart of their problem. Though they are zealous, their enthusiasm is misdirected. Instead of accepting the righteousness that comes from trusting in God, they imagined that they *could* keep the Law and in that way become righteous and acceptable to God, i.e. saved. In doing this, they have not seen their need for God's life-line to all and so have rejected Christ. Verse 4 spells out their mistake. The Law was always supposed to point beyond itself, to a time when God Himself would make people right with Himself (see OT notes), and this plan has been fully revealed in Christ. 'Christ is the end of the Law' in two senses: He is the end (or fulfilment) to which the Law points, as Paul will go on to explain in v. 5, and yet He is also the termination of the Law, in that the Law is now irrelevant for salvation, because now anyone may be made righteous if they believe in Christ.

## 5–13 THE OLD TESTAMENT TEACHES THAT RIGHTEOUSNESS IS BY FAITH, NOT THE LAW

Verses 5–13 spell out the point made in v. 4, concerning the difference that Christ has made, in enabling all people to be made righteous. Paul goes to passages in Leviticus and in Deuteronomy to show the impossibility of obtaining righteousness by trying to keep the Law and, by contrast, the easy availability of the righteousness that God gives, to those who have faith in Christ.

◆ **Righteousness-by-Law says, 'Salvation depends upon obedience' (v. 5)**
In Leviticus 18:5, Moses states the principle undergirding the Law, that God's blessing is contingent upon our obedience (see

OT notes). Yet we know that righteousness is unobtainable by trying to keep the Law, simply because no-one can do so perfectly. We are rebels at heart, as the Old Testament testifies and as Paul has shown in chs 1–3.

◆ **Righteousness-by-faith says, 'Trust in God's revealed word, namely Christ' (vv. 6–10)**

Turning to words from Deuteronomy 30, Paul explains that righteousness is now readily available. His overall meaning is straightforward enough: he is assuring his readers that righteousness by faith is not beyond anyone's grasp. Jesus has now come down from heaven and has already been raised from the dead, and therefore we do not have to go to impossible lengths – i.e. keeping the Law – in order to be saved. This is the gospel that Paul is proclaiming (v. 8b). It is now a simple matter of trusting, both personally and publicly, in the salvation that Christ has made available (vv. 9–10).

The difficulty for us is to see how Paul can obtain this meaning, as expressed in v. 8, from the original context. Moo suggests (pp. 650–1) that Paul is starting his quotation with words from Deuteronomy 9:4, where Israel is warned against attributing their future possession of the land to their own righteousness. This would demonstrate the existence of an underlying assumption about blessing being contingent upon obedience, i.e. that obedience is not the key thing, but that, rather, God is fully responsible for their enjoyment of any blessings. In vv. 8–9 Paul goes on to explain that righteousness (and so life) does depend upon God and that we obtain it through faith in Christ.

Also significant is the fact that the verses that Paul quotes from Deuteronomy 30, vv. 12–14, follow on after God's promises, in vv. 1–10, that, despite Israel's inevitable rebellion in the future and their consequent judgment, He will call them back to Himself and circumcise their hearts, so they may live with Him in love and obedience. This is the language of the new covenant that we saw in Romans 2:29. Despite the solemn call to obedience, the Law always had in mind God's plan of making people righteous through His grace.

◆ **Therefore anyone, Jew or Gentile, who calls on Christ will be saved (vv. 11–13)**
The means by which righteousness is given – through trusting in Christ – is now available to anyone; the door of salvation has been thrown open. Paul shows that this is what scripture has always said. He quotes from both Isaiah 28:16 and Joel 2:32, where God has promised that all who trust in Him, calling out for His help, will be saved. Although both promises were made to Israel, the terms of the promises mean that all people may benefit, for indeed Jesus is Lord of all, irrespective of race.

## 14–17 FAITH COMES FROM ACCEPTING THE PREACHED WORD ABOUT JESUS. BUT ISRAEL WOULD NOT ACCEPT IT
If anyone who calls on Christ may be saved, why are so many Jews not saved? Paul addresses this question by tracing the steps that they must take in order to believe.

◆ **The significance of preaching the good news (vv. 14–16)**
As Paul considers, in reverse order, the chain of events that are necessary – calling upon God, believing, hearing, preaching and sending – we are made aware of the significance of the good news of salvation being preached in the first place. The quotation from Isaiah 52:7, concerning the time when Isaiah himself was sent by God to preach His message of redemption to exiled Israel (Isaiah 52:9), confirms that this was as true in the past as it is now.

◆ **But Israel did not accept the promise about Jesus (vv. 16–17)**
The quotation, from Isaiah 53:1, is taken from the beginning of God's promise of rescue by His suffering servant. The verse tells us, however, that the chain of events described in 10:14–15 was not completed in the case of most Israelites; they did not accept God's offer of salvation. Since saving faith comes through accepting the message about Christ (v. 17), Israel's rejection of Him has excluded them from receiving God's salvation. How did this happen?

## 18–21 ISRAEL HEARD AND WAS ABLE TO UNDERSTAND, BUT THEY CONTINUED TO REJECT GOD, SO GOD TURNED TO SAVE GENTILES INSTEAD

The rest of the chapter looks more closely at Israel's history and reveals the point at which the chain (see above) was broken.

◆ **Israel has heard, both through creation and through the Law (v. 18)**

Paul asks whether it is possible that those who are unsaved did not hear the message preached (v. 14), but immediately answers that they must have heard. He supports this answer by quoting from Psalm 19:4 which talks of God's general revelation to all people in creation. This seems like a peculiar answer, but it works on two levels. First it reminds us of 1:18–21 and the truth that, from creation, all people know that God, in His power and divinity, should be honoured and depended upon. Second, however, the context of this quotation in the psalm also points to the knowledge of God uniquely given through the Law, which brings reward and encourages trust in God (Psalm 19:14). The Jews have no excuse at all.

◆ **Israel could understand from the Law and the prophets (vv. 19–20)**

Having established that Israel had the opportunity of hearing the message, Paul goes on to ask whether it is possible that they didn't understand what they heard. Instantly, however, he shows how both the Law and the prophets eliminate this possibility.

First, he quotes from the song that Moses taught the Israelites shortly before he died (Deuteronomy 32:21; see OT notes). This song stands as a witness against them, foretelling Israel's rejection of God, and stating that because they have made God jealous and angry, His judgment will be to make *them* jealous and angry, as He turns to bless other nations who do not share their privileges. Israel, therefore, have no excuse; they know that they should not have rejected God. (NB: God is free to do this without being unfaithful because Israel have broken the covenant.)

Paul then quotes from Isaiah 65:1–2, which shows that the prophet had given Israel the same message. Isaiah tells of how God will judge Israel for their sin and turn instead to those who do not seek Him. Israel, therefore, cannot plead ignorance in their defence. Scripture testifies that Israel will reject God and that Gentiles will believe.

◆ **Israel has been stubborn and rebellious (v. 21)**
The reason why Israel did not accept God's offer of salvation is spelt out in the quotation from Isaiah 65:2. Here, God is portrayed as an anguished father who is constantly rejected by those He longs to embrace. This is the reason why Israelites are not being saved: their constant rebellion and refusal to turn to Him has brought God's judgment on them, such that most are heading for destruction (Isaiah 65:6–7).

# Key themes and application

◆ **The Law always pointed to salvation by faith**
The Law states that if you obey it, you will be blessed and if not, you will be cursed. Israel took this as the sole purpose of the Law and so worked hard to obey it. Yet even as the Law was given, God indicated that His people would not keep it, that they *would* rebel against Him, and that their only hope of being right with Him was to trust *Him* as her rescuer. The point of the Law, therefore, was always to point beyond itself, to show that there is no possibility of our reaching God's standard of perfection, and that we therefore need God Himself to make us righteous. Ultimately, as God revealed, this could only come through faith in Christ.

Although we probably feel a long way from the nation of Israel, we should beware our natural tendency to try to get right with God by keeping laws and commands. *Salvation comes solely through trusting in God's work*. It is therefore inappropriate, and misguided, to think that we can ever earn God's favour by, for example, keeping the Ten Commandments or following the Sermon on the Mount. Although these revelations from God tell us how we should live in His world, they should always be understood as pointing us towards our need for rescue and thereby encouraging us to trust in Jesus, the rescuer. Furthermore, when we feel that we are failing God, the fact that salvation is all about God's grace through Christ, and not about works, should be a great comfort to us.

### ◆ Israel's unbelief is not God's fault; it comes from Israel's rebellion

The overwhelming message of this passage is that the Jews' exclusion from God's people is their own fault. First, they rebelled by trying to obtain a right status with God by keeping the Law, ignoring the fact that the Law pointed beyond itself to the necessity of looking to God Himself for righteousness. Second, this rebellion became more apparent when they were judged at the exile; at that time they were given a clear promise of rescue through the coming Messiah. Still they refused to trust God, and thus they remain under judgment. This should also be a lesson for us. The fact that salvation is not about works does not let us off the hook concerning our rebellion against God. Like Israel, we are still culpable for our sin.

The previous passage told us about God's absolute sovereignty in choosing those whom He wishes to save, while this passage teaches us that we are culpable if we reject God's message of salvation. The Bible asserts, equally, both His sovereignty and our responsibility to trust Him in order to obtain righteousness, and it shows us to be without excuse if we do not do this. As Paul has already stressed in his letter, everybody knows that they should not reject God. We cannot, therefore, blame God if we do not believe, and nor can we blame Him if other people do not believe; each one of us has an active role to play in turning to God for salvation.

### ◆ Salvation by faith in Christ is available to all people

Since a right standing with God comes not through keeping the Law but through faith in Christ, this status cannot be restricted to the Jews. Rather, those who acknowledge Christ, putting their trust in Him, may be assured of salvation. The fact that salvation is freely available has far-reaching implications for evangelism. We often come up against the view that spreading the gospel is sometimes inappropriate, on account of the background, experience or lifestyle of the individual unbeliever. Yet the wonderful truth is that everyone may be saved by faith in Christ, so it is appropriate to tell everyone. A secondary point from this passage is the importance of preaching the message; if anyone is going to be saved he must first hear the message of the gospel.

Scripture thus upholds the urgency of the task of evangelism. We should put great effort into faithfully proclaiming the message of salvation to all people, in a relevant and engaging way.

## Unanswered questions

◆ Are rebellious Jews now without hope? Has God fully turned instead to the Gentiles?

## The aim of this study

To see that the reason why so few Jews believe is that they continue to rebel, refusing to trust God for their salvation. And yet, God's message is that salvation through Christ is available to anyone who believes.

## Suggested questions

◆ Do you blame people if they don't believe in Jesus? Why? Why not?
◆ What is the key question that Paul has been answering since 9:1?
  – What answer is given in 9:1–29?

### 9:30–10:4 UNLIKE THE GENTILES, THE JEWS HAVE NOT OBTAINED RIGHTEOUSNESS BECAUSE THEY TRIED TO DO SO THROUGH OBEDIENCE TO THE LAW INSTEAD OF THROUGH FAITH

◆ What surprising situation are we left with, in 9:30–31?
  – Why is it surprising?
  – To what question does it lead?
◆ What reasons does Paul give, in 9:32–10:4, as to why Israel have not obtained righteousness?
  – How have they gone wrong with regard to the Law?
  – How have they 'stumbled over the stumbling–stone'?
  – Why is their zeal insufficient for their salvation?
  – In what way is Christ the end of the Law?
◆ 'God will look favourably on me – I follow the Ten Commandments.' How should we respond?

## 5–13 THE OLD TESTAMENT TEACHES THAT RIGHTEOUSNESS IS BY FAITH, NOT THE LAW

◆ In the light of Leviticus 18:5, which Paul quotes in 10:5, why might someone still claim that Israel's failure to obtain salvation is God's fault?

◆ How does Paul argue that this is not the case? How does Paul use the quotation from Deuteronomy? What is the implication of the word being 'in your mouth and in your heart'?

  – What have Israel failed to understand?

  – How hard is it for Jews to be saved?

  – What is required for anyone to be saved?

  – What effect should this teaching have on our day-to-day Christian lives?

◆ Christians are sometimes attacked for trying to evangelize people from other religions. How can we defend our actions?

◆ Summarize Paul's answer regarding Israel's unbelief so far.

## 14–17 FAITH COMES FROM HEARING THE MESSAGE OF SALVATION

◆ What do vv. 14–15 tell us about the chain of communication that is necessary? Describe all the necessary stages by which the Israelites might call on the Lord for salvation.

  – And yet, what is Israel's situation?

## 18–21 ISRAEL HEARD BUT DISOBEYED, SO GOD JUDGED THEM AND SAVED GENTILES INSTEAD

◆ What possible excuse does Paul suggest for Israel not accepting God's offer of salvation?

  – How do we know that Israel heard?

  – How do we know that Israel understood?

  – Why, then, did Israel not accept the message of salvation?

## SUMMARY

◆ What does this passage add to the previous one, in answering the question as to why so few from the nation of Israel believe?

  – Can we blame Israel for not believing?

– Can people be blamed today if they do not believe? How should this passage affect our relationships with those who do not believe?

◆ How will this passage affect our attitude to the Old Testament?

# ROMANS 11:1–36

## Context

So far, in addressing the issue of the Jews' apparent unbelief, Paul has explained what has happened from two perspectives. In 9:1–29 we saw God's perspective. Paul has shown us that God's people have always been defined by His choice, rather than through ancestry or human worthiness, and that God has always said that many Jews were not chosen. Then, in 9:30–10:21, we saw Israel's failure from the human perspective. Israel made the error of trying to obtain righteousness through obeying the Law (9:32), by their own efforts. By doing this they failed to trust God and rejected His promise of rescue through Christ, to whom the Law pointed for salvation. Although salvation was now readily available through Jesus, they would not accept it, and because of their rebellion God turned to other nations instead.

This, however, is not the end of the story for the Jews. Paul first shows that there are, as there always have been, a few Jews whom God has preserved; from among those who are hardened, there are some who will be saved (although Paul does not say who they are or when this will be). He also explains that the Jews have been hardened so that the gospel may go the Gentiles.

This chapter picks up the idea that Paul wrote about in 9:6, that the nation of Israel and God's chosen people (the true Israel) are two different things. The nation is no longer the locus of God's activity. God does have a plan of salvation for both Jews and Gentiles, and by this plan He will save a fixed number of each (11:25–26).

Paul ends this section of his letter, which began at 9:1, by praising the God whose ways are infinitely higher than ours.

## Structure

**11:1–6** God has not totally rejected His people: there is, as there always has been, a remnant

**11:7–10** The others have been hardened in judgment

**11:11–32** But the Jews still have an important part to play in God's plan, so saved Gentiles must not be arrogant

**11:33–36** Praise God for His unfathomable wisdom and purposes!

## Old Testament background

**Elijah:** He was a prophet in Israel at a time of great national apostasy under King Ahab (1 Kings 16:29–33). Ahab's wife, Jezebel, threatened to kill Elijah because he had had the prophets of Baal killed, after the confrontation at Mount Carmel (1 Kings 18:16–40), and so he fled for his life. He spoke to God in despair, believing himself to be the last remaining faithful Israelite (1 Kings 19:10), but God replied with the words quoted in Romans 11:4.

## Text notes

### 1–6 GOD HAS NOT TOTALLY REJECTED HIS PEOPLE: THERE IS, AS THERE ALWAYS HAS BEEN, A REMNANT

Chapter 10 ended with an image of Israel under judgment, refusing to turn to the God who had offered her salvation (10:21). Paul begins ch. 11 by asking whether God has consequently given up on the nation of Israel altogether. This possibility Paul immediately denies, providing two instances to demonstrate that the opposite is true.

◆ **Paul himself has been chosen (vv. 1–2a)**
First Paul points to himself. He is a Jew and a direct descendent of Abraham, yet God has clearly not rejected him, apostle that he is! God has not turned away from all Jews; some, such as Paul, He has chosen. (See notes on the meaning of 'foreknew' on p. 143.)

### ◆ Elijah was not the only faithful Israelite (vv. 2b–6)

Next, Paul appeals to the Old Testament, to the account of the time when all Israel seemed to have blatantly rebelled against God, turning to the false god, Baal, and wanting to kill Elijah, God's faithful prophet (1 Kings 19:10, 14). In reply to Elijah's cry of despair, God told him that He had preserved a remnant of seven thousand Israelites who had not turned away to worship Baal (1 Kings 19:18). (NB: In the Bible the numbers 7 and 1,000 are often used symbolically, to denote completeness.) Paul asserts that the same is still true: although there appear to be almost no believing Jews, God has preserved a relatively small, but definite, number. Lest we think, however, that they may have done something to deserve this, we are reminded that it is by God's grace alone.

## 7–10 THE OTHERS HAVE BEEN HARDENED IN JUDGMENT

Having established that a remnant of Jews have been chosen by God's grace, Paul concludes that most of the nation that was so zealous has been hardened by God. As we have seen, their error was to seek righteousness by their own works (9:31). This passage restates the realities described in 9:1–10:21 in order to prepare for the question coming in v. 11: are those who are now hardened, hardened for ever? Paul is again quoting from the Old Testament to show the predicament of rebellious Israel.

Verse 8 is an amalgam of Deuteronomy 29:4 and Isaiah 29:10, and it echoes Isaiah 6:9. Each of these passages tells of how the people of Israel are unable to understand because God has not given them understanding. Indeed, the Isaiah passages say that God has blinded and deafened them in judgment for their hard-heartedness.

In vv. 9–10 Paul then quotes from Psalm 69. This is David's prayer that his enemies, his 'brothers' among them (see v. 8) – and David sees them as God's enemies also, since he is God's anointed king – will meet with disaster. By quoting this prayer Paul implies that Israel have now become God's enemies because they have rejected Him. The imagery suggests the loss of security – 'their table', a place of domestic stability, becomes a place of danger – and the fate of being plunged into blindness and slavery for ever. This is the punishment deserved by those who reject their God: to be made incapable of ever being saved.

**11–32 BUT THE JEWS STILL HAVE AN IMPORTANT PART TO PLAY IN GOD'S PLAN, SO SAVED GENTILES SHOULDN'T BE ARROGANT**

Verse 10 is shocking. This quotation causes Paul to ask whether David's prayer, for God to judge His enemies, was answered in the case of Israel: does the fact that these Jews have been hardened mean that they cannot now be saved? He answers by showing the place of the Jews in God's plan of salvation. In doing so He addresses what seems to have been an issue in the Roman church – Gentile Christians being arrogant towards Jewish ones (see Section Notes). It appears that some Gentile Christians, aware that God had turned to the Gentiles in the face of Israel's rejection of Him (10:19–20), consequently thought too much of themselves and looked down upon Jewish Christians, considering them to be less welcome in the body of believers. Understanding God's plan, however, should lead to the elimination of all such arrogance.

◆ **The role of the Jews in God's process of salvation (vv. 11–16)**

Paul denies the suggestion that Jews are beyond salvation. Instead, he points to the bigger picture of God's purposes in history. He explains both the process that God is following and also the part that he, as an apostle, is playing in it.

***God's pattern of salvation (vv. 11–12):*** God's hardening of Israel does not mean the end of His plans for them. Israel's rejection of the gospel has caused the good news to be taken to the Gentiles (v. 12) who are now being saved. (We can see this happening in Acts, e.g. 13:46 and 18:6.) Yet God's purpose goes beyond this: it is that, as the Gentiles receive salvation and benefit from the blessings and promises that God gives to His people, some Jews will become envious (v. 11) and, as a result, will respond to the gospel and so be saved (as Paul envisages in v. 14).

As he considers this prospect, Paul anticipates how great will be the implications of God's plan in the future, when all the appointed Jews do respond to the gospel. If, through Israel's rejection of the gospel, God has brought salvation to the Gentiles (the rest of the world), we will marvel over the 'greater riches' (v. 12) that will follow when they do accept it. These 'greater riches' are referred to, in v. 15, as 'life from the dead', i.e. resurrection day.

(NB: By using the words 'their fulness' (v. 12), Paul is not fore-seeing God's acceptance of every member of the nation of Israel; in his own generation, he expects only 'some' to be saved (v. 14). Instead, this phrase denotes the acceptance of a complete number of Jews.)

This is the sequence of events, or the overall pattern of God's plan, that Paul has been describing:

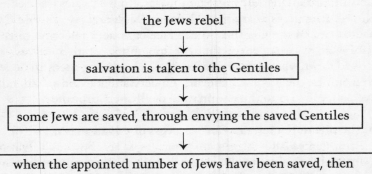

We might ask why the salvation of a certain number of Jews should signal the completion of God's salvation plan. As if in answer to this question, Paul gives two illustrations, in v. 16, concerning these appointed Jews, whose salvation is to be the indication that God has saved everyone He intends to save – He will have made up the full complement of His people. These Jews will be like the first part of the dough which, when ready, indicates that the whole batch is ready, and also like the healthy root which shows that the branches are healthy. Once God sees these Jews believing, He will know that everyone who is appointed has been saved and will therefore commence judgment day and glorify His people with Jesus.

***Paul's role in God's pattern of salvation (vv. 13–14):*** Paul speaks of his own place in God's purposes, and addresses the Gentiles in particular (v. 13). In the context of Gentile Christians boasting over the Jewish Christians (see above), Paul stresses that his efforts as apostle to the Gentiles are not because the Gentiles are more important, but because, in addition to reaching them, he wants to save some of his own race, according to God's saving process.

### ◆ Further reasons why saved Gentiles should not be arrogant (vv. 17–24)

Paul continues with the imagery of a tree, with roots and branches, but now he uses this image to teach the Gentile Christians why they must not boast over Jews.

***The source of the Gentiles' salvation is Israel (vv. 17–18):*** First, the Gentiles must remember that the root of their faith is Jewish. Verse 17 reminds us of the Jews who have been broken off from God's people because they wouldn't trust God for their salvation (9:30–10:21). But it follows that if Gentiles ('wild olive shoots') have subsequently been grafted in, they have no grounds for feeling superior over unsaved Jews; there would be no salvation for the Gentiles were it not for the Jews.

***Gentiles will be cut off, as the Jews were, if they do not continue to believe (vv. 19–22):*** Although it is true that Jews were broken off specifically to enable the salvation of Gentiles, Paul retorts that this provides no grounds for arrogance either, reminding the Gentiles that they were not grafted in on merit, but by faith (by trusting in God's promise to save them when they couldn't save themselves). Furthermore, just as the Jews were cut off because they did not continue to trust God, so will the Gentiles be cut off, should they turn away from His grace; there will be no difference. Paul urges them not to focus on themselves, but on the character of God Himself, by whose kindness they stand in their faith, but who also deals severely with those who cease to depend upon Him for salvation.

***It is easier for Jews to be re-grafted in (vv. 23–24):*** Since salvation depends only upon calling on Christ (10:13), it is no more difficult for a Jew to be saved than for a Gentile: he needs only to turn back to God from his unbelief to become one of God's holy people. Indeed, since this is only what the Jews were always supposed to do in the Old Testament, Paul suggests that this is easier than the grafting in of godless pagan Gentiles.

## ◆ God will save all elect Jews just as He will save all elect Gentiles (vv. 25–29)

In v. 25, Paul returns to the big picture of God's plan for salvation history, that he outlined in vv. 11–16, and teaches the Gentile Christians about the implications of this plan.

Gentiles shouldn't be conceited, with regard to the Jews, since some Jews have been hardened in order that 'the full number' (the same as 'fulness' in v. 12) of Gentiles might be grafted in to God's people. In other words, part of Israel has been hardened for the Gentiles' benefit. Yet God's overall plan means that a further number of Jews will be saved – indeed, they must be for the plan to be completed.

Paul's teaching in vv. 25–26, and in particular the phrase, 'And so all Israel will be saved', has caused much controversy over the years and opinion is much divided over its meaning. Our preferred interpretation (that of Calvin) takes 'all Israel' to refer both to elect Jews and to elect Gentiles. Here is a suggested paraphrase: 'The nation of Israel is experiencing a partial hardening, in the sense that some Jews, who are appointed for salvation, are temporarily broken off, but this is happening so that the full number of elect Gentiles may come in (i.e. come in to Israel by being grafted in). However, once all the elect Gentiles have been saved, the hardening of any appointed Jews will end and so, in this way, all of the true Israel – the true people of God, comprising the Jewish remnant, the grafted Gentiles and the regrafted Jews – will be saved.'

*(NB: Stott, among others, suggests that Paul cannot change the meaning of 'Israel' between v. 24 and v. 25, as suggested above, but in 9:6 that is exactly what the apostle has done. Both Moo and Stott conclude that v. 26 points to a great number of Jews being saved in the last generation. [For extensive debate on this subject see Stott, pp. 303–5 and Moo, pp. 719–26.] But for Paul to add such a dramatic extra ingredient at this stage of his argument would mean interrupting the flow of a passage which he seems to be concluding. Also, such a meaning would fuel Jewish pride, which Paul has done so much to counter (2:17–21). In addition, such a meaning would not do justice to the phrase 'and so', which means 'in this way'. It is possible that 'Israel' in v. 26 could refer to all the elect Jews, but*

*this still does not mean that a large number will be saved at
the end.)*

Paul shows how scripture testifies to this, the completing of
God's plan, by quoting from two passages in Isaiah (59:20–21 and
27:9), and possibly also from Jeremiah 31:33–34, in which we
find God's promises about how He will turn the Jews away from
their rebellion.

Once Gentiles understand God's plan, as outlined in vv.
25–26, they should see why it is inappropriate to boast over
Jews. As far as the good news of salvation is concerned, the Jews
are currently enemies, so that salvation may come to the
Gentiles (literally 'for your sake'), but as far as being chosen for
salvation is concerned, elect Jews are saved 'on account of the
patriarchs'. This means that they are loved like Abraham, who
had faith in God's promise (4:20), like Isaac, who was one of
God's children by virtue of God's promise (9:8), and like Jacob,
who was chosen by God (9:11–12). God's gift of righteousness
and His sovereign election cannot be changed.

***Jews and Gentiles are, equally, disobedient people to whom God
shows mercy (vv. 30–32):*** Finally, Paul shows that God's plan of
salvation means that Jews are saved in precisely the same way
that Gentiles are. Both receive mercy against a background of
disobedience. There is nothing more worthy about the Gentiles
who are grafted in. For all people God's purpose is the same.
Verse 32 is a summary of the gospel for the world.

*(NB: The context of Romans will not allow v. 32 to be teach-
ing universalism, the idea that God will save absolutely everyone. The content of vv. 30 and 31 suggests that 'all' refers to all
types of people, i.e. both Jew and Gentile.)*

## 33–36 PRAISE GOD FOR HIS UNFATHOMABLE WISDOM AND PURPOSES

Finally, Paul comes to the end of his exposition of God's plan of
salvation through the gospel, which he started in 1:16. Having
answered the matter of Israel's unbelief, he now has absolutely no
reason to be ashamed of the gospel. And the assurance given to all
believers, as he described in 8:28–39, is now shown to be certain
beyond question, because God really has been faithful to what He
promised. Paul's response is to fall on his knees and praise the God

who has done all of this. Some key themes of the gospel are seen in his doxology.

◆ **God's wisdom is unsearchable (vv. 33–34)**

One of the great lessons we learn, as we hear of God's purposes, is that His wisdom and His ways are higher than ours. He is not a God whom we can neatly define or easily explain, and the things that He does reveal to us often leave us speechless (9:19–20). In v. 34 Paul quotes from Isaiah 40, in which the prophet announces God's plan to save Israel from exile in Babylon: with Isaiah, he acknowledges God's unfathomable wisdom.

◆ **God is no man's debtor (v. 35)**

Revealing Himself as the almighty creator, God tells Job (in Job 41:11, which Paul alludes to here) that He owes nothing to anyone, since everything belongs to Him. The gospel hammers this point home to us. We deserve nothing from God (except His wrath) and can demand nothing from Him, neither mercy nor, even, answers.

◆ **God is at the centre of His plans (v. 36)**

Contrary to our self-centred ideas, God's work does not revolve around us. It is His gospel (1:1) which reveals His righteousness (3:26), such that He will exalt the name of His Son (8:29). He alone is worthy of eternal glory.

# Key themes and application

◆ **Israel and the Jews**

The lessons that we learned in ch. 9 need to be reinforced here. God's true people are not the same as the Jews as an ethic group, nor are they the nation-state of Israel, but rather they are those who 'believe', i.e. who trust in God for their salvation. *This* is God's holy people Israel, comprising those of both Jewish and Gentile origin. God does not have a different plan of salvation for the Jews, as many teach; the Jews, as much as anyone else, need to respond to the gospel. We must therefore evangelize Jews just as much as Gentiles. To do so is not anti-Semitic but, in fact, the most loving action it is possible to take. An extra dimension that we see in this passage is that the conversion of Gentiles is a significant way in which God reaches out to Jews, since Jews will become envious of the blessings that Gentiles enjoy when they are saved.

◆ **Do not boast**.

Just as Paul told the Jew, in ch. 2, that he could not boast, so here he warns Gentiles against boasting over Jews. This was clearly a vital issue in the Roman church, but the principle still applies today. If we are Gentile believers, we should have no sense of superiority over Jews; our faith has stemmed from the root of Israel and we have been made true Jews ourselves. This has only happened through God's mercy and if we cease to trust God we will be treated as God treated faithless Jews. In any case, God fully intends to include Jews as well as Gentiles in His elect, rescuing them from disobedience as He did us. Instead of focusing on ourselves, we should focus on the character of God, on His kindness to us and also on His sternness towards rebels. And so we should concentrate on continuing to trust Him.

◆ **Praise God**

Paul's response, in vv. 33–36, should be shared by all believers. Once we start to consider the scope and magnificence of God's plan of salvation, we should acknowledge Him for who He is and what He has done. We should bow before His infinitely superior wisdom and be humbled by His overwhelming generosity.

We always put ourselves first and see ourselves at the centre of God's plans, but we need to acknowledge that at the heart of God's gospel is God Himself, and that He alone is worthy of our praise and glory.

## Unanswered questions

◆ How should our lives be changed by what God has done?

## The aim of this study

To understand God's plan of salvation. This understanding should include the realization that God has not turned away from all Jews, and also that Gentile believers should be humble, not boastful towards Jews. Such an understanding should cause us to be amazed, at God Himself and at His astonishing plan for the rescue of His people.

# Suggested questions

◆ What are Christians sometimes accused of, in their evangelism to Jews?
◆ From what we have read in chs 9 and 10, why might the Gentile Christians in Rome have looked down on the Jews, both inside and outside the church?
  – Why might it appear that God has rejected His historic people (11:1)?

## 1–6 GOD HAS NOT TOTALLY REJECTED HIS HISTORIC PEOPLE: THERE IS, AS THERE ALWAYS HAS BEEN, A REMNANT

◆ How does Paul show that God has not totally rejected His historic people?
  – How do his two examples support his answer?
  – What makes Elijah such a good example?
  – What is Paul's conclusion, in the light of these examples?
  – People often speak of a 'faithful remnant'. Why wouldn't Paul use this phrase?

## 7–10 THE OTHERS HAVE BEEN HARDENED IN JUDGMENT

◆ What has happened to those who are not part of the remnant?
  – How do vv. 8–10 summarize what Paul has said so far about the Jews?

## 11–32 THE JEWS STILL HAVE AN IMPORTANT PART TO PLAY IN GOD'S PLAN, SO SAVED GENTILES SHOULDN'T BE ARROGANT

◆ What question is Paul asking in v. 11?
*(Leader: This is a long passage, so take it in small parts, one at a time.)*
**Read vv. 11–16**
◆ Write out the stages in God's overall plan of salvation.
  – How does Paul work in accordance with God's plan?
  – So can Jews who are currently unsaved no longer be saved?
  – What important place do Jews have in salvation history? How does v. 16 illustrate this?
**Read vv. 17–24**

◆ What reasons does Paul give the Gentiles as to why they should not boast over Jews?
  – In what way are the Gentile Christians supported by a Jewish root?
  – Why should they not boast over Jews who were cut off?
  – What should we do about the warning in vv. 21–22?
  – Why is it easy for God to bring Jews back to Himself?
  ***Read vv. 25–32***

*(Leader: This is a dense and difficult passage, so don't get bogged down in detail. Make sure you set aside a good amount of time for vv. 33–36.)*

◆ In v. 25, Paul returns to the subject of God's overall plan of salvation.
  – Why have some Jews been hardened? How should this stop Gentiles from being conceited?

◆ Paul's statement in v. 26, 'And so all Israel will be saved', has caused much difficulty for generations of commentators – so don't be surprised if you can't tie up the loose ends now!
  – From what we have seen in Romans so far, why can this not mean that every single Jew will be saved?
  – Try to write out your own version of vv. 25b–26a. (Hints: (a) In 9:6, Paul used the word 'Israel' in two senses. (b) 'And so' in v. 26 means 'in this way'.)

◆ Looking at the whole of vv. 25–32, what reasons does Paul give the Gentiles for having a right attitude towards Jews?

◆ How should this passage change the attitude of the Gentile Christian towards Jews? How should it change our attitude and practice regarding evangelism to Jews?

## 33–36 PRAISE GOD FOR HIS UNFATHOMABLE WISDOM AND PURPOSES

◆ Paul has come to the end of the argument that he began in ch. 1. For what does he praise God, and why?
  – What does he emphasize about God?

◆ To what extent have *you* learned to praise God for these things, having read Romans this far?
  – How has your attitude to God been challenged? Of what do we need to remind ourselves as we think about Him?

# SECTION NOTES:
# Romans 12:1–15:13

In this part of his letter, Paul teaches the Romans how the gospel of salvation, which he has explained in 1:18–11:36, should impact both their own lives as individuals and also the life of the church in Rome as a whole. He sets out the principles that should govern all their behaviour and attitudes, and then expands upon these principles to show how they apply in a number of important areas: relationships within the church; attitudes to governing authorities; friction between believers over disputable matters. It is striking that all these areas are relational, which suggests that the greatest impact that the gospel should have upon believers is in the challenging and changing of their relationships.

## The place of chapters 12:1–15:13 in Romans

Since these chapters contain a great deal of practical application, it is tempting for us to seize on Paul's teaching without seeing how it relates to the rest of his letter. Yet it is, in fact, rooted in what has gone before. Several particular connections should be mentioned.

◆ **Response to the gospel**
The most important factor, in understanding the context of these chapters, is to see that all Paul's exhortation flows out of the gospel. His opening words, in ch. 12, urge the Romans to respond 'in view of God's mercy', so we must not focus on Paul's

teaching here as if it were purely a treatise on church practice. Everything he encourages them to do he presents as being the fitting response of justified sinners to God's compassion and salvation.

◆ **Do not conform but be transformed**

Since Paul gives his instructions against the backdrop of the gospel that has saved us, we see in this section many contrasts between the way that Christians should now live and the way we used to live, when we lived in rebellion, as described in 1:18–3:20.

◆ **Offering your bodies to God**

In chs 6–8, Paul explained what it means to be a justified person. Our present experience is dictated by the fact that we live in the overlap of the realms of Adam and of Christ (since God has not yet brought the realm of Adam to an end – see Section Notes for chs 5–8). On the one hand, God has transformed us in our inner beings, such that we are no longer rebels at heart, but now delight in God's Law (7:22), because our minds are controlled by the Holy Spirit (8:5). Paul refers to this in 12:2 as (literally) 'the renewal of your minds'. Yet on the other hand, our mortal bodies (which include our thinking and impulses) remain influenced by the sinful realm of Adam and will therefore instinctively rebel against God until they are resurrected (8:11).

This teaching, from earlier in the letter, is the reason why Paul urges the Romans to offer their 'bodies' to God, as he begins to give them instructions for living their new life in Christ. As they wait for their resurrection, Christians are to bring the rest of their lives into line with the transformation that God has brought about within.

◆ **Jew/Gentile tension in the church**

Once again, we see the issue of Jews and Gentiles refusing to accept one another completely as Christian brothers and sisters. The reason for the tension, here, appears to be that Christians from a Jewish background are struggling to come to terms with the freedom that the gospel gives them in regard to food laws and festival days. It seems that their background made it hard for them to accept that they could be godly without observing these rituals. As a result, Gentile Christians were looking down on them judgmentally because of their scruples and Jewish Christians were condemning the Gentiles for doing what they perceived to be sinful. Paul calls for both groups to accept one another fully, and particularly calls for the Gentiles to watch their practice for the sake of their Jewish brothers.

◆ **Love as the fulfilment of the Law**

It is striking that love appears time and again as the key principle which should inform Christians' relationships in all contexts. In 13:10, Paul says that 'love is the fulfilment of the Law', and this saying picks up a loose end from ch. 7. There, Paul told us that through being united in Jesus' death, we have been set free from the Law (7:4–6). In that context he meant that, through Christ's sacrifice, we have been set free from the *power of the Law to condemn us to death*, which we deserve because we are all Law-breakers. But later in ch. 7 Paul maintained that, as a Christian, he delights in God's Law and is still a slave to it (7:22, 25). How can this be? The answer comes in ch. 13. The Law is still to dictate our behaviour *in the sense that* Christians are called to love all people, and love is the principle that stands behind the whole Law. In loving others, Paul says, we thereby fulfil the Law.

# Structure

**12:1–2  Key principles**
In the light of God's mercy, give your bodies to God. Do not conform to the world, but be transformed by your new mind.

**12:3–13:14  Relationships revolutionized by the gospel**

**12:3–21** Think soberly of yourself and humbly serve one another
Let your relationships with God, one another and those who oppose you be hallmarked by sincere love and humility

**13:1–14** Submit to the governing authorities because God has established them
Do not stop loving one another and live in the light of the future

**14:1–15:13** **An important case of the relationships revolution: Relating to Christians with whom you disagree over disputable matters**

14:1–12 Do not pass judgment on disputable matters. Remember who is Lord and judge

14:13–15:13 Limit your freedom for the sake of others. Like Christ, do not please yourself, but consider God's plan of salvation which is for all

# ROMANS 12:1–2

## Context

The beginning of ch. 12 is a pivotal point in Paul's letter to the Romans. It represents a major shift, as he turns from instruction to exhortation. Although chs 1–11 are not without exhortation, they are mainly taken up with Paul's systematic explanation of the gospel as 'the power of God for the salvation of everyone who believes: first for the Jew, then for the Gentile' (1:16). Now, in this last main section of his letter (12:1–15:13), Paul will focus on various areas of day-to-day living, and the outworking, in those areas, of the principles that should hallmark a Christian life, i.e. a life lived in obedience to the gospel that he has just been explaining (see Section Notes).

The first two verses of ch. 12 are the key to the whole section. First, they link Paul's exhortation about daily living with all that he has written earlier. Thus, 'in view of God's mercy' refers to the theme of all the previous eleven chapters – the gospel. Then, these verses outline the essence of the Christian's response to God's mercy, a response that will be the theme for the rest of the section. At the heart of this response is a transformation, and this should happen within the life of a believer as a result of the new mind that he has been given. This idea picks up on an important issue that was discussed in chs 6–8. At his very heart the Christian is no longer a rebel, but rather, through God's work in his life, he now delights in God's law in his inner being (7:22). Yet he still needs actively to offer God *his body* (as Paul insisted in 6:13), a body that remains influenced by the sinful realm of Adam and which will, therefore, still rebel instinctively against God (7:23, 25) until it is resurrected (8:11). So now we see the reversal of the situation described in ch. 1: when we were rebels, fundamentally, against God, our bodies were given over to sinfulness (1:18–32), but now that God has given us new minds, by giving us His Spirit, we are to give the rest of ourselves back to God.

## Structure

**12:1** In the light of God's mercy, give your bodies to God
**12:2** Do not conform to the world, but be transformed by your new mind

## Old Testament background

**Sacrifice:** The concept of sacrifice lay at the heart of Israel's life, and God had given detailed instructions on how various sacrifices should be made (e.g. Leviticus 1–7). A sacrifice might have one of a number of functions, such as the making of atonement for sin (Leviticus 16), but in essence it was a gesture of wholehearted devotion to God. For a sacrifice to be made, an animal (typically) would be set apart for God and His glory; once given, it no longer belonged to the giver. It would have been a new idea to take the language of sacrifices and apply it to a person being devoted to God, but there is an Old Testament precedent for this in 1 Samuel 1:27–28.

**A new mind:** In Jeremiah 31:33 and Ezekiel 36:26–27 God had promised faithless Israel that when He rescued them, He would give them new hearts with His Law written on them, so that they would be able to obey Him. Paul has already shown, in chs 6–8, that these promises have been fulfilled in the gospel (7:22, 25; 8:5–6, 9), and in 12: 2 he returns to the idea of a mind being renewed.

# Text notes

## I IN THE LIGHT OF GOD'S MERCY, GIVE YOUR BODIES TO GOD

The 'therefore', with which Paul begins the chapter, is highly significant: Paul will build all that he is about to say, in 12:1–15:13, upon all that he has already said in 1:18–11:36.

### ◆ In view of God's mercy

The whole of 1:18–11:32 is summarized by the phrase 'in view of God's mercy', which reads literally 'the mercies of God'; these words are loaded with meaning. Their immediate context is 11:31–32, concerning God's plan of salvation, His intention to show mercy to both Jews and Gentiles. Paul's response to this, at the end of ch. 11, was to praise God for His unfathomable wisdom and purposes, but here he spurs us on to make our whole lives a response to what God has done, for we cannot consider God's plan without seeing our own place in it.

In the broader context of Romans (from 1:18), Paul has been teaching of the wonder of God's mercy shown to individuals who believe. First, in 1:18–3:20, he taught that each of us deserves only to face God's righteous anger, because of our rejection of Him. Starting at 3:21, however, he explained how God stepped in to make us righteous, through the substitutionary sacrifice of His Son, and how this righteousness is appropriated through trusting in His promises (3:27–4:25). Then, from 5:1 to 8:39, he showed us the consequences of our justification: our freedom from the ruling power of sin and death, and the unbreakable promise we have of a certain future, when we shall be glorified with Christ for ever. We deserve none of this, yet God has graciously given it to us out of His mercy. In view of all that He has done and promised, it is fitting that our lives should be devoted to Him in wholehearted gratitude.

### ◆ Offer your bodies to God

Having reminded us of God's overwhelming mercy, Paul now uses the language of temple and sacrifice to describe the total dedication of a life given to God. His words, about our bodies being living sacrifices that are 'holy and pleasing to God', are reminiscent of the instructions given to the Israelites (see OT notes and, e.g., Leviticus 1:17; 2:10). Paul's command is that we should take action with regard to our 'bodies'. God has transformed us in our inner beings, yet we are still waiting for the resurrection of our bodies which will, until that day, still be inclined to follow rebellious impulses. (See Section Notes for chs 5–8, noting especially the meaning of 'body', i.e. that it includes our thinking and our impulses.) Knowing this, and in view of what God has already done and promised, Paul tells us to offer our bodies totally to God. They are no longer for our sole use, nor should they be 'instruments of wickedness' (6:13), but they are to be dedicated entirely to Him. In this way, we are to bring our bodies into line with our inner beings, which are now controlled by the Spirit, so that our whole lives are devoted entirely to God.

◆ **This is true worship**

Giving ourselves to God in this way is what Paul describes as spiritual worship. To worship God is to live in such a way as to give Him His full worth and value, acknowledging all that He is and all that He has done. (See Psalm 95 for an Old Testament example of this.) The Christian does this by giving God the only thing he can offer – his mortal body, i.e. his life in this world. The Greek word translated as 'spiritual' is difficult to define, but it can equally mean 'wholehearted' or 'reasonable', in the sense of being 'appropriate for human beings as rational and spiritual creatures of God' (Moo, p. 752). True worship is thus the Christian's appropriate response of devoting his or her whole life, in this world, to God.

## 2 DO NOT CONFORM TO THE WORLD, BUT BE TRANSFORMED BY YOUR NEW MIND

What does it mean to worship God in this way? Paul goes on to explain the means by which we may continually offer our bodies to God, giving first a negative and then a positive. The whole principle of what he is saying is rooted in what we have already seen in chs 1–11.

### ✦ Do not continue to conform to the world

Looking back towards the beginning of Paul's letter, we find a clear exposition of what it means to be conformed to the pattern of the world. He describes how the world has turned against its creator in rebellion, thinking wrongly about God, and refusing to glorify Him or thank Him (1:18–23). So God has handed the world over to wrong actions and every kind of sinful behaviour, as we see around us (1:24–32). This is true of all people (5:12) and it used to be true of every Christian, but believers have been transferred from the realm of sin and are now slaves to God (6:22). We should no longer, therefore, allow ourselves to be squeezed into the world's rebellious mould. We should refuse to think as the world thinks or act as the world acts.

### ✦ Be transformed by your new mind

Paul is *not* telling us to change our minds *gradually* but, rather, he is restating what he has already told us. Our minds *have already been changed*, at conversion – a more accurate translation of the phrase would be 'by the *renewal* of your mind' – and they are now 'set on what the Spirit desires' (8:5). We now delight in God's Law in our inner beings (7:22) and, at the deepest level, we are no longer set in rebellion against God. Paul is telling us to live, now, in the light of what we know – teaching that he has previously given us in ch. 6. Since we have been given new minds, i.e. new inner beings that delight in God's ways, we need to bring the rest of ourselves, i.e. our thinking and behaviour, into line with our minds. Such a transformation will be a lifelong battle for us, but this is what it means to offer our bodies as living sacrifices.

### ✦ Then you will be able to approve God's will

'God's will' (v. 2b) is usually understood to mean His moral will, i.e. His behavioural code by which He wants His people to live distinctive lives, or His specific guidance, e.g. on whether or not one should pursue a certain career or a particular relationship. But it would be better to let the context of Romans steer our thinking on this matter. For Paul has already taught us that God's will for all people is that they should obey the gospel and trust in His promises of salvation through Christ (1:5). Then, Paul has also told us of God's revealed plan and purpose to take

Christians to glory (8:27b–30), and to have mercy on all people (11:32). So we should understand God's will to be His *overall* will for our lives and His plan of salvation for the world.

*(NB: Concerning the two alternatives mentioned above: God's moral will is part of His overall will for our lives. So, as we submit to Christ and trust in God's promises, we will be changing our behaviour in various ways, some of which are outlined in chs 12–15. But as to specific guidance for us as individuals, there is nothing in the rest of the letter to suggest that Paul is referring to this.)*

As we allow ourselves to be transformed by the new minds that God has given us, Paul says we will be able to 'test and approve what God's will is'. The Greek word for 'approve' means acknowledging the rightness of God's will, such that we 'understand and agree that it is right to put it into practice'. This contrasts with the mind we used to have which, because we rejected the knowledge of God, was 'depraved' (see 1:28, where the opposite word is used) and unable to judge what was right. With a new mind, however, and living out a new life, the believer will understand and demonstrate the value and importance of obeying God's word, of trusting the gospel, and of living in the light of God's plans, acknowledging that His way is good, pleasing and perfect.

# Key themes and application

### ◆ Motivated by mercy

All that Paul calls us to do, in these verses and in the rest of chs 12–15, is rooted in a knowledge and an understanding of God's mercy, both as expressed to the individual who is saved and as shown in His plan of salvation, revealed for the benefit of the whole world. All Christian living and ethics are ultimately rooted in a deep gratitude for what God has done for us. A true understanding of His mercy will inevitably bring about an acknowledgement of our sin, since we know we deserve only His wrath. And it will give us an overwhelming thankfulness for what He has done for us through Christ.

The danger for all Christians is that we move away from this basic truth, either because we forget it or because we want to move on from it. But Paul sees it as the constant motivation for all that we do. Every decision and every action should be a response to His mercy. If we are to remain spiritually healthy, we need to remind ourselves and one another of these amazing truths each day. Western culture is losing the ability to think deeply, always wanting instead some new source of mental stimulation, but Christians need to go against the flow. To remind oneself of the truths that God has revealed, so that they become the heartbeat of one's Christian life – this is true biblical meditation. And it should lie at the heart of all Christian gatherings. We should always be seeking to remind one another of what He has done for us, through hearing the Bible read and explained, through singing, praying, discussing, etc.

◆ **True worship**
Worship is defined here as offering the whole of one's life back to God. It means that we need to offer up our mortal bodies, constantly, for His use and glory – something that will be a daily affair until we are resurrected. It is critical that we have this Christian understanding of worship. Worship is no longer confined to any particular place, or associated with a particular person or activity, as it was in the Old Testament. It is not the activity that goes on in church, and nor is it related especially to singing or music. To think of worship in any of these ways is to go back to Old Testament temple thinking. True worship extends to *all places* and *all activities* and is possible for anyone who has turned to Christ. It will mean putting God first in every area of one's life, which, in practice, means putting Him at the centre of every decision and every action. This is how we will bring honour to Him.

◆ **Do not conform to the world, but be transformed by your new mind**
This is all to do with how, in practice, we should worship.

First, we should consciously resist being influenced by the principles and standards of a world that has rejected God. The world tries to squeeze us into its mould in many different ways, some blatant, some insidious, and we need to beware of the world's lies. Currently, the media is one of the world's most powerful and effective weapons, since the images and values of advertising and Hollywood, for example, surround us constantly.

We should not underestimate the pull they exert on us; we need to be alert to their influence, on us and on others too.

Behaviour that is obviously rebellious is not the only way of conforming to the world; we should also be aware of the ways in which we conform to the world by what we do *not* do, e.g. by not praying.

Second, we should allow our new minds, informed by the gospel and controlled by the Spirit, to shape and influence our thinking and behaviour. We now know how God wants us to live and we should not quench our minds as we battle with the desires of our mortal bodies. This too will involve reflection on God's mercy to us, in the gospel, so that we are motivated to live differently.

These principles should shape our lives in every area. One example is the area of money. In the West, most of us have enough money to be presented with real choices as to how we spend it, and it is in these choices that the world urges us to conform, in countless ways, to its value system. It tells us, for example, that money gives us the power to do what we want, and that, since this is a great source of happiness, we should seek to gain as much as we possibly can. It tells us that status symbols are important for our self-worth, and so we should spend our money on those things that will give other people the desired impression. And it convinces us that money will provide the security we need for the future, and so we should store it away for our own comfort in years to come. With our new minds, however, we know that putting ourselves and our desires at the centre of our lives is the reason for God's anger and judgment on mankind (1:18–32). We also know that our worth is found not in the value of our assets, but in the fact that, while we were still sinners, Christ died for us (5:8). We know that death is inevitable, but that our future security goes beyond the grave, for we will share in Christ's inheritance and, even more, we know that nothing can stop God from glorifying us. Understanding all of these things through the gospel, our attitude to money should be distinctively different from that of the world. When we have provided for the essential needs of ourselves and our dependants, we should seek to be generous to others and to use our money for the sake of the gospel and the extension of God's kingdom.

Other areas worth considering are: conversations; work; priorities for our children; relationships, sex and marriage; how we use our homes; how we spend our free time, and how we plan for the future.

# Unanswered questions

◆ How will this transformation be seen in practice?

# The aim of this study

To be so aware of God's overwhelming mercy towards us that we give ourselves wholeheartedly to Him.

# Suggested questions

◆ *(Before reading the passage)* How would you define 'worship'?
◆ *(After reading the passage)* In what way is this a turning point in Paul's letter?

I IN THE LIGHT OF GOD'S MERCY, GIVE YOUR BODIES TO GOD

◆ What does Paul mean when he says 'in view of God's mercy'?
  – What is the extent of God's mercies that we have seen in Romans so far? How is His mercy seen, having regard to the state from which we were rescued? And to the way He rescued us? And to the future He has in store for us?
◆ What response, from God's people, does Paul call for? What does this mean? Why is the language of sacrifice so appropriate?
  – Why does he specify 'your bodies'?
  – In your own words, what will this response look like?
◆ What is our honest response to this instruction?
  – Where does Paul say we should look for our motivation?
  – What effect will it have on our Christian lives if we do not focus on God's mercy?
  – How can we, in practice, allow God's mercy to motivate us? How can we help one another in this?

◆ What name does Paul give to such a response to God's mercy?
  – How is the term 'worship' generally used?
  – According to Paul, what is wrong with these views?
  – What is dangerous about confining worship to activities in a church building?
  – How might the right definition help us avoid this danger?

## 2 DO NOT CONFORM TO THE WORLD, BUT BE TRANSFORMED BY YOUR NEW MIND

◆ How does Paul say we should worship God?
◆ In Romans terms, what does it mean to conform to the world?
  – How does the world encourage us to conform?
  – How might it encourage middle-class Christians/teenagers/students/young parents/senior citizens to conform? *(Use the example that best fits your group. Be as specific as possible, so that Paul's teaching is closely applied to real life.)*
◆ Is Paul suggesting that, as Christians, our minds will change gradually? What have we been told about having a new mind?
  – What do our new minds tell us when we face pressure to conform?
◆ Choose one (or maybe two) of the following areas and discuss what it will mean, in that area, to avoid conforming and, instead, to have an outlook transformed by our new minds: money; our conversations; work; priorities for our children; relationships, sex and marriage; how we use our homes; how we spend our free time; the way we plan for the future.
◆ According to Paul, what will be the result of living in this way?
  – What has Romans told us about God's will? (See 1:5; 8:27–30; 11:32.)
  – How will we 'test and approve what God's will is', when we devote our whole lives to Him?
  – How does this contrast with the way we used to be? (See 1:28.)

◆ This is a great passage to inform and encourage our prayers. How should we pray in the light of what Paul teaches here?
  – For what can we thank God?
  – Is there anything we need to confess?
  – For what do we need to ask Him for help?

# ROMANS 12:3–21

## Context

Paul began ch. 12 by exhorting us to live in the light of the gospel, the gospel he had spread out for us in chs 1–11. In response to God's overwhelming and undeserved generosity to us in Christ, we are to give the whole of our lives back to Him, for His use and for His glory. Putting this into practice will mean resisting the pressures and attitudes of a world that lives in rebellion against God and, instead, allowing our new minds to transform everything we think, say and do.

As he continues, Paul now starts to explain what will be the results of such a transformation, and focuses first on the impact that the gospel should make upon our relationships. In this passage, he shows how we should have a sober view of ourselves, as individual members of God's people (vv. 3–8). Then he moves on to our relationships with others, describing how our attitudes, to both believers and unbelievers, should be revolutionized by the gospel (vv. 9–21).

## Structure

**12:3–8**   Think soberly of yourself as one part of the body of Christ

**12:9–21**   The body of Christ is marked by revolutionized relationships

# Old Testament background

**God saving a people:** When God first made promises of blessing to Abraham, in Genesis 12, He promised him not only numberless descendants, but also that He would make him and his descendants into a great nation, i.e. into a people, with a corporate identity, who would live in harmony. This is why, throughout the Old Testament, we see God dealing not just with individuals but also with Israel as a nation, giving her the Law and the sacrificial system so that she might become distinct among all the peoples of the world (Exodus 19:5–6).

    **God equips His people:** The idea of God giving people specific gifts is not unique to the New Testament. We see the same idea, for example, in the account of the construction of the Tabernacle (Exodus 35:30–36:2) where God gave the craftsmen particular gifts and skills for their work.

# Text notes

### 3–8 THINK SOBERLY OF YOURSELF

At the heart of our rebellion against God lies wrong thinking, and one of our greatest temptations is to boast about ourselves and over others – this was obviously an issue between Jews and Gentiles in Rome, at the time when Paul was writing to them (see 2:17; 3:27; 11:18). Now, however, addressing each individual with the full authority of his apostleship (v. 3, cf. 1:5), he commands his readers to have a correct view of themselves. His point comes over even more strongly in the Greek, which reads, literally, 'Do not *think* of yourself more highly than you ought to *think*, but rather *think* of yourself with sober *thinking*.' There is no room for pride in the believer, and for this Paul gives two clear reasons.

◆ **... according to the gospel (v. 3)**

    First, we are to view ourselves in accordance with the 'measure of faith' that God has given us (v. 3). This phrase may be translated in a couple of ways, but the context of Romans does not allow it to mean 'the *quantity* of faith that individuals are given'. The faith that Paul has written about previously is the faith of Abraham, the kind of faith by which people are saved; in other words, it is a firm trust in God's promises which people either do or do not have (4:20–24). The phrase in 12:3, therefore, must mean 'the measure that is faith'. Accordingly, Christians should evaluate themselves in the light of the gospel (see Cranfield, pp. 300–1, and Moo, p. 761). When we see ourselves in the perspective of God's mercy (12:1), in the honest and unflattering light of the gospel as taught in 1:18–11:36, we see that we are sinners who have been saved by grace alone and that all boasting, therefore, must end.

◆ ... as one of many parts of the body of Christ (vv. 4–8)
Paul's second reason, in v. 4 (which, in the Greek, is linked to v. 3 by the word 'for'), is that individual Christians are parts of a greater whole, the church. Paul uses the analogy of the body (also seen in 1 Corinthians 12:12–31 and Ephesians 4:1–16) to teach humility and interdependence. Just as the body has, and needs, different members with different functions, so the church has, and needs, people with different gifts. Furthermore, these gifts do not belong solely to the individual, but rather to the whole of the church. If we understand that this is our position, we will not think too highly of ourselves. Just as we are to give ourselves fully to God (v. 1), so we are to give ourselves fully to one another.

Then, in vv. 6–8, Paul lists examples of the different kinds of gift that God gives His people. His focus is not on the nature of the gifts that he mentions – these gifts are just examples. (So this is not the place to get stuck into a debate about prophecy!) Instead, his emphasis is on our interdependence and our responsibility towards each other. God has given different gifts to different people; so, whatever gifts we have, by grace, been given, we should use each one in a manner that is appropriate to the gift, in order to serve the rest of the 'body'.

## 9–21 THE BODY OF CHRIST IS MARKED BY REVOLUTIONIZED RELATIONSHIPS

Having addressed the Roman Christians as individuals and established their places within the body, Paul now gives his instructions to the Christian community as a whole. In doing this he is reflecting the pattern we find in the Old Testament, of God dealing with a people as well as with individuals (see OT notes). The rest of the passage comprises a catalogue of over twenty brief instructions, most of them given without elaboration, regarding the ways in which God's people should relate to one another, to God and to the unbelieving world. It is difficult to see any particular organization in this list of commands, although key themes do emerge from it – love, sincerity, humility and peace. And there seems to be a shift in emphasis, at v. 17, from the believers' relationships with each other to their relationships with people in the outside world: note the vocabulary change from 'one another' (vv. 10, 16) to 'everybody' and 'everyone' (vv. 17, 18).

As we look at the negatives and positives in these verses, we see that there is a strong element of not conforming to the pattern of the world; our relationships are to be quite different and, in fact, transformed. Another thing that will impress us, in Paul's description of the changes that should result from our having new minds, is the striking contrast with the selfishness and destructiveness that come from living in rebellion against God, as was outlined in 1:21–32.

| **12:9–21** | **1:21–32** |
|---|---|
| Loving (12:9–10) | Heartless (1:31) |
| Hate evil (12:9) | Approving of evil-doers (1:32) |
| Serving the Lord (12:11) | God-haters (1:30) |
| Do not be proud/conceited (12:16) | Arrogant and boastful (1:30) |
| Live in harmony and peace (12:16, 18) | Strife (1:29) |
| Repay no-one for evil (12:17) | Malice (1:29) |
| Overcome evil (12:21) | Inventors of evil (1:30) |

## ◆ A new relationship with God

Previously, we related to God only in outright hostility. We rejected Him as creator, giving Him none of the honour and gratitude that His name deserved, and worshipped, instead, things He had created in His world (1:18–25). Now, however, because of all that He has done for us, we belong to Him and our lives are to be given in service to Him (12:1). Yet Paul goes further, for we are not to be reluctant or dutiful servants: rather, we are to be distinctly and enthusiastically His, constantly maintaining a passion for Him (v. 11) and focusing on the future that He has in store for us (v. 12).

◆ **New relationships with one another**

When we remember that God's plan is to make us into a large family for His Son (8:29), we can understand why there is such a focus on right relationships. Just as He rescued the *people* of Israel (see OT notes), so now God does not just save individuals to relate to Himself, but a 'family' or 'body' of believers who are to live interdependently, for the sake of one another. Members of the church should therefore be genuinely and deeply concerned for one another's physical, emotional and spiritual well-being, showing a love that is both wholehearted (v. 10) and practical (v. 13).

◆ **New relationships with your enemies**

Our love is not to be restricted to one another, but is also to be extended to those who oppose us. (NB: Paul may well have in mind the hostility that could come from others within the church – for example, the ill-feeling between Jews and Gentiles – as well that coming from outside.) We are bound to face hostility from the world, since we have turned to God in a world that has fundamentally rejected Him, but the gospel teaches us to react to it in a new way. Four times Paul tells us not to retaliate, but to seek the good of our enemies (vv. 14, 17, 19–20, 21).

Revenge is not an option, because we know that this is the right and prerogative of God alone (v. 19); He will judge and bring justice to bear. Instead, we are to show genuine love for our enemies. This, as v. 20 suggests, will put them to shame and may even, perhaps, provoke them to repentance.

## Key themes and application

◆ **Right thinking about ourselves**

The gospel should revolutionize the way that we think about ourselves. Previously we were full of pride, even thinking it fit to reject our creator, but now, having been saved from His righteous wrath by His wonderful mercy, we know that we are merely sinners saved by grace. We have no reason to think of ourselves highly, since we contributed absolutely nothing to our salvation. God owes us nothing, and we have no rights before Him. Pride is a great enemy of the gospel and a great danger for the Christian. We open ourselves to pride the moment we take our eyes off God and His work through Christ – here again we see the importance of meditating on these essential gospel truths.

A further reason that Paul gives for viewing ourselves soberly is the fact that we are now part of a body, the church. And so we should not pride ourselves on account of the gifts we have been given because they do not belong to us *for our use*, but were given for the good of God's people. Instead, therefore, we should thank God for the gifts and consider how we can best use them for the sake of other Christians.

One of the hallmarks of the modern mindset is individualism. We instinctively focus on the freedom and the right of the individual to do or say whatever he or she chooses. This attitude has inevitably spread into Christian culture, where my commitment to God's people has been replaced by the idea that a church should serve and fulfil me, providing the teaching, music, friendship and sub-culture that I desire. Yet really, this is only an expression of our sinfulness, a way of putting ourselves at the centre of our own lives. When God rescues people, however, He puts them together to live for the benefit of one another. This means that my greatest concern should not be how a church could serve me, but how I may best serve that church, using the gifts that God has given me.

◆ **Right relationships**

Paul expects the gospel to transform the way that we treat other people, both within and without the church. When we were in rebellion against God, we found ourselves set against one another, but now that we have peace with God (5:1) we are to seek right relationships, also, with those around us. God has put believers together in one body and each member is to live for the sake of the whole. Our love for others is to be genuine, whole-hearted, practical and indiscriminate. Even more radical than this is the new attitude that we should have towards those who oppose us: we are to respond to hostility with love and forbearance, leaving justice to God alone.

Relationships that have been transformed in these ways by the gospel will inevitably attract some unbelievers. This, perhaps, is one of the things that Paul sees as provoking some Jews to envy and so on to salvation, but, in any case, the appeal of relationships that are characterized by devotion and harmony, rather than by malice and duplicity, should not be underestimated; such relationships should make any onlookers desire the same for themselves.

The commands in vv. 9–21 call for these same characteristics to be demonstrated in all relationships. Rather than skim over the whole list of Paul's instructions, it is probably more profitable, here, to concentrate on a few of them. First, in each case, we will face the challenge of how much we may, in fact, be following the world's pattern in this area, and then we will consider how our behaviour might be transformed by our new minds. Here are some initial thoughts ...

*'Never be lacking in zeal' (v. 11):* This command is a challenge to all Christians, but especially, perhaps, to those who have been believers for some time. It is easy to slip into a more comfortable and moderate Christianity, attributing the overt enthusiasm of recent converts to the zeal of youth or to naivety. In this, Christians in the West are also influenced by a culture that is increasingly cynical and suspicious of strong emotions and convictions. Yet Paul specifically tells us to maintain our spiritual fervour, remembering whom we are serving. To maintain one's enthusiasm for God's glory must surely be a fitting response to His mercy and, in fact, a sign of maturity rather than immaturity.

*'Practise hospitality' (v. 13):* This essential principle of community life is also, like our membership of a local church (see above), under attack from individualism, particularly when this is blended with materialism. The home at the beginning of the twenty-first century has become a private possession, set up to serve the pleasure of the individual or the small family unit. Again, we need to be reminded that God has saved us to be members of a people, and that everything He gives us is to be used for the benefit of the whole body. True hospitality will

involve opening our homes to others, not just for the showpiece dinner party, but also at times when people around us are in need. Such giving may be sacrificial, but even so, we will be giving the merest fraction of what God has given us (11:35).

*'If your enemy is hungry, feed him' (v. 20):* We should not overlook the radical difference between the attitudes in this list and those of the world. It is popular to be tolerant, but tolerance lasts only so long as people do us no harm. What Paul is describing here is an unconditional love which can only come from understanding that we too were once enemies of the God who nevertheless rescued us. We need to consider how we might go about loving those who ignore or ridicule us for our faith, or those from within the church who may oppose us, and how, instead of merely gritting our teeth, we might actually go out of our way to seek their good. We should pray for them, serve them and consider how we can tell them God's gospel.

## Unanswered questions

◆ How does the gospel change our relationships with governing authorities?

## The aim of this study

◆ To see ourselves rightly, as saved sinners who belong to the body of Christ, and so to go about serving one another, responding to all with love and humility.

## Suggested questions

◆ Write down, in a sentence, why you go to church.
◆ To summarize the last study, explain what true worship looks like, according to Paul in 12:1–2.

### 3–8 THINK SOBERLY OF YOURSELF

◆ How does Paul want us to think of ourselves? What does he mean by this? In what way will this be a contrast with the way we used to think of ourselves, before we received God's mercy?

◆ 'The measure of faith' is the faith that God has given us, i.e. our trust in the gospel. How does the gospel teach us to think of ourselves soberly?
   – Why do we have no reason to think of ourselves highly?
   – Why is pride a great danger to the Christian? How can we keep ourselves humble?
◆ What reason is there, in vv. 4–8, to think soberly of ourselves?
   – How does the illustration of the body back up Paul's point?
   – How should this influence the way we view our gifts?
   – Returning to our answers to the first question: do we go to church for the right reasons? How should we change our attitudes? To what extent does our culture affect our attitude to church?
   – How should these verses shape our time together as Christians?

## 9–21 THE BODY OF CHRIST IS MARKED BY REVOLUTIONIZED RELATIONSHIPS

◆ What should be the governing principles for all our relationships?
   – What contrasts do you see with the behaviour described in 1:18–32?
◆ In 12:2, Paul told us not to conform to the world, but to be transformed by our new minds. How do these principles work out in our relationship with God? With other Christians? With those who oppose us?
◆ Pick out three of Paul's instructions (one for each of the three kinds of relationship mentioned above), and discuss what it would mean if we were to put them into practice. (Try not to be glib in doing this, but instead be as thorough and practical as possible.)
   – In what areas do we need God's help? For what should we pray?

## Study 20

# ROMANS 13:1–14

## Context

Chapter 13 continues the theme that began in ch. 12, that of out-lining what it means for God's people to give their earthly lives back to Him, as living sacrifices and in response to His mercy (12:1–2). So far Paul has explained how our view of ourselves and also our view of other people, i.e. our relationships, are both to be transformed; this will happen through our understanding of the fact that we are saved sinners and, as such, part of the body of the church. We are not to think too much of ourselves, but we should serve one another with the gifts that God has given us, showing our genuine love for others (particularly for believers) in every aspect of practical daily living (12:3–21).

At the start of ch. 13 Paul turns to the Christian's relationship with the governing authorities. He commands everyone to submit to the governing authorities, explaining that they are established by God to rule in the world.

In the second half of the chapter, Paul returns to the subject of our obligation to love one another and stresses the urgency of this in the light of the future return of Christ.

## Structure

**13:1–7** Submit to the governing authorities under God
**13:8–14** Do not stop loving one another, in the light of the future

# Old Testament background

**Submission to authorities:** There are two examples, of God's people relating to the governing authority, to be found in the book of Daniel. Daniel, Shadrach, Meshach and Abednego lived under pagan rule when the southern kingdom of Judah was exiled to Babylon. Most of the time they lived under Babylonian authority, accepting, for example, the new names that they were given (Daniel 1:7). But when obedience would mean disobeying God, or not being able to give Him honour, they refused (Daniel 3 and 6). When this meant that they got into trouble, they quietly submitted to the punishment they were given.

# Text notes

### 1–7 SUBMIT TO THE GOVERNING AUTHORITIES UNDER GOD
The Christians in Rome were living, at the time of Paul's letter to them, under a pagan but largely beneficent Roman rule, but the principles that Paul outlines in these verses are not specific to a particular time, and should therefore apply to Christians in any era. He gives each individual in the church the clear command to submit to the governing authorities, a command based on the fact that these authorities are set up by God to keep order and to establish justice in His world.

Paul's teaching, here, has added many extra pages to the commentaries! The discussion, mostly, is on the question of how his teaching should be applied under corrupt, malevolent or totalitarian regimes. Yet, while such discussion is important, it can easily obscure, behind a heap of qualifications, the essential point that Paul is making, which *will* apply in most circumstances. *All* governing authorities are bound to be sinful, and yet we are still called to submit to them. The exception comes only when they ask us to sin, in which case we have a duty to obey God, who is our higher authority. Should this happen, we need to be prepared to submit to the consequent punishment.

God's people have wrestled with these issues at many different times throughout history. Two notable times are recorded in the book of Daniel (see OT notes) and in the book of Acts, concerning the time when the gospel was spreading in the early days of the church (Acts 4:18–20).

◆ **Submit because God establishes all authority (vv. 1–2)**
The Christian is wrong to think that living under the lordship of Christ gives him the right to disregard earthly rulers, because of the simple fact that God Himself has put all rulers in their position. And so, says Paul, rebellion against them constitutes rebellion against God, which inevitably brings judgment.

*(NB: The word 'submit' sometimes carries very negative con-notations about the abuse of power, but the word means, liter-ally, 'subordinate yourself to'. God has established a particular order or hierarchy of authority and it is fitting that we should acknowledge our place in it.)*

◆ **Authorities are God's servants to commend or to punish, so do good! (vv. 3–5)**
God establishes governing authorities for particular purposes – to commend those who do good and to punish those who do evil. In this, though they may be unaware of the fact, they are serving God by establishing law and order in the world. Our obvious responsibility, therefore, is to do good; if we do this we will not need to fear our rulers. We tend, naturally, to think that freedom comes from ignoring authority and doing what we want, but in fact true freedom comes from a proper submission, which will leave us with nothing to fear from those in authority. The only people who need fear the authorities, as a general rule, are those who deserve to face their punishment.

Is Paul saying, 'Submit or else!'? No, he isn't, for he goes on to say that we should always do so, in any case and regardless of the possibility of punishment, because we should never do what our conscience tells us is wrong (cf. 2:14–15).

◆ **Give taxes and honour to God's servants (vv. 6–7)**
Since the governing authorities are God's servants and work full time for our benefit, part of our submission will involve the pay-ment of tax (v. 6). But this specific application sits under the general principle in v. 7. We are to give to everyone what we owe them, and this will mean not only the paying of taxes, but also having a right attitude of respect and honour towards those whom God has put in authority over us.

## 8–14 DO NOT STOP LOVING ONE ANOTHER, IN THE LIGHT OF THE FUTURE

Here, Paul starts to sum up a segment of his letter which began at 12:3, and in which he has examined the impact that the gospel should have upon various relationships. He returns to the fundamental principle of love, which ought to underlie all our relationships, and then urges his readers to live in the light of Christ's return.

### ✦ A life-long obligation (v. 8a)

Verse 8 acts as a bridge between two points. First, it summarizes v. 7, as believers are instructed to pay all their debts, but then Paul continues by making one exception to this rule: the one debt that we cannot pay in full is our obligation to love one another. Though we may like to live as though we were quite independent of others, the truth is that we will always owe one another the wholehearted devotion outlined in 12:9–21.

### ✦ Love fulfils the Law (vv. 8b–10)

If we do love one another in this manner (i.e. according to 12:9–21), Paul says that we will be fulfilling the Law. In this, he follows the example of Jesus, who identifies the commands to love God and to love one's neighbour as the underlying principles that govern all the individual commandments (Matthew 22:37–40). Those who genuinely love other people will not commit adultery or steal or covet, and so will satisfy the demands of the Law. Though ch. 7 of Romans has told us that we are free from the Law, i.e. that we are free from the Law's condemnation (7:4–6), this does not mean that the Law is irrelevant for us; we still delight in its goodness (7:22) because we know it expresses the character and will of God. Paul's point is that we are bound to what have always been the Law's essential principles: love for our neighbour as well as love for God (see Leviticus 19:18).

### ✦ Live in the light of the coming day (vv. 11–14)

Paul began this part of his teaching, about the believer's new perspective on relationships, by pointing back to the past, to the believer's rescue from spiritual death through God's mercy, because the believer's motivation must be grounded in his understanding of God's mercy towards him (12:1–3). Here, Paul rounds

off his teaching on this subject by pointing believers to the significance of the future and Christ's return. As in chs 5–8, he refers
to two realms, using the imagery of night and day, darkness and
light, to illustrate our position. We are approaching the dawn of
our glorification, in accordance with God's promise to make us
like Christ (8:28–30). Meanwhile, we are to live as those who
belong to the day and not as those who belong to the night.

In practical terms, the imminence of this event – 'the day is
almost here' (v. 12) – demands urgent action. The language of putting off and putting on corresponds to the idea of not conforming
but being transformed, as in 12:2; it is also often used in the New
Testament to describe repentance. The patterns of behaviour
from which we must turn are those which characterize all people
in their state of rebellion against God, rebellion that has caused
God to 'give them over' to their sins (1:24–32). Though we have
been saved from final punishment, our sinful nature (our flesh)
will continue to have sinful desires (7:25c), but Paul warns us
against dwelling on, or planning how to feed, these sinful desires
(see also 8:12–14) and tells us to clothe ourselves with Christ
instead. As we consecrate our lives to Him we will 'put on His
likeness'; and since, in the future, we are going to be part of His
glorified family, when we are conformed to His likeness (8:29), no
other way of living in the present can be acceptable.

# Key themes and application

### ♦ Submission to authorities
Christians are called to submit to governing authorities because
they are established by God to keep order, and so prevent anar-
chy in His world.

The great danger with this issue is that we could spend all our
time discussing the cases where it may not apply, instead of considering the normal circumstances of our own lives, where it
certainly does. We are to acknowledge all those who are in
authority over us, subordinating ourselves to what God has put
in place, both in principle and in detailed practice. The principle
applies not only to the government and the law, but also to
every hierarchy in which we find ourselves, whether this is at

work or college or within any other organization. Many Christians have made the mistake of thinking that their new obedience to God excuses them from having to obey anyone else, but this is to ignore the fact that all authority is given by God Himself. But it is not sufficient to be compliant yet grudging: our attitudes should be affected too.

For most of the history of Christendom, submission to ruling authorities has been the most sensible course of action for those wishing to avoid reprisals, and yet today subordination is less clear. The increased concern with the rights of the individual and the evolution of political protest mean that people will often choose not to submit to their rulers. To many, nowadays, our sense of obligation and our willingness to acknowledge authority will seem old-fashioned and even to be an encouragement to those who could abuse their power. Yet, although protest is now an option, it doesn't change our obligations. (To give an authentic example: in Britain Christians should have paid the poll tax and, if they had wished to protest about it, they should have done so legally.)

Difficulties with this command arise when the authorities in question are particularly corrupt or oppressive, i.e. when they require their subjects to go against God's Law. Is it right to follow orders, when they would lead us to sin? It is not possible to legislate for every conceivable circumstance, but it would be fair to assert several principles. Clearly this passage tells us that God Himself is our ultimate authority, so it must be right to obey Him first, for ultimately we will face His judgment. If, however, obeying God rather than man gets Christians into trouble, they should be prepared to face the consequences as, for example, did Daniel (see OT notes). Where corruption is rife, the role of Christians is to do all that they can, respectfully and legally, to bring about change. Christians should not, however, be involved in revolutionary activity – our message to the world is not one of rights and freedom, but the gospel.

### ✦ Love one another

As in ch. 12, Paul reminds us of our obligation to love those around us. This is a debt we should constantly repay: there will never be a day when we can say that we have loved enough. But such teaching, of course, is entirely counter-cultural today. We should not miss the important significance of Paul's emphasis on love: being inherently selfish, we dislike the idea of being under an obligation to one another, preferring to be free to suit ourselves, but Paul says that our lifelong focus should be on people. In this, however, we should note that the love being called for does not mean seeking the greatest happiness of others, but rather their greatest good before God. We are to love according to the reality of Christ's return, and so challenge and confrontation may often be necessary.

◆ **Live in the light of the future**

Our whole lives, and in particular our relationships, are to be governed by an awareness of the future that God is bringing into being. Our full and final salvation, when our bodies will be resurrected and glorified, should be the factor that constantly motivates us, as we consecrate our lives to God. By nature we will follow the world, which is preoccupied with the concerns of the present, but we know that a greater reality is approaching, when God's rule will be fully established. We should therefore bring our lives into line with His rule, seeking to rid ourselves of the sinful behaviour that characterizes the world and, instead, living lives of obedience in response to the gospel of Jesus.

It is easy for the church to rest on its laurels, confident of its salvation in the future, but Paul calls us to be alert. Being ready for Christ's return will involve discipline, hard work and vigilance, but it is vital that we be pro-active in this; a sleepy church quickly slips into pagan behaviour. We are to live distinctively and radically, in keeping with our destination.

## Unanswered questions

◆ How do we love those in the church with whom we disagree?

## The aim of this study

To understand that we must submit to authority, and that we must love one another wholeheartedly, since we belong to God's future.

# Suggested questions

◆ In this passage, Paul tells the Roman Christians to submit to governing authorities. How does that instruction make you feel? Why?

◆ Why has Paul included this instruction at this point in his letter? Where are we in Romans? How is this passage linked to what has come before?

## 1–7 SUBMIT TO AUTHORITIES UNDER GOD

◆ Looking through vv. 1–7, what different reasons does Paul give as to why we should submit to governing authorities?

– Why is the fact that they are established by God a reason to submit to them? How does this point correct our wrong thinking?

– How does the role that God has given them relate to our submission to them?

– Why does Paul bring in conscience as a reason for submitting?

– Why should we pay taxes?

◆ What impact should this teaching have on us?

– How does it apply when the governing authorities command their subjects to sin? Does this passage have any principles to guide us? What should Christians' reaction be if they face punishment for refusing to obey, because it would cause them to sin?

– Can a Christian protest if he or she lives under a corrupt government?

– It is easy to talk about cases where Paul's teaching doesn't apply, but in most cases it should. What stops us wanting to submit? How can this passage help us to have a right attitude?

## 8–14 DO NOT STOP LOVING ONE ANOTHER, IN THE LIGHT OF THE FUTURE

◆ How does Paul link v. 8 with what has gone before?

– Why does Paul describe our love in this way?

– How does this challenge our normal attitude and the attitude of the world? Do we love in this way? Why not? How can we change?

– In what way does love fulfil the Law?

◆ It would be easy to resent both having to submit to authorities and also having to keep on loving one another. How should vv. 11–14 change our perspective?
  – How does Paul view the present?
  – How should we live? What should our attitude be in the present?
◆ Looking back over chs 12 and 13, what kinds of things should characterize Christians in their relationships?
  – In what areas, within your local church setting, do your relationships most need to change? Where will your motivation come from? For what do you need to pray?

**Study 21**

# Romans 14:1–12

## Context

Since 12:1, Paul has been describing how Christians should wholly consecrate their lives to God, in response to His mercy, and has focused particularly on the transformation that should be seen in their relationships. Whereas once we were set against God and lived in enmity with one another (1:24–32), now, having been reconciled to God, we are to love one another humbly and wholeheartedly throughout our lives (12:9–16; 13:8–10). In 14:1–15:13, we are told that this love is to be extended, also, to those in the church with whom we disagree on disputable matters. This is the context in which Paul now examines the relationship between the 'weak' in faith and the 'strong'.

It appears that there were some in the church in Rome who were uncertain as to the freedom they had to observe, or to ignore, certain customs and rituals, and that this was giving rise in some believers to feelings of superiority over other believers (because they themselves could enjoy their freedom in the gospel), and also in another group of believers to feelings of condemnation towards their fellow believers (because they themselves felt more strongly about following certain patterns of behaviour). Almost certainly, this was a Jew/Gentile issue (see Text Notes), and in tackling it Paul is reverting once again to a major theme in his letter, the fact that the gospel is for both Jew and Gentile (1:16). The two groups have already been warned against boasting over one another (2:17–21; 11:16–32), and they have been taught that, in the light of the gospel, their relationship is to be characterized by love and humility. In spite of their differences the 'strong' and the 'weak' are to accept one another fully as Christian brothers and sisters.

## Structure

**14:1–4** Do not judge others who belong to God
**14:5–9** Live to the glory of Christ, the Lord
**14:10–12** Do not judge. It is God who will judge us all

## Old Testament background

**Food laws and special days:** God gave the Israelites detailed instructions about what they could and could not eat (e.g. in Leviticus 11) so that they might be set apart ('consecrated' or 'holy' – Leviticus 11:44) as His people. He told them to observe both the Sabbath and a series of feasts in order to commemorate their rescue from Egypt, and also to offer a number of sacrifices. These commands and rituals became, therefore, some of the clearest external factors by which the Jews were distinguished from the surrounding nations. Even when they were in exile we see God's people seeking to observe these regulations. Daniel, for example, when in Babylon, insisted that he be fed only on vegetables, so that he could keep the Jewish food laws (Daniel 1:8–16). The same scrupulous thinking may lie behind the abstinence of some of the Roman Christians (v. 2). We should note, however, that in the gospels Jesus declares that all food is clean (Mark 7:14–19), and also that He is Lord of the Sabbath (Mark 2:27–28).

## Text notes

### 1–4 DO NOT JUDGE OTHERS WHO BELONG TO GOD

It seems clear from this passage that problems were arising between Jews and Gentiles in the church, with regard to food laws and special days. Those whose faith was weak were almost certainly Jewish Christians whose background caused them to struggle over putting these restrictions and rituals aside, even though the gospel made them free to do so. They were not people whose salvation was under threat, nor were they 'morally' weak, in the sense of being more liable to 'gratify the desires of the sinful nature' (13:14). Rather, vv. 2, 5 and 14 suggest that they were 'Jewish Christians whose weakness consisted in their continuous conscientious commitment to Jewish regulations regarding diet and days' (Stott, p. 356).

They cannot have been insisting that their religious observance was essential for salvation, for although Paul clearly considers their thinking to be wrong (14:14), he does not condemn them as he does the Judaizers in Galatians (see Galatians 1:8–9). But they were weak in their 'assurance that one's faith permits one to do certain things' (Cranfield, p. 341). And so, 'disputable matters' are seen to be issues that are not essential (or said to be essential) to the message of salvation, but are secondary matters over which believers disagree.

◆ **Welcome the weak in faith without passing judgment on disputable matters (v. 1)**
The Greek word for 'accept' means 'to welcome into one's fellowship and into one's heart': Paul wants the weak in faith to experience Christian love that is unhindered by other people's reservations regarding their personal scruples. Passing judgment will naturally exclude and marginalize those who are accused, whereas God's people are to live in harmony with one another (12:16). Paul is not calling for what Western society calls 'tolerance', i.e. a dutiful acknowledgement of others' rights to believe whatever they wish, but rather he is saying that we should treat the weak as equal members of God's family, without allowing minor differences of opinion to damage our fellowship.

◆ **Do not judge those whom God has accepted (vv. 2–3)**
Although the major problem seems to have been the treatment of the weak by the strong (15:1), it's possible that friction had developed on both sides. While the strong were considering the weak to be inferior, the weak had accused the strong of having a slack attitude towards personal godliness. Both points of view are forbidden, however, for they negate God's acceptance of all Christians. The gospel teaches us that none of us is better than any other believer; we are all rebels whom God has justified. If

God has thus welcomed us all into His family, how can we look down on our brothers and sisters? Quite the opposite should be true – we are called to hold one another in higher regard than ourselves (12:10).

◆ **They belong to God (v. 4)**
If we look down on another believer, we suggest that we somehow stand in authority over that person, forgetting that our 'stronger' or 'weaker' brother or sister is actually responsible to Christ and not to us. On these matters, therefore, Paul tells us that we are in no position to pity, or to condemn, those who belong to Him.

◆ **The Lord can and will enable the weak to stand (v. 4)**
It is not our place to judge another Christian's relationship with God, as the Roman Christians were doing, apparently, on account of these matters. It is God's work, and only His, to enable His people to survive to the end. Moreover, He has promised that He will do so (8:28–30) and nothing can get in His way (8:31–39).

## 5–9 LIVE TO THE GLORY OF CHRIST, THE LORD

In these verses, Paul takes up the theme of Christians being answerable to their Lord and impresses it equally upon both the weak and the strong, so as to prevent them from judging one another.

◆ **Do everything to the Lord (vv. 5–6)**
The days that Paul mentions are likely to be Jewish festival days, or even the Sabbath (see OT notes). On these secondary issues, one might say, 'It doesn't matter what you believe, but what you believe must matter to you.' In other words, though issues may be disputable, the things we do must still be done as 'to the Lord', i.e. wholeheartedly and for His honour (12:11). Individuals must not offend their own consciences but, instead, seek to honour Christ, acknowledging Him, through thanksgiving, in whatever they choose to do.

◆ **For Christ is Lord of all (vv. 7–9)**
In doing everything 'to the Lord', the Romans will be acknowledging a deeper issue, which is that all Christians belong to

Christ; it is in response to God's mercy towards them, demonstrated in Christ, that they are to give every aspect of their lives back to Him (12:1), for His glory. Jesus has demonstrated His right to ownership and authority over us through His death and resurrection, which proved His identity as God's anointed ruler of all (1:4). If He *is* Lord of all, then each of us has a responsibility to live in a way that constantly brings honour to His name. And if this is our priority, we are less likely to judge others over the way in which they honour Him.

## 10–12 DO NOT JUDGE. IT IS GOD WHO WILL JUDGE US ALL

In v. 10, as in v. 4, Paul challenges the Christian who accuses a fellow believer, whether it is the weak judging the strong or the strong looking down on the weak. This time, however, his challenge is made in the light of the final judgment. All petty squabbling and resentment are insignificant when seen from the perspective of judgment day. Paul quotes from Isaiah 45:23, where God proclaims to the nations that every single individual will bow before Him. When we put other believers in the dock, we are forgetting that we too will be included when all people have to face God on judgment day and give an account of their lives. We are in no position to pass judgment ourselves.

# Key themes and application

## ◆ Accept one another without passing judgment

Behind this passage lies a clear Jew/Gentile conflict which is now rarely seen in the church. Yet the principles that Paul teaches the church in Rome can still guide us where similar disputes occur today. The closest examples will therefore be those where, as in Rome, the cultural background of some believers is causing them to have doubts over their freedom in the gospel, regarding particular practices. Other Christians, who understand the freedom that the gospel permits, may ask how they should treat these 'weak' fellow believers. Paul's answer is simple: they should treat them no differently from any other Christian brother or sister, but embrace them fully in the love and personal commitment of the Christian community. Put negatively, the 'strong' should not judge the weak or think any the less of them.

Following this teaching will mean going against all our sinful inclinations, because naturally we love to promote ourselves, and condemning others is an effective way of doing so. But it will help us if we remember what the church is: we are like a body, put together by God, and each of us, as one part of that body, is to live for the benefit of the rest, the other parts of the body. Disputes over secondary issues will only divide us. 'We are not to turn the church into a debating chamber, whose chief characteristic is argument, still less into a law court in which weak persons are put in the dock, interrogated and arraigned' (Stott, p. 360).

Paul gives two reasons that ought to bring about the necessary change in attitude. First, if we are 'strong' we should remember that our weaker brothers are answerable only to Christ, who is Lord of all – this point is developed below. Second, we should not judge, because it is God's job to judge, and when He does, we will face Him too.

### ◆ We are not our own, we belong to the Lord

Part of Paul's appeal stems from the fact that weaker Christians, whom we may be tempted to judge, are not answerable to us but to their own Lord – which reminds us that Jesus is our risen Lord as well. The implication of this is that we should do all things for His honour and glory.

Paul stresses that, as members of the body of Christ, we do not live to ourselves alone, a fact that strikes at the heart of our desire for independence. The world tells us that we are free to live our lives without reference to anyone else, and that our decisions are therefore of no consequence to anyone else. This appeals to our selfishness, although by implication it also robs us of the opportunity to make decisions that have intrinsic value. Paul's teaching turns this on its head. The fact that we are answerable to God means that all our actions and decisions *are* truly significant. Thus we always have a responsibility to act according to our consciences and, at the same time, we have the possibility of doing all things, however mundane, for the glory of God.

## ✦ Disputable matters

What constitutes a disputable matter today? The following guidelines may be helpful.

1 **The principles apply to behaviour or to practice, but not to doctrine:** Paul applies his teaching to a context of differing opinions regarding Christian behaviour. He is not encouraging Christians to disagree freely over the assertions of scripture, and nor, having already laid out eleven chapters-worth of doctrine, is he inviting contradiction! Rather, this passage relates to disagreements among Christians over the *ways* in which they should give their lives to God, in response to His mercy, the mercy that Paul has explained in chs 1–11.

2 **For a matter to be disputable, there must be no clear, relevant commands:** When it comes to Christian behaviour, God has given His people clear indications about the behaviour that will be pleasing and acceptable to Him. There is therefore no place for applying this passage to, say, the issue of homosexual practice. Within the boundaries that God has laid out, Christians are free to behave as they choose. Some, however, may wish to abstain from something that the Bible permits because their cultural context causes them to associate such behaviour with sin (e.g. drinking alcohol in a culture where it is everywhere associated with violence and debauchery).

   Genuine disputable matters usually tend to be related to tradition or culture, such as the style of music in church, the means of baptism, churchmanship, the use of particular gifts, etc. The danger for the church is that we become flexible on indisputable gospel issues, but totally intractable when it comes to matters in which we have total freedom.

3 **All issues are disputable except gospel issues:** This means that Christians have total freedom in the way that they live out their lives to God's glory, *unless something additional to gospel truth has come to be viewed as essential to salvation.* In this case, it becomes a gospel issue of the kind that Paul condemns in Galatians 1:8–9. Because of this, any disputable matter can become a gospel issue the moment it is insisted upon as necessary for salvation.

# Unanswered questions

◆ How should this teaching influence our behaviour?

## The aim of this study

To commit ourselves wholeheartedly to loving and accepting Christians with whom we disagree on non-gospel issues.

## Suggested questions

◆ While travelling abroad, you spend time in a church where the Christians think you are sinning because you drink alcohol. How would you react in this situation? What would you think of them?

◆ What was the main point of chs 12 and 13? Are there any themes which carry over to ch. 14?

◆ Read through the passage. What is going on in the church in Rome?

### 1–4 DO NOT JUDGE OTHERS WHO BELONG TO GOD

◆ Who are the 'weak in faith'? What does it mean to be 'weak'?

◆ How are the strong and the weak tempted to act towards each other? Why?
  – What does Paul instruct them to do instead?
  – What different reasons does he give?

### 5–9 LIVE TO THE GLORY OF CHRIST, THE LORD

◆ What is Paul saying in these verses?
  – Why does he include these verses in his argument?

◆ Why should we 'live to the Lord'?
  – What will it mean for us to live like this?

### 10–12 DO NOT JUDGE. IT IS GOD WHO WILL JUDGE US ALL

◆ Why do you think we like to pass judgment on one another?
  – Why should we not do so? What misunderstanding on our part does it indicate?

◆ Returning to the first question, what lessons should you learn from this passage?
◆ In what circumstances do these lessons about disputable matters apply? What kind of issue are the Romans facing?
   – In what circumstances do these lessons not apply? Why?

◆ Summarize how Christians should treat one another with regard to disputable matters.

## Study 22

# ROMANS 14:13–15:13

## Context

In this passage, Paul is still explaining to the Christians in Rome what it means to live lives that are transformed in response to God's gospel. He continues the line of argument, begun at 14:1, that he is addressing to the 'strong' and the 'weak', i.e. to believers who find themselves in dispute over one another's views and practices regarding food and special days.

As a result of God's saving work through the gospel, a new community, consisting of believers, is created, with its members brought together to live interdependently as one body. The Christians belonging to this new community in Rome have been told by Paul that their relationships should be characterized by devotion to one another (12:9–16), but there is a danger that their disagreements will divide what God has brought together. Paul's central message, therefore, is that the strong and the weak are to accept one another fully as Christian brothers and sisters, without passing judgment on non-gospel matters over which they disagree. So far, he has grounded this instruction in the fact that all Christians have been accepted by God, through the gospel, and so belong to Him, being answerable to Him alone. This truth also means that each of us must do what we are convinced before God is right.

In this passage Paul gives further reasons for the need to accept others who disagree with us over non-gospel issues: the Romans, he reminds them, have an obligation to love their fellow

Christians and so to behave considerately towards them, and also they should keep in mind the priorities of God's kingdom which are far more important than their disagreements. Paul's words, in these verses, are addressed particularly to 'the strong', but he also continues to urge mutual acceptance within the church.

## Structure

**14:13–23**  Limit your liberty for the sake of the kingdom

**15:1–6**  Follow Christ's example in not pleasing yourself

**15:7–13**  Accept one another, so as to bring praise to God and be in accord with the goal of His plan of salvation

## Old Testament background

**The salvation of the Gentiles:** On account of mankind's rebellion against God (Genesis 3), men and women are cut off from their creator, facing death under His judgment. The story of the Old Testament is of how God makes promises to rescue humankind, and begins to fulfil them (although most of these promises are unfulfilled by the time the New Testament begins). In His mercy, He chooses one man, Abraham (see Genesis 12), whose descendants will be His people. Throughout the Old Testament the people of Israel, Abraham's physical descendants, are seen to be distinct from all other nations, having a unique relationship with God. They are to be 'holy', set apart by their way of living in obedience to the LORD. Indeed, the food laws and the observance of festivals (the presenting issues within the church in Rome) were two explicit ways in which they as a people came to be distinguished from the Gentiles.

Yet, even at the time when God made His promise to Abraham, He had said that *all peoples* (i.e. all kinds of people) would be blessed through him (Genesis 12:3). This promise is later developed, as recorded in the writings of the prophets (e.g. Isaiah 56:3–8). And so the inclusion of the Gentiles among God's covenant people is the fulfilment of His promise to rescue a people from the whole of humankind – and this is the goal towards which God is working throughout history.

# Text notes

## 14:13–23 LIMIT YOUR LIBERTY FOR THE SAKE OF THE KINGDOM

Paul began his address to 'the strong' and 'the weak' by focusing on their attitudes to one another, and his main point, so far, is summarized in 14:13a: they must stop judging one another for their different opinions about disputable matters. In v. 13b, however, he tells the strong that they are to consider the consequences of their behaviour in front of the weak. (The fact that Paul is primarily addressing the strong, from 14:13b onwards, may be seen from his focusing on those who eat all foods and so cause the weak to stumble.) The strong understand their liberty in the gospel, but they need to appreciate that the expression of that liberty could cause those with scruples to be confused about what God wants, and thus be caused to sin. Furthermore, this kind of upset will undermine God's work of creating a family of believers who are united in their love for each other.

◆ **Instruction: Do not put anything in your brother's way (vv. 13b–15a)**

Paul calls for those who are 'strong' to make a firm resolution not to allow their behaviour to cause problems for their weaker brothers or sisters. On disputable matters, even the fact that they may be right (v. 14) must not take precedence over the conscience of the individual believer. If a Christian whose faith is weaker believes that their behaviour is sinful, the strong must put aside the freedom that they know the gospel gives them, so that the weaker believer may not feel discouraged in his or her Christian discipleship.

Next, Paul encourages the strong to remember a key element of their response to God's mercy, the response that he began to explain in ch. 12: their relationships with each other are to be transformed according to the central, governing principle of love (12:9–16). He wants them to recognize that causing distress to a member of the Christian family is a way of ignoring this principle, which is in fact their greatest obligation (13:8).

◆ **The principle: the kingdom comes first (vv. 15b–18)**

In order to persuade the strong to love the weak as they should,

Paul raises the stakes. It is not merely a question of the weak being offended; the reality is that they could be 'destroyed' by the behaviour of the strong. Although commentators are divided over whether it is possible for a weak person to lose his salvation, the strength of Paul's language suggests that he does envisage such a disastrous possibility. The thoughtlessness of the strong could devastate (the word can mean 'ruin' or 'spoil') someone else's relationship with God: Christians who see fellow-Christians sinning – or so it seems to them – could feel confused about what it means to offer one's life to God (12:1), and discouraged from persevering in the Christian life; they may feel at odds with their heavenly Father, and so be put on a path towards giving up altogether. It would then be apparent that the strong, whose behaviour had caused such trouble, had had scant regard for the high price paid by Christ to save their brothers or sisters.

But does the liberty of the strong have no value, therefore? The strong might understand Paul to be devaluing their freedom in Christ, when he commands them to restrict their liberty. No, v. 16 corrects this idea and supplies a further reason that we should avoid offending 'the weak'. This is that they (or others looking on and seeing us give offence to our Christian family) will condemn what we know to be a great blessing of the gospel, i.e. our freedom, and we should not allow God's work to be devalued in this way.

In v. 17, Paul shows that both these instructions will involve a change of perspective. Rather than focusing on these minor disputes, we need to put first the eternal priorities of God's kingdom. These are 'righteousness, peace and joy', the consequences of justification by faith, as Paul has laid out in 5:1–5. Compared with these, our differences of opinion over disputable issues are an irrelevance, and so, serving Christ 'in this way' (i.e. putting people's salvation before the expression of our liberty) will please God because we will be putting His concerns before our own. Not only this, but also such selfless concern for the well-being of others will not go unnoticed by people around us.

◆ **Conclusion: Build up, don't tear down! (vv. 19–21)**
When the stakes are as high as this (see above), the full force of the instruction in v. 13b should be felt, so Paul again articulates

our responsibility (v. 19). The word for 'destroy' in v. 20 is different from that used in v. 15; it means 'to tear down' and is used of the destruction of the temple (Matthew 24:2). If God's work is to unite a family in the likeness of Christ and to put together one body, we should not tear down what He is doing. Far from letting our careless behaviour undermine our brothers and sisters, we should be channelling all our time and energy into building one another up in our mutual faith.

Paul's conclusion is categorical: if someone's choice of behaviour in a disputable matter causes problems for a fellow believer, 'it is wrong ... ', 'it is better not to ... '. Having stated in v. 20 that all food is clean, Paul demonstrates how something that is right (the freedom to eat any food) becomes wrong if the faith of God's people is going to be put at risk.

◆ **Keep your liberty to yourself for the sake of others (vv. 22–23)**
As he views the importance of God's kingdom, and also the dangers of undermining individual believers or the body of the church, Paul advises the strong not to parade their freedom before others. Although, by appreciating their freedom in the gospel, they are blessed in such an understanding, they must beware. For if they should cause a weaker believer to behave in a way that he has doubts about, that believer would be doing wrong because he would not be acting out of faith; he would therefore be living in a spirit of rebellion against God, a way of life condemned by God. Again we see how God's honour and His kingdom are to take precedence over everything.

## 15:1–6 FOLLOW CHRIST'S EXAMPLE IN NOT PLEASING YOURSELF

For the first time Paul identifies those who understand their liberty in Christ as the 'strong' and identifies himself as being among their number, but the essence of his instruction remains the same. Although he sees the scruples of the weak over food and special days as 'failings', he stresses once again the responsibility that the strong should have towards the weak.

◆ **Bear with the weak (15:1a)**
It would be easy for the strong to patronize the weak, or to show frustration at their immaturity. This, however, would not reflect

the life-long debt of love for one another that Paul has stressed in 13:8. Instead, therefore, the strong are to bear with the weak, gently supporting and strengthening them in their faith. Those who are mature enough to enjoy their freedom in the gospel need to work at being sufficiently godly to bear with the struggles of others and, more, to seek their good.

◆ **Please others, not yourself (vv. 1b–2)**

The inclination to ride roughshod over the interests of those with whom we disagree comes out of our selfish desire to do what we wish, but the gospel should bring about a revolution in our understanding and our relationships, so that we think of ourselves with humility (12:3) and are concerned for one another's good (12:10). The goal of each Christian should be the good of others, but what does this mean? The 'good', described already by Paul, is that of being built up, such that believers will one day be conformed to the likeness of Christ (8:28–29).

◆ **Follow Christ's example in this (v. 3)**

In seeking the good of others we have the supreme example of Jesus to follow. Both in His life and in His death we see that He was concerned to please His Father and to work for our good, instead of considering His own benefit (Mark 14:35–36). Paul quotes, however, from Psalm 69 and applies to Jesus the words of a righteous man who endures insult and scorn for the sake of God's glory. By comparison with the scale of His personal sacrifice, the restriction of our liberty for the sake of our weaker brothers and sisters is trifling.

◆ **Encouraged by scripture … (v. 4)**

Having quoted scripture himself, Paul pauses here to remind the Romans of the importance of the Old Testament. Far from being of limited value to Christians, the record of all God's dealings with His people in the past has been deliberately preserved for our practical benefit, so that we will keep going until we receive all that God has promised when we are raised.

◆ **A prayer for the unity that will glorify God (vv. 5–6)**

At this point, Paul demonstrates the need to depend on God as he prays according to the principles that he has just been teaching. In the light of God's plan to unite believers as a body, and in view of the potential that these disputable matters have to cause division, Paul asks God to give the Roman Christians the desire and the ability to be united, as they follow the example of Christ in living for the good of one another. Moreover, since division among God's people would bring dishonour to His name, the goal of Paul's prayer is that the Romans should glorify God as a united body.

## 15:7–13 ACCEPT ONE ANOTHER, SO AS TO BRING PRAISE TO GOD AND BE IN ACCORD WITH THE GOAL OF HIS PLAN OF SALVATION

Paul now begins to sum up this part of his letter, using the same command that he gave at its beginning: the Romans are to accept one another completely (cf. 14:1), in the light of their own acceptance by God through the gospel. In vv. 8–13, however, he gives a further reason for accepting one another. He shows that this mutual acceptance between Jews and Gentiles is an essential outworking of God's great plan of salvation for the whole of history (see OT notes). Moo comments, 'He sets the local conflict in Rome against the panorama of salvation history in order to stimulate them to obedience' (p. 874).

The grammatical structure of vv. 8–9a is uncertain and is discussed by most commentators. What seems clear, however, is that Paul is holding up to these Jews and Gentiles in Rome, who are in danger of falling out of fellowship with one another, the servant attitude of Christ, as follows:

◆ **Christ has fulfilled God's promises to save the nations (vv. 7–9a)**
Christ came as a Jew to demonstrate the faithfulness of God in keeping the promises of salvation He had made to Abraham, and also in order to bring blessing and salvation to the Gentiles, as Paul described in 11:11. This being so, how can the Jews condemn those to whom God has shown mercy? On the other hand, the Gentiles should remember that their salvation stems from a Jewish root (cf. 11:18).
◆ **So Christ brings praise to God for His mercy, as scripture testifies (vv. 9b–12)**
Paul reinforces the truth about the Gentiles being included among God's people by quoting four times from the Old Testament, taking one quotation from each of its parts: v. 9b

comes from 'the former prophets' (2 Samuel 22:50), v. 10 from
'the Law' (Deuteronomy 32:43), v. 11 from 'the writings' (Psalm
117:1), and v. 12 from 'the latter prophets' (Isaiah 11:10). These
verses show that the whole of scripture testifies to the inclusion
of the Gentiles, and thus to God's purpose of uniting people of
every kind under His rule (see OT notes), in order to bring praise
to His name. If the believers in Rome truly understand that this
is what God is doing throughout history, they will recognize
that their unity as the body of Christ must come before their
minor differences of opinion.

Paul finishes this part of his letter, on the strong and the weak,
with a prayer (v. 13), asking God to make the Romans thoroughly
gospel-minded. He wants them to be focused on the priorities of
God's kingdom (5:1–5; 14:17) and, in particular, on the future that
God has in store for them. In the light of the riches of the gospel,
their disagreements fade into nothing.

# Key themes and application

## ◆ Putting the kingdom and others before our liberty

Paul urges the strong to be careful so that, as they live out their
freedom in the gospel, they do not cause others who may have
scruples to become compromised or discouraged, and thereby
threatened in their faith. Rather than holding on to their liberty,
he says, the strong should see God's kingdom and His work of
glorifying a family of believers (8:30) as their highest concern,
and encourage each other to grow in the Lord.

For us, this will mean watching the way our behaviour affects
others. We may be aware of the freedom that we have in the
gospel – and we are right to appreciate it – but the welfare of our
Christian brothers and sisters matters much more, ultimately,
than our freedom. We should also be aware, therefore, of the
disputable matters (see notes on 14:1–12 for definitions) that
may be significant to others in our fellowship (e.g. the Sabbath,
alcohol). In these matters, if our practice will cause other
Christians to be confused or distressed then it is wrong to go
ahead. This principle goes very much against the pattern of the

world, where the rights of individuals to practise their beliefs are almost sacred, so we need to be ready to resist the tide of worldly thinking. We have higher principles which must govern our behaviour: our devotion to one another, the selfless example of Christ, and the honour of God's name which is upheld when and where His people are united.

It is not necessarily wrong to seek to educate the weak in their understanding, but this passage tells us that it must be part of a greater desire to build them up. Such a course of action might be particularly necessary if a weaker Christian were holding the church to ransom over one particular issue which offended them (e.g. insisting on following traditional church practices which are alienating the unbeliever). In cases like these, the priorities of the kingdom (and His greater plan of salvation for many) must come first.

### ◆ The priority of building one another up

Effectively, Paul's message is, 'Don't tear down, but build up!' Christians need to take seriously their responsibility towards one another. Previously, we were self-centred and self-serving, but now we have been brought together and, in response to God's mercy towards us, we are to be devoted to one another. Instead of causing ruin, we are to consider how we may strengthen one another in our faith. This is more than a call to be harmless; we should be actively involved in spurring one another on in faith and in love. With the phrase 'for his good, to build him up' Paul has qualified his instruction to 'please' our neighbour (15:2), i.e. we are to please him or her, not for their pleasure, but for their good.

### ◆ Unity that glorifies God

As Christians accept one another, Paul says that God is glorified and His name is praised. As God reaches out to people in salvation, not only does He reconcile them to Himself, but He also reconciles them to each other in a family; they become one body in which the different members are devoted to one another. When God's people allow secondary issues to divide them, the reputation of the gospel is tarnished. Not only do others suffer, but also God's name is not given the honour it deserves. Again, we need to live differently; instead of being concerned for ourselves, as would be natural in our individualistic culture, we should refuse to promote ourselves above the priorities of God's kingdom. When we are divided, our practice obscures our witness in the world, whereas a group of believers with different backgrounds, cultures and experiences, who are united through the gospel and who remain united even when they differ on secondary matters – such a group is living proof of God's plan and His power to unite a family for ever under Christ.

## Unanswered questions

◆ Why should the Romans, and why should we, listen to Paul?

## The aim of this study

To be willing to restrict our freedom for the sake of others and, instead, to be committed to building up one another, in order to glorify God.

## Suggested questions

◆ Looking back to the previous study:
  – What was going on in Rome? How were the strong and the weak treating one another?
  – What was Paul's main point? What reasons did he give?

### 14:13–23 LIMIT YOUR LIBERTY FOR THE SAKE OF THE KINGDOM
Paul is addressing a Jew/Gentile issue in Rome, but here is a modern equivalent. Imagine you move to a new church. The congregation is comprised of committed believers, but soon you discover that some of the older members are offended by the way you dress, because they think it shows a lack of respect for God.

◆ In the above scenario, what advice might you be given by today's society? How do you think you would react?
◆ What does Paul say are the potential dangers?
  – In what way could a believer be 'destroyed' by what you wear?
  – What is the work of God that could be destroyed?

◆ What are Paul's instructions?
  – What reasons does he give?
  – How does he encourage us to think differently? What new priorities does he give us?

## 15:1–6 FOLLOW CHRIST'S EXAMPLE IN NOT PLEASING YOURSELF

◆ How does Paul say the strong should behave?
  – Why does he give Jesus as an example?
  – How would these verses apply to the above scenario?
◆ How does Paul's prayer fit in with his teaching?

## 15:7–13 ACCEPT ONE ANOTHER, SO AS TO BRING PRAISE TO GOD AND BE IN ACCORD WITH THE GOAL OF HIS PLAN OF SALVATION

◆ How does Paul, in 15:7–13, challenge the Romans' perspective on their disputes?
  – What was the dividing issue in Rome?
  – How do vv. 7–9a address this issue?
  – Why does Paul use these quotations from the Old Testament?
◆ What is God's overall plan of salvation?
  – How should this influence our thinking when we are divided over disputable matters?
◆ How have you been challenged to think differently about:
  – yourself?
  – other Christians?
  – God?

# ROMANS 15:14–16:27

## Context

Having dealt with the issue of potential division among the Roman Christians, Paul brings his letter to a close. He follows the convention of finishing his letter with a mixture of greetings, warnings and prayers, but within these verses we also find reference to some of the major themes of his letter. In addition to these we find that Paul returns to the themes with which he opened his letter (in 1:1–17), with the result that the main body of his letter is set within the context, or frame, of these themes: his relationship with the Romans, the nature of his ministry and the wonderful power of God's gospel.

Paul's purpose here is to point his readers back into his letter and to the good news of salvation. He first explains why we should listen to his message by authenticating his ministry as the apostle to the Gentiles. He also includes a warning against listening to teaching that is different from what he has taught. Finally, he gives the assurance that the good news that God has revealed is the means by which He saves people and makes them His own for ever.

## Structure

15:14–33  Paul's ministry to the Gentiles
  16:1–16  Greetings
16:17–20  Warnings against false teachers
16:21–23  Messages

**16:25–27** Glory to God who can keep you through my gospel

# Old Testament background

**Isaiah 52:15:** The words that Paul quotes in 15:21 come from one of the Servant Songs in Isaiah. These songs foretell the coming of God's suffering servant who will deal with His people's sin. Here, Isaiah tells of how God's servant will bring salvation to nations other than Israel. The Old Testament always envisaged that God's message of salvation would go to those who hadn't previously heard.

# Text notes

### 15:14–33 PAUL'S MINISTRY TO THE GENTILES

There appear to be two good reasons why Paul should want to tell the Romans about his ministry in the past and his plans for the future. First, he wants to explain why he has not previously visited this important church, and then, why his planned stay with them will only be 'for a while'. Second, he wants them to have confidence in him and his ministry, not only so that they will abide by his teaching, but also so that they will get behind his missionary plans.

◆ **Paul and the Romans (vv. 14–15a)**

It may be that, having written them a long letter full of strong argument, Paul anticipates that the Roman Christians might be offended by his teaching (e.g. on universal condemnation outside the gospel, or on equality between Jew and Gentile within the gospel). Does the apostle, who has never met them, have doubts about their faith? Whatever the reason, Paul goes out of his way to assert his confidence in them. Addressing them as his brothers, he assures them that he is convinced that they are 'full of goodness, complete in knowledge and competent to teach one another'. Such a description may seem like an exaggeration – 'a little harmless, diplomatic hyperbole' (Stott, p. 378) – or, Paul may be thinking more specifically. First, he may have in mind the transformation that has come about since they were 'filled with every kind of wickedness, evil, greed and depravity' (1:29).

Second, he may be referring to their minds, already renewed (12:2), which now enable them to encourage one another in the gospel they have been taught. In any case, his 'bold' letter was not written to address their faults, but to 'remind' them of what they know already, for all that he has taught them is in accordance with the essential message of salvation.

◆ **Paul, the apostle to the Gentiles (vv. 15b–22)**

Though he wishes to reassure the Romans, Paul makes no excuse for writing to them as he does. He explains that he has the right to write to them 'boldly' for they, like all Gentiles, are his responsibility, since God has appointed him to be the apostle to the Gentiles. In these verses we get a unique insight into Paul's understanding of his own work, the work that has prevented him from coming to Rome before.

*A priestly ministry (vv. 15b–16)*: In the Old Testament, the Gentiles were excluded from any kind of relationship with God, being barred from access to the holy places of the temple and being regarded, by the Jews, as defiled. But now Paul can write of how the Gentiles may be offered to God, as an offering that is sanctified and fully acceptable to Him. Because he has been involved in bringing about this great change, Paul describes his role as a 'priestly duty'. In this, however, he is completely different from the Old Testament priests who mediated between the people and God by offering sacrifices, so that people could relate to God (albeit in a limited way). Paul's role is to proclaim the gospel of God, which itself is powerful to save the Gentiles (1:16). Paul mediates only in the sense that he preaches God's gospel, that he carries the gospel from God to the Gentiles. It is *God* who makes people acceptable to Himself, through *His* gospel and by *His* Spirit.

*Glorying in Christ (vv. 17–19a):* Paul's role was unique in the history of salvation and pivotal in the growth of the church, yet he always turns the spotlight on to Christ. The word for 'glory' is the same as that translated 'brag' in 2:17, 'boast' in 3:27, and 'rejoice' in 5:1–11. This is permissible boasting, as Paul acknowledges that everything he has achieved has been accomplished by Christ, through the power of the Spirit, and confirmed – because he is an apostle – by signs and miracles (see 2 Corinthians 12:12).

*A pioneer (vv. 19b–22):* Paul's desire to find new territory in which to preach the gospel explains his plan to go to Spain (v. 24); he has nowhere else to preach in the eastern Mediterranean. Yet his 'ambition' is not an absolute rule and does not make his proposed visit to Rome inconsistent. It was fitting that he should visit the seat of the empire that had such an influence on the Gentile world.

*The trip to Spain via Rome:* Paul's time in Rome will be a time of blessing and refreshment (vv. 29, 32) through the mutual encouragement he mentions in 1:12, but it will not be very long. His desire to take the gospel into new territory will take him on to Spain. As he goes, however, he wants the Romans to 'assist' him practically. This word usually denotes the giving of money and provisions, and Paul is writing in advance, to ensure that they understand his mission and purpose. Having gone to great lengths to explain the gospel to them fully, he looks to them to share his convictions and therefore to get behind the spread of the good news. Even in the case of an apostle, gospel work is presented as a team effort.

*The trip to Jerusalem:* First, however, he is going to Jerusalem. This is more than just an example of 'sharing with God's people who are in need' (12:13); rather, it picks up a major theme of the letter – the debt that Gentile Christians owe to their Jewish roots (11:18; 15:8–9). By telling the Romans about this visit, and by asking them to support him in prayer (v. 31), Paul is stressing his commitment to Jewish Christians and so discouraging the division between Jew and Gentile that seems to be occurring in the church. Instead, he promotes unity and mutual devotion within the body of the church.

## 16:1–16 and 21–23 GREETING AND MESSAGES

In a group Bible study, it is not really appropriate to examine these greetings in great detail. The verses remind us that Romans was a personal letter that would have been read out in the church; the greetings from Paul (vv. 1–16) and from others (vv. 21–24) are very specific to that context. The reason for the large number of greetings may be found, perhaps, in the fact that Paul has not yet visited the church and so wishes to demonstrate his personal concern for the Romans.

It is noteworthy, however, that in a church whose faith Paul has com-
mended (1:8; 15:14), we find many of the marks of true fellowship
that Paul calls for as part of an obedient response to God's mercy
(12:9–16): Mary, in v. 6, for instance, 'who worked very hard for you',
has already understood Paul's injunction in 12:10, that Christians
should be devoted to one another in brotherly love. Various commentators have also highlighted the fact that most of the names
mentioned in these greetings are Gentile names, which sheds further
light on Paul's commands to Gentiles not to boast over Jews
(11:13–32) or pass judgment on them (14:1). These commands would
have been all the more important if the Jews were a minority.

## 16:17–20 WARNINGS AGAINST FALSE TEACHERS

The list of greetings is interrupted by a stern warning about false
teachers. Throughout the time of the New Testament church,
there seems to have been the threat of false teachers, such as those
who taught that it was necessary for Christians to obey the Old
Testament Law. The particular group that Paul has in mind is not
identified here, but their characteristics are clear: they are divisive,
they teach what is contrary to the gospel, they are self-serving, and
they persuade people through flattery. This last characteristic
could be a particular danger for the Roman Christians, whom
Paul has already warned against boasting (11:18) and thinking too
highly of themselves (12:3).

We should note that Paul takes a very different line on the divisions caused by false teachers, compared with his line on divisions
over disputable matters. Regarding such disputes, he teaches the
Romans to accept one another fully within the fellowship, but
with false teachers he is fiercely unequivocal: 'Keep away from
them' (v.17). The apparent maturity of the Romans does not mean
that they are immune to such dangers. And since being complete
in their knowledge (15:14) demands only an understanding of the
gospel, any involvement with false teaching is to be avoided (v.19).
In this context, it is likely that the promise in v. 20a is an incentive to let God Himself deal with those who oppose Him and His
gospel, for He surely will.

## 16:25–27 GLORY TO GOD WHO CAN KEEP YOU THROUGH MY GOSPEL

Paul finishes his letter to the Romans by praising God. To a certain extent these verses mirror the opening verses of the letter, as he refers to the gospel about Jesus (v. 25, cf. 1:3) being revealed by God, so that all nations (v. 26, cf. 1:5) might believe and obey God (v. 26, cf. 1:5).

As he finishes, however, Paul's main purpose is to give the Romans confidence in the gospel he has explained, and thereby to encourage them to stand by it.

◆ **God can keep you by my gospel (v. 25a)**
The Romans should have no doubts about the significance of the teaching contained in Paul's letter, for Paul proclaims that God is able to establish them through it. In the context of the letter, this surely means that as they trust His promises of salvation through Christ, God will keep them secure, even though they may suffer in this world, and that He will certainly complete His plan to conform them to the likeness of Christ (8:28–39). The Romans must abide by Paul's gospel about Jesus Christ, for it is the way that God will secure them for glory.

◆ **This gospel has now been made known (vv. 25b–26)**
The importance of abiding by Paul's gospel becomes even clearer as the apostle highlights how privileged the Romans (and we) now are. God's gospel of salvation through Christ was previously hidden, such that salvation was not easily available to all, but now God has revealed everything so that everyone may believe and call on Christ for salvation (cf. 10:8–13).

◆ **Praise God (v. 27)**
In the light of the fact that God has graciously revealed the gospel, by which the Romans and all people may be 'established', Paul praises God for His unique wisdom. Though it is Paul who has brought this gospel to the Romans, eternal glory belongs to God alone.

If God in His wisdom has revealed His powerful gospel of salvation, which can establish the Romans as God's children for ever, and if this is the gospel that Paul has proclaimed in his letter, then surely they, and we, must hold on to all that he has taught.

# Key themes and application

In a passage like this, which is very specific to the Romans and to Paul's unique ministry, it is important that we apply Paul's teaching correctly. We must *not* take passages that are *descriptive* of a particular situation, and see them as *prescriptive* for us. With this caveat in place, however, it is possible to make some significant observations as well as drawing out some principles.

## ◆ The apostle Paul

More than anywhere else in Romans, this passage shows us the nature and authority of Paul's ministry as the apostle to the Gentiles. The first application for us, therefore, is that we ourselves should acknowledge his authority and accept his teaching. It has become fashionable to disagree with, or dislike, Paul, but here we are reminded that he was appointed by God Himself, so that the Gentiles might be made holy and acceptable to God. We also see both his humility and his commitment to God's gospel. We should be grateful to God for Paul's ministry, of which we are beneficiaries, and obey his gospel message.

An important question concerns the extent to which his ministry is a model for ours. It would be an error to see ourselves in Paul's position: we have not been set apart by God as he was (15:16), we cannot expect our preaching to be accompanied by signs and miracles (15:19), and we are not bound to preach where Christ is not known (15:20). These aspects of his ministry are unique to his place in salvation history. From the wider context of Romans, however, we know that the message that Paul proclaims (15:16) is God's gospel (1:1) which is itself powerful to save all who believe (1:16). But this is not dependent upon Paul but upon God, and so we too may be involved in people becoming acceptable to God (15:16) as we preach His gospel (cf. 10:14). Furthermore, as we do so, we may be fully confident that the good news of salvation is available to all people.

Another principle that comes through the whole passage is that of partnership in the gospel. We see it in Paul's call for the Romans to join him in his struggle by praying to God for him (15:30–32), and also in the way that he mentions the names of many in Rome who have served him, or worked hard 'in the Lord'. We all have an obligation to support the work of the gospel. Even if we struggle, or are not in a position to tell others ourselves, we should support our brothers and sisters who do.

◆ **Keep away from false teachers**

Paul's strong warning, about those who cause divisions by teaching what is contrary to the gospel, should not be lost on us. Our society's preoccupation with tolerance will mean that Christians may often be urged to toe the line by being 'open-minded' and seeing alternative views as valid. Paul's approach could not be more different. As in other parts of the New Testament (e.g. 2 Timothy 2:16–18), we are told to keep away from anything that is different from the apostolic gospel. Although this may sound closed-minded in today's world, the truths and consequences of the gospel mean that the stakes are too high for us to dabble in what is, by definition, evil (16:19).

◆ **The gospel by which God can establish us**

Paul's letter concludes with praise to God for His revelation of the good news of Jesus Christ, so that all people might have saving faith. As ever, we need to be reminded to remove ourselves from the centre of our thinking and, instead, to acknowledge the God who has revealed His plan of salvation and will establish His people in the gospel. It is, of course, fitting that the note on which we end our study of Romans should be, like Paul's, one of praise, and yet his words should also compel us to go deeper into the gospel that he has just explained. We need to be reminded of the gospel just as much as the Romans did (15:15). We live in a culture which is always looking for something new, or for a different perspective, but Paul teaches us that it is God's gospel that will establish us in our faith, such that we will be saved as part of God's family for ever. We should not think that we have done with the message of Romans and so can move on to new things. As Paul has done, we should long to go deeper into God's great news of salvation.

# The aim of this study

To accept Paul's authority as God's apostle, and therefore to accept his teaching, keep away from false teachers and trust in the gospel to keep us for ever.

# Suggested questions

◆ Why is it tempting to skim over final passages like this one?

## 15:14–33 PAUL'S MINISTRY TO THE GENTILES
◆ What are the major ingredients of 15:14–33?
◆ How does Paul make sure that the Romans do not think his letter has been written to address their deficiencies?
◆ List the different things that Paul tells us about himself, under the headings of 'his role', 'his mindset' and 'his plans'.
  – Why does he tell the Romans about these things?
◆ Many today would say that Paul's teaching is a product of his background and the culture of the time, and that therefore we need no longer accept his teaching. What do these verses tell us?
  – What should be our proper response to Paul and his teaching?
◆ What are the dangers of taking Paul's ministry as a model for our ministry?
  – What *general principles* could we apply to our ministry?

## 16:1–16 and 21–23 GREETINGS AND MESSAGES
◆ Why might Paul have included such a long list of greetings?

## 16:17–20 WARNINGS AGAINST FALSE TEACHERS
◆ Against what does Paul warn the Romans?
  – What are the characteristics of these false teachers?
◆ Paul also talked about 'divisions' and 'obstacles' in 14:1–15:13. How and why is his approach different here?
  – How does Paul's approach to false teaching differ from ours? How does v. 20 fit in with his approach?

## 16:25–27 GLORY TO GOD WHO CAN KEEP YOU BY MY GOSPEL

◆ For what does Paul praise God at the end of his letter?

  – In the context of Romans, what is Paul likely to mean when he says that God can 'establish you'?

  – Why are the Romans, and we, so privileged to live when we do?

◆ What should be our next move, having come to the end of Romans?

◆ Having studied Romans, for what do you want to praise God?

# GROUP PREPARATION
# QUESTIONS

## An overview

Read through the whole of Romans fairly rapidly.

◆ Divide the letter into sections (maximum seven). What is each
  section about, approximately?
◆ What major themes did you identify?
◆ How does Paul present the Christian message?
◆ How does Paul describe the Christian life?

If possible, read the whole book through again one or two times
before starting the individual studies.

## Study I

# 1:1–17

◆ What do we learn about Paul and what do we learn about the Romans in this passage?

◆ How is Paul's summary of the gospel in vv. 1–6 different from what we might say?

◆ What do we learn about Paul's relationship with the Roman citizens?

◆ Why is Paul so eager to preach the gospel to the Romans? (There is more than one answer to this question.)

## Study 2

# 1:18–32

◆ Why is God angry?


– Is His anger justified?


◆ What does mankind do wrong?


– What is God's response?


◆ What do most people think is mankind's biggest problem?


– How does this passage challenge that view?


◆ How should this passage influence our message in evangelism?

## Study 3

# 2:1–29

◆ To whom is Paul talking
  – in 2:1–16?


  – in 2:17–29?


◆ What is his argument:
  – in 2:1–16?


  – in 2:17–29?


◆ Why does this section follow 1:18–32?


◆ What does this passage teach us about God's judgment?

# 3:1–20

◆ What are the potential objections that Paul raises in vv. 1–8? Why do they matter?

  – How does he answer these objections?

◆ What is the purpose of the Old Testament quotations in vv. 9–18? (Do look up some of them.)

  – How do vv. 9 and 19 help us to understand them?

◆ What is the verdict on the human race by 3:20?

  – How should this affect our attitude towards ourselves?

  – How should this affect our attitude towards those who aren't Christian?

**Study 5**

# 3:21–26

◆ Why is 3:21 so significant in the context of Romans so far?

◆ What different things do we learn about this 'righteousness from God'?

◆ Read Leviticus 16 (the background on the Atonement).

– Summarize what happened and why.

– How does this help us to understand Romans 3:25?

◆ How does the solution in these verses solve the problem explained in Romans 1:18–3:20?

**Study 6**

# 3:27–4:25

◆ Divide up the passage and give each part a title.

◆ How does 3:27–31 relate to the previous study (3:21–26)?

◆ What does Paul intend to prove from Abraham's story (4:1–25)?

◆ What are the main lessons that we learn about Abraham?

◆ What is the nature of Abraham's faith? How is our faith like his?

## Study 7

# 5:1–11

◆ What are the consequences of being justified through faith?

◆ Why is having 'peace with God' so remarkable?

◆ How does Paul change our perspective on suffering and on the future?

◆ How do you know that God loves you? Is Paul's reason different?

◆ How can a Christian say that he or she is definitely going to heaven?

# 5:12–21

◆ Divide this passage into parts and give each a heading.

◆ Why does Paul compare Christ with Adam? How are they similar?

◆ How are Christ and Adam different?

◆ Throughout, Paul talks of two 'realms'. What are they, and what are the features of each realm?

◆ How does this give us great confidence that we will be saved, as taught in 5:1–11?

## Study 9

# 6:1–14

## vv. 1–11

◆ Why does the question arise in v. 1? Write it in your own words.

◆ What has happened to Christians in the past?

◆ What will happen to Christians in the future?

◆ What is God's intention for His people?

## vv. 12–14

◆ How do these instructions make sense, in the light of vv. 1–11?

**Study 10**

# 6:15–7:6

## 6:15–23

◆ How is the question in v. 15 different from the question in 6:1?

◆ If we refuse to obey God in one area of our lives, what does that say about us?

◆ What does Paul say has happened to the Christian?

◆ How does Paul motivate us to obey God?

## 7:1–6

◆ What is the point of Paul's illustration from marriage?

◆ Contrast the life lived under the Law with the life that belongs to Christ.

**Study 11**

# 7:7–25

◆ Why is the question in 7:7 there?


– Why does it matter?


◆ How do the Law and sin relate to each other?


◆ How is Paul struggling in vv. 1–25? Why?


◆ What lessons does this passage teach us about the Christian life?

**Study 12**

# 8:1–17

◆ To what does the 'therefore' in v. 1 refer?

◆ Explain, in your own words, why there is 'no condemnation'.

◆ What do vv. 5–11 tell us about:
  – non–Christians?

  – Christians?

◆ What does this passage teach us about the Holy Spirit, who He is and what He does?

◆ What reassurance is there here for the Christian who is frustrated because he or she can't stop sinning? (cf. 7:24)

## Study 13

# 8:17–30

◆ What are 'our present sufferings' (v. 18)?

◆ How is our experience related to that of creation?

◆ What should our perspective be on:
  – the present?


  – the future?

◆ How does God help us now?

◆ What is God's will for Christians?

## Study 14

# 8:28–39

◆ From vv. 29–30 what do we learn about God's purpose?

◆ How does Paul show that God's plan is unstoppable?

◆ How does Paul show that God is for us (v. 31)?

◆ Why can the Christian have such confidence that God will complete His plan?

◆ Read Psalm 44, from which Paul quotes in v. 36. What can we learn from the attitude of the people in the psalm?

◆ What does this passage teach us about the perspective that Christians should have in the face of suffering?

**Study 15**

# 9:1–29

◆ How does this section (chs 9–11) follow on from ch. 8? Why does Paul have to explain why so few Jews are saved?

◆ What point is Paul making by using the Old Testament examples in vv. 6–13? How do they explain v. 6?

◆ How does Paul answer the questions in vv. 14 and 19?

◆ What truths about God does Paul teach here, and why do we find them hard to accept?

**Study 16**

# 9:30–10:21

◆ How is this passage related to 9:1–29?

◆ Why did the Jews not obtain righteousness? (9:30–10:4)

◆ What does this teach us about the Law?

◆ What do vv. 5–13 teach us about righteousness by faith?

◆ What reasons *cannot* be given for Israel's unbelief?

◆ What reasons does Paul give?

**Study 17**

# 11:1–36

◆ Divide the chapter into parts and give each a heading.

◆ How does Paul show in vv. 1–10 that God has not totally rejected His people?

◆ From vv. 11–16, what are the stages in God's overall plan of salvation?

◆ What different reasons does Paul give the Gentiles as to why they shouldn't boast over the Jews? (vv. 17–32)

**Study 18**

# 12:1–2

◆ How has Paul conveyed the extent of God's mercy in chs 1–11?

◆ What does Paul mean by 'offer your bodies as living sacrifices'?

◆ What do these verses teach us about worship? What is it not? What is it?

◆ How does the world try to make us conform to its pattern?

◆ How should our new minds transform us?

◆ What is 'God's will' (v. 2b)?

**Study 19**

# 12: 3–21

◆ How does Paul call for us to be transformed in the way that we think of ourselves?

◆ How should the illustration of the body affect our attitude to ourselves? And to the church?

◆ How does the behaviour outlined in vv. 9–21 contrast with that in 1:21–31?

◆ What do you find to be the most challenging practical implications of this passage?

**Study 20**

# 13:1–14

◆ What different reasons does Paul give as to why we should submit to the governing authorities?

◆ What are the implications for our lives?

◆ How should we apply this teaching in areas where Christians live under corrupt or oppressive regimes?

◆ What does it mean to love one another as Paul commands in v. 8?

◆ What do vv. 11–14 teach us about having a right perspective?

– How should this challenge us personally?

## Study 21

# 14:1–12 (read up to 15:13)

◆ To whom is Paul referring as the 'weak' and the 'strong'?

◆ How are the weak and the strong in danger of treating one another wrongly?

◆ How are they to see one another? Why?

◆ How are both the strong and the weak to see themselves?

◆ How would you define a 'disputable matter' (v.1)?

◆ What disputable matters are in danger of dividing us today?

**Study 22**

# 14:13–15:13

◆ Divide the passage and give each part a title.

◆ What are Paul's main instructions? How do they differ from those in 14:1–12?

◆ What main arguments or principles does Paul employ to back up his instructions?

◆ In vv. 7–13, how does Paul conclude his teaching on the strong and the weak?

◆ How does this teaching challenge the thinking of the world? In what ways should we be challenged personally?

## Study 23

# 15:14–16:27

◆ Note down everything that Paul writes about himself: role, motivation, strategy, plans.

◆ Everything that Paul mentions about himself has some relevance to the Romans. Why does he tell them each thing?

◆ What should be our response to Paul and his teaching?

◆ What are the characteristics of the false teachers in 16:17–20? What is Paul's approach to them?

◆ For what does Paul praise God in 16:25–27?

◆ What should be our main responses, having come to the end of Romans?

# ROMANS REVIEW STUDY

Before the study, read right through Romans again, maybe two chapters per day, and think again about the things you have learned.

◆ What has been the single biggest lesson that you have learned from Romans this year?

◆ What have you learned about:
  – God?

  – yourself?

  – the Christian life?

  – Christians?

  – your non-Christian friends?

◆ What have you found to be the most challenging passages? Why?

◆ How will you try to ensure that these lessons are not forgotten?

◆ For what do you want to thank God at the end of Romans?

# BIBLIOGRAPHY

C. E. B. Cranfield, *Romans – A shorter commentary* (T. & T. Clark Ltd., 1985)

Douglas Moo, *The Epistle to the Romans* in the series 'The New International Commentary on the New Testament' (Eerdman Publishing Co., 1996)

Leon Morris, *The Atonement* (IVP, 1983)

Anders Nygren, *Commentary on Romans* (Fortress Press, 1949)

S. Olyott, *The Gospel as it Really is* (Evangelical Press, 1979)

David Peterson, *Possessed by God A New Testament theology of sanctification and holiness* in the series 'New Studies in Biblical Theology' (Apollos, 1995)

David Seccombe, *Dust to Destiny* in the series 'Reading the Bible Today' (Aquila Press, 1996)

John R. W. Stott, *The Cross of Christ* (IVP, 1986)

— *The Message of Romans* in the series 'The Bible Speaks Today' (IVP, 1994)

# TRAINING DAYS AND TAPES

The Proclamation Trust runs **Read Mark Learn** Leaders' Training Days for small group Bible study leaders. For details please contact:

The Proclamation Trust
Willcox House
140-148 Borough High Street
London SE1 1LB
England

Tel:     020 7407 0561
Fax:     020 7407 0569
e-mail:  pt@proctrust.org.uk

Tapes of the Training Day material are also available from the Proclamation Trust Tape Ministry at the same postal address. Other details are as follows:

Tel. (voice-mail):  020 7407 0563
e-mail:  tapemin@proctrust.org.uk